THE TESLA
FBI FILES

DISCOVERY PUBLISHER

2015, Discovery Publisher
All rights reserved.

No part of this book may be reproduced in any form or by any electronic or mechanical means including information storage and retrieval systems, without permission in writing from the publisher.

Author when not written otherwise : Nikola Tesla
Editor in Chief : Adriano Lucca

DISCOVERY PUBLISHER

616 Corporate Way
Valley Cottage, New York, 10989
www.discoverypublisher.com
books@discoverypublisher.com
facebook.com/DiscoveryPublisher
twitter.com/DiscoveryPB

New York • Tokyo • Paris • Hong Kong

TABLE OF CONTENTS

INTRODUCTION ... 2

FREEDOM OF INFORMATION RELEASE ON SUBJECT: NIKOLA TESLA ... 4

LETTER TO J. E. HOOVER ... 4
2/12/1937

FBI FOIPA—DELETED PAGE INFORMATION SHEET ... 7
UNDATED

FBI MEMORANDUM—DEATH RAY ... 8
1/11/1943

LETTER TO FBI—EXPERIEMENTS AND RESEARCH OF NIKOLA TESLA ... 9
1/21/1943

LETTER FROM J. EDGAR HOOVER ... 10
UNDATED

LETTER FROM FBI—ALIEN ENEMY CUSTODIAL DETENTION ... 12
3/19/1943

FBI—SAVA M. KOSANOVICH ... 13
3/29/1943

FBI—ESPIONAGE ... 17
10/17/1945

LETTER TO ALIEN PROPERTY CUSTODIAN ... 21
1/30/1943

LIST OF PERSONS ASSOCIATED WITH NIKOLA TESLA ... 29
UNDATED

MEMORANDUM FOR MR. WHITSON ... 40
6/8/1949

FBI—SAVA N. KOSANOVIC, INTERNAL SECURITY 4/3/1950	41
MEMORANDUM—TESLA ESTATE 4/17/1950	44
FBI—YUGOSLAVIAN CONSULATE 12/1/1948	46
ACTIVITIES OF CONSULATE EMPLOYEES UNDATED	47
NIKOLA TESLA MONUMENT, NIAGARA FALLS 8/2/1976	49
FBI—YUGOSLAVIAN CONSULATE, INTERNAL SECURITY 2/19/1953	56
LETTER FROM CLARENCE M. KELLEY, DIRECTOR 7/7/1975	59
ENGINEERING MANAGEMENT SOCIETY 6/27/1983	60
LETTER FROM ROGER S. YOUNG 7/25/1983	61
CURRENT BIOGRAPHY UNDATED	63
RED AMBASSADORS, SAVA KOSANOVICH UNDATED	68
FBI—INTERNAL SECURITY REGISTRATION ACT 2/2/1946	73
FBI—INTERNAL SECURITY REGISTRATION ACT 11/7/1947	76
FBI—INTERNAL SECURITY REGISTRATION ACT 3/4/1945	79
FBI—INTERNAL SECURITY REGISTRATION ACT 5/8/1945	82
YUGOSLAVIAN ACTIVITIES IN THE US 8/30/1946	83

YUGOSLAVIAN ACTIVITIES IN THE US — 85
11/18/1947

FBI—DELETED PAGE INFORMATION SHEET — 88
UNDATED

FBI—AMERICAN SLAV CONGRESS — 89
11/18/1942

FBI—AMERICAN SLAV CONGRESS — 96
11/5/1943

FBI—AMERICAN SLAVE CONGRESS — 102
11/5/1943

NIKOLA TESLA, THE SLAVIC AMERICAN — 110
UNDATED

SAVA KOSANOVISH, ALLEGED COMMUNIST — 121
11/13/1943

MEMORANDUM—WESTBROOK PEGLER — 123
1/30/1951

MEMORANDUM—INTERNAL SECURITY — 126
8/30/1946

FBI—ALLEGATIONS — 127
6/19/1952

THE UNITED AMERICAN YUGOSLAV CLUB OF NEW YORK — 131
9/8/1975

FBI—LOYALTY OF EMPLOYEES OF THE UNITED NATION — 133
3/28/1960

FREEDOM OF INFORMATION RELEASE ON SUBJECT: NIKOLA TESLA — 139

LETTER TO J. EDGAR HOOVER — 140
9/24/1940

DEATH RAY FOR PLANES — 141
9/22/1940

LETTER FROM J. EDGAR HOOVER — 142
10/1/1940

FBI NYC DIRECTOR VEST UNSUBS
1/12/1943
143

FBI NYC DIRECTOR, UNKNOWN SUBJECTS
1/9/1943
145

FBI MEMORANDUM
1/11/1943
147

FBI MEMORANDUM FOR MR. LADD
1/12/1943
149

LETTER TO J. E. HOOVER
4/16/1948
150

LETTER FROM J. E. HOOVER
4/22/1948
152

LETTER FROM J. E. HOOVER
4/3/1950
153

DIRECTOR, FBI—INTERNAL SECURITY MEMO
4/17/1950
154

LETTER TO DIRECTOR, FBI
UNDATED
155

REQUEST TO FBI
8/18/1952
156

LETTER FROM J. E. HOOVER
8/26/1952
158

OFFICE MEMORANDUM
5/5/1953
159

OFFICE MEMORANDUM
8/19/1954
161

THE LIFE AND WORK OF DR. NIKOLA TESLA
2/3/1954
162

PRODIGAL GENIUS
UNDATED
163

REGISTERED MAIL
2/5/1954
164

LETTER TO GEORGE SCHERFF   166
2/3/1954

IMPORTANT ANNOUCEMENT   168
UNDATED

SPECIAL DELIVERY—LETTER TO GEORGE SCHERFF   169
UNDATED

INTERNAL SECURITY   170
3/10/1954

LETTER TO J. E. HOOVER   171
6/25/1955

STRANGE GENIUS   173
5/1955

RECOGNITION FOR TESLA   174
UNDATED

INFORMATION CONCERNING ESPIONAGE   175
6/29/1955

LETTER TO SWEZEY   177
6/30/1955

LETTER TO J. E. HOOVER   178
8/1/1955

LETTER FROM J. E. HOOVER   179
8/11/1955

LETTER TO J. E. HOOVER   180
9/10/1955

LETTER FROM J. E. HOOVER   181
9/20/1955

RECOGNITION FOR TESLA   182
7/13/1955

THE GENIUS WHO WALKED ALONE   183
6/1955

RECOGNITION FOR TESLA   188
10/7/1955

$2000 PUBLIC AID SOUGHT 10/26/1955	189
TESLA STATUE FUNDED $UNKNOWN 1580	190
LETTER TO FBI 6/23/1956	192
LETTER FROM J. E. HOOVER 6/29/1956	193
OFFICE MEMORANDUM—FLYING SAUCER 7/25/1957	194
LETTER TO J. E. HOOVER 3/18/1958	198
LETTER FROM J. E. HOOVER 3/14/1958	199
LETTER TO FBI—REQUEST FOR INFORMATION 6/24/1959	200
LETTER FROM J. E. HOOVER 7/2/1959	201
LETTER TO FBI—ACCESS TO RECORDS 12/6/1960	202
REPLY FROM FBI 2/14/1961	203
LETTER FROM J. E. HOOVER 2/23/1961	204
LETTER FROM FBI—PAPERS FOR EXAMINATION 11/21/1962	205
LETTER FROM J. E. HOOVER 11/27/1962	206
LETTER TO FBI 3/18/1964	207
LETTER TO FBI—TESLA PAPERS 3/10/1964	208

LETTER FROM J. E. HOOVER 209
3/8/1964

LETTER TO FBI—IS IT TRUE? 210
6/23/1964

LETTER FROM J. E. HOOVER 211
6/22/1964

LETTER TO FBI—OREGON STATE UNIVERSITY 212
3/28/1967

LETTER FROM J. E. HOOVER 213
4/2/1967

LETTER TO J. E. HOOVER—TESLA FILES 214
6/23/1964

LETTER TO FBI—EDISON: IT WOULD NEVER WORK 216
2/25/1969

LETTER FROM J. E. HOOVER 217
3/4/1969

LETTER TO FBI—TESLA'S PERSONAL EFFECTS 218
4/8/1970

LETTER FROM J. E. HOOVER 219
4/14/1970

LETTER TO FBI—FOREIGN AGENTS 220
7/8/1970

LETTER FROM J. E. HOOVER 221
7/15/1970

LETTER TO FBI—HAVE THEM IN JAIL 222
12/6/1971

LETTER FROM J. E. HOOVER 223
12/14/1971

LETTER TO FBI—RECORDS LOCKED UP 224
UNDATED

LETTER FROM L. PATRICK GRAY III, ACTING DIRECTOR 225
10/31/1972

LETTER TO FBI—RESUMING TESLA'S WORK 4/1/1973	226
LETTER FROM L. PATRICK GRAY III, ACTING DIRECTOR 4/11/1973	227
LETTER TO FBI—MICROFILM 6/20/1973	228
LETTER FROM WILLIAM D. RUCKELSHAUS, ACTING DIRECTOR 6/27/1973	229
UNITED STATE SENATE TO FBI 6/26/1973	230
LETTER TO SENATOR PACKWOOD—ALASKA MILITARY CONTRACT 6/27/1973	231
LETTER FROM WILLIAM D. RUCKELSHAUS, ACTING DIRECTOR 7/5/1973	232
LETTER TO FBI—WHY? 7/20/1973	233
LETTER FROM WILLIAM D. RUCKELSHAUS, ACTING DIRECTOR 7/19/1973	234
LETTER TO FBI—ALIEN PROPERTY CLARIFICATIONS UNDATED	235
LETTER FROM CLARENCE M. KELLEY, DIRECTOR 8/2/1973	237
LETTER TO FBI—IMPOUNDED MATERIAL 6/9/1975	238
LETTER FROM CLARENCE M. KELLEY, DIRECTOR 7/7/1975	239
LETTER TO FBI—BAD PUBLICITY 11/13/1975	240
LETTER FROM CLARENCE M. KELLEY, DIRECTOR 11/26/1975	241
ROUTING SLIP 10/21/1975	242

LETTER TO FBI—NATIONAL SECURITY 10/17/1975	243
LETTER FROM CLARENCE M. KELLEY, DIRECTOR 11/10/1975	244
LETTER TO FBI—MICROFILMS RECORDS 4/20/1976	245
FUSION ENERGY UNDATED	247
TESLA TRIES TO PREVENT WORLD WAR II UNDATED	249
LETTER FROM CLARENCE M. KELLEY, DIRECTOR 4/3/1976	253
UNITED STATE SENATE 6/16/1976	254
LETTER TO FBI—UNPUBLISHED PAPERS UNDATED	255
LETTER FROM CLARENCE M. KELLEY, DIRECTOR 6/23/1976	257
LETTER TO FBI—HOTEL NEW YORKER 7/26/1979	258
LETTER FROM CLARENCE M. KELLEY, DIRECTOR 8/6/1979	259
MEMORANDUM—DR. TESLA UNDER THE FOIA 2/25/1980	260
FBI INTERNAL ROUTING ACTION SLIP 10/10/1979	261
EVERY CASE IN "PREPROCESSED" UNDATED	262
MEMORANDUM FOR THE DIRECTOR, FBI 2/9/1981	263
LETTER FROM ROGER S. YOUNG 3/10/1981	264

IN THE CUSTODY OF ALIEN PROPERTY 3/23/1981	**265**
LETTER FROM ROGER S. YOUNG 4/1/1981	**268**
LETTER TO FBI—UNDERGROUND SAN FRANCISCO PAPER 7/21/1981	**269**
LETTER FROM ROGER S. YOUNG 8/7/1981	**271**
LETTER TO FBI—AIR FORCE AERONAUTICAL SYSTEM DIVISION 8/18/1983	**272**
TESLA: MAN OUT OF TIME UNDATED	**276**
FBI—RECORDS/OPERATIONS SECTIONS 8/26/1983	**318**
FBI—SEARCH SLIP 8/26/1983	**321**

The FBI's FOIA Library contains many files of public interest and historical value. In compliance with the National Archives and Records Administration (NARA) requirements, some of these records are no longer in the physical possession of the FBI, eliminating the FBI's capability to re-review and/or re-process this material. Please note, that the information found in these files may no longer reflect the current beliefs, positions, opinions, or policies currently held by the FBI.

Some material contained in this book may contain actions, words, or images of a graphic nature that may be offensive and/or emotionally disturbing. This material may not be suitable for all ages. Please view it with discretion.

THE TESLA
FBI FILES

INTRODUCTION

One of the more controversial topics involving Nikola Tesla is what became of many of his technical and scientific papers after he died in 1943. Just before his death at the height of World War II, he claimed that he had perfected his so-called "death beam." So it was natural that the FBI and other U.S. Government agencies would be interested in any scientific ideas involving weaponry. Some were concerned that Tesla's papers might fall into the hands of the Axis powers or the Soviets.

The morning after the inventor's death, his nephew Sava Kosanovic hurried to his uncle's room at the Hotel New Yorker. He was an up-and-coming Yugoslav official with suspected connections to the communist party in his country. By the time he arrived, Tesla's body had already been removed, and Kosanovic suspected that someone had already gone through his uncle's effects. Technical papers were missing as well as a black notebook he knew Tesla kept—a notebook with several hundred pages, some of which were marked "Government."

P. E. Foxworth, assistant director of the New York FBI office, was called in to investigate. According to Foxworth, the government was "vitally interested" in preserving Tesla's papers. Two days after Tesla's death, representatives of the Office of Alien Property went to his room at the New Yorker Hotel and seized all his possessions.

Dr. John G. Trump, an electrical engineer with the National Defense Research Committee of the Office of Scientific Research and Development, was called in to analyze the Tesla papers in OAP custody. Following a three-day investigation, Dr. Trump concluded:

His [Tesla's] thoughts and efforts during at least the past 15 years were primarily of a speculative, philosophical, and somewhat promotional character often concerned with the production and wireless transmission of power; but did not include new, sound, workable principles or methods for realizing such results.

Just after World War II, there was a renewed interest in beam weapons. Copies of Tesla's papers on particle beam weaponry were sent to Patterson Air Force Base in Dayton, Ohio. An operation code-named "Project Nick" was heavily funded and placed under the command of Brigadier General L.C. Craigie to test the feasibility of Tesla's concept. Details of the experiments were never published, and the project was apparently discontinued. But something peculiar happened. The copies of Tesla's papers disappeared and nobody knows what happened to them.

In 1952, Tesla's remaining papers and possessions were released to Sava Kosanovic and returned to Belgrade, Yugoslavia where a museum was created in the inventor's honor. For many years, under Tito's communist regime, it was extremely difficult for Western journalists and scholars to gain access to the Tesla archive in Yugoslavia; even then they were allowed to see only selected papers. This was not the case for Soviet scientists who came in delegations during the 1950s. Concerns increased in 1960 when Soviet Premier Khrushchev announced to the Supreme Soviet that "a new and fantastic weapon was in the hatching stage."

Work on beam weapons also continued in the United States. In 1958 the Defense Advanced Research Projects Agency (DARPA) initiated a top-secret project code-named "Seesaw" at Lawrence Livermore Laboratory to develop a charged-particle beam weapon. More than ten years and twenty-seven million dollars later, the project was abandoned "because of the projected high costs associated with implementation as well as the formidable technical problems associated with propagating a beam through very long ranges in the atmosphere." Scientists associated with the project had no knowledge of Tesla's papers.

In the late 1970s, there was fear that the Soviets may have achieved a technological breakthrough. Some U.S. defense analysts concluded that a large beam weapon facility was under construction near the Sino-Soviet border in Southern Russia.

The American response to this "technological surprise" was the Strategic Defense Initiative announced by President Ronald Reagan in 1983. Teams of government scientists were urged to "turn their great talents now to the cause of mankind and world peace, to give us the means of rendering these nuclear weapons impotent and obsolete."

Today, after a half-century of research and billions of dollars of investment, the SDI program is generally considered a failure, and there is still no realistic means of defense against a nuclear missile attack.

For many years scientists and researchers have sought for Tesla's missing papers with no apparent success. It is conceivable that if Nikola Tesla knew a means for accurately projecting lethal beams of energy through the atmosphere, he may have taken it to the grave with him.

The FBI claims that despite longstanding reports and rumors, it was not involved in searching Tesla's effects, and it never had possession of his papers or any microfilm that may have been made of those papers. Since 1943, the FBI has told a consistent story to all who have asked. Reports to the contrary appear to be based on an initial confusion of FBI agents with other government officials—especially Alien Property Office personnel. These rumors have long been repeated in biographies and articles on Tesla without double-checking the facts as reported in their files.

This book contains all files released by the FBI concerning Nikola Tesla.

February 12, 1937

Mr. Edgar Hoover, Director,
Federal Bureau of Investigation,
Washington, D.C.

My dear Mr. Hoover:

I do not know whether or not the recent series of air crashes on the west coast has attracted the attention of your department, or whether, if investigation were indicated, the jurisdiction would be your own. An idea as to the cause of these crashes has occurred to me, however, and I thought it might bear a bit of checking up.

If you will check newspaper files as far back as 1934, I believe you will find that the earliest of the unexplained (and apparently unexplainable crashes) occurred about that time.

As I remember the events, it was during that year that three small planes exploded in the air over Texas and southwestern Kansas and Oklahoma. These crashes were not accounted for, either by subsequent investigation where the plane occupants were killed or by the experience of surviving plane occupants in one case.

Following these tragedies there came a lapse of about a year, after which there occurred (likewise without apparent reason) the series of crashes which cost the lives of a senator, of Knute Rockne, and a number of others. All crashes again occurred in the South and Southwest.

Again there was a lapse of time, this one not quite a year, and there started the worst series of air disasters the country has yet seen. One plane lost in the Southwest and not yet accounted for. One plane crashes into a mountainside within sight of its airport. And now the most recent incident, the falling of a United liner into San Francisco Bay while circling its airport, preparatory to landing.

Now in this most recent incident, the experience of the radio operator at the airport seems to me to be highly illuminating. This operator reported a soft buzz interrupting his communication with the liner ... a loud roar such as produced by the worst imaginable static ... then silence. The plane had dropped into the bay like a plummet.

- 2 -

Crack pilots do not suddenly become rank hams and bungle in handling a ship. Nor do the three motors (or even two) on the large airliners, stop simultaneously without extremely sufficient reason. These things might happen once or even twice in a lifetime. They do not happen six and eight times a year. It is not logical that they should.

To digress for a moment, I recall reading an article in a magazine a year or two ago, written by Nikola Tesla, the inventor. The article dealt with a new invention of Mr. Tesla's ... a giant induction coil which would project power (high voltage) through the atmosphere without the use of transmission wires. Mr. Tesla devoted some space to the possible social benefits that would result to the public should his invention be perfected and become practical.

I have not heard of Mr. Tesla now in two or three years. Perhaps he has left the country. Perhaps he is still here. He might still be working on the invention described in the above-mentioned article. It might have been stolen from him.

In any case, his views on the ideas presented by these two unconnected subjects, would be well worth while having. And if I had the money and the time, I should certainly make an effort to smoke him out myself.

The thing is simply this: if one man can make an instrument that will project power through the air for even so short a distance as 500 yards (the then-practical limitations of Mr. Nikola's device) it is entirely possible for another to project power for several hundreds of miles. And the effect of such uncontrolled power on metallic objects in its path is entirely unpredictable.

Please do not think me a "crank" letter writer. I have never before written a letter of this type to anyone. But the idea seems to me so within the bounds of possibility that I most sincerely feel it will bear some practical study.

Yours very respectfully,

Passaic, N.J.

UNDATED

4-750 (Rev. 9-29-95)

XXXXXX
XXXXXX
XXXXXX

FEDERAL BUREAU OF INVESTIGATION
FOIPA
DELETED PAGE INFORMATION SHEET

6 Page(s) withheld entirely at this location in the file. One or more of the following statements, where indicated, explain this deletion.

☑ Deletions were made pursuant to the exemptions indicated below with no segregable material available for release to you.

Section 552

☑ (b)(1)
☐ (b)(2)
☐ (b)(3)

_____
_____
_____

☐ (b)(4)
☐ (b)(5)
☐ (b)(6)

☐ (b)(7)(A)
☐ (b)(7)(B)
☐ (b)(7)(C)
☐ (b)(7)(D)
☐ (b)(7)(E)
☐ (b)(7)(F)
☐ (b)(8)
☐ (b)(9)

Section 552a

☐ (d)(5)
☐ (j)(2)
☐ (k)(1)
☐ (k)(2)
☐ (k)(3)
☐ (k)(4)
☐ (k)(5)
☐ (k)(6)
☐ (k)(7)

☐ Information pertained only to a third party with no reference to the subject of your request or the subject of your request is listed in the title only.

☐ Documents originated with another Government agency(ies). These documents were referred to that agency(ies) for review and direct response to you.

_____ Pages contain information furnished by another Government agency(ies). You will be advised by the FBI as to the releasability of this information following our consultation with the other agency(ies).

_____ Page(s) withheld inasmuch as a final release determination has not been made. You will be advised as to the disposition at a later date.

_____ Pages were not considered for release as they are duplicative of _____

_____ Page(s) withheld for the following reason(s): _____

☑ The following number is to be used for reference regarding these pages.
65-30311-237

XXXXXXXXXXXXXXX
X Deleted Page(s) X
X No Duplication Fee X
X for this page X
XXXXXXXXXXXXXXX

XXXXXX
XXXXXX
XXXXXX

FBI/DOJ

FBI MEMORANDUM—DEATH RAY

1/11/1943

JOHN EDGAR HOOVER
DIRECTOR

Federal Bureau of Investigation
United States Department of Justice
Washington, D. C.

13818

January 11, 1943

JBL:ed

Mr. E.A. Tamm
Mr. Clegg
Mr. Glavin
Mr. Ladd
Mr. Nichols
Mr. Rosen
Mr. Tracy
Mr. Carson
Mr. Coffey
Mr. Hendon
Mr. Kramer
Mr. McGuire
Mr. Harbo
Mr. Quinn Tamm
Tele. Room
Mr. Nease
Miss Beahm
Miss Gandy

MEMORANDUM FOR MR. LADD

RE: UNKNOWN SUBJECT;
EXPERIMENTS AND RESEARCH
OF NIKOLA TESLA (Deceased)
ESPIONAGE - M

    In a teletype from the New York Office dated January 9, 1943, the Bureau's advice is requested as to what action should be taken in connection with this matter. It is to be noted that Tesla died January 7, 1943, and resided at the Hotel New Yorker. He was one of the world's outstanding scientists in the electrical field and has been conducting many experiments in connection with wireless transmission of electrical power and what is commonly referred to as the "Death Ray".

    Sava Kosanovich, a distant relative intensely disliked by Tesla, is taking steps to get possession of these important documents and plans. Kosanovich on January 7, 1943, with George Clark, in charge of the Museum and Laboratory for RCA, and Kenneth Swezey of Brooklyn, New York, entered Tesla's rooms in the Hotel New Yorker and, with the aid of a locksmith, broke into a safe containing some of Tesla's valuable papers, including important electrical formulae, designs, et cetera.

    Tesla is reported to have completed and perfected his experiments in the radio transmission of electrical power and to have conceived and designed a revolutionary type of torpedo not presently in use by any nation. It is reported that Kosanovich may possibly make this material available to the enemy.

ACTION:

    I called Mr. Donegan of the New York Office at 12:30 P.M. and pointed out the apparent burglary violation on the part of Kosanovich. I told him this matter should be discreetly discussed with the State's Attorney in New York City with a view to locating Kosanovich and apprehending him on a burglary charge in order to determine the nature of the material he took from Tesla's safe. I pointed out the necessity for the State's Attorney keeping any action most secret in view of the highly confidential nature of the plans involved. I also suggested that the New York Office contact the Surrogate Court in order that Tesla's effects as well as the contents of his safety deposit boxes might not be entered without the presence of a Bureau Agent in order that we may endeavor to preserve the secrecy of any plans or items essential to the conduct of the war and national security.

65-47953-1

FSP:AB

January 21, 1943

SAC, New York

Re: UNKNOWN SUBJECTS; SAVA KOSANOVICH;
EXPERIMENTS AND RESEARCH OF NIKOLA TESLA (Deceased)
ESPIONAGE (M)

Dear Sir:

Reference is made to a teletype dated January 9, 1943, from the New York Field Office and to a phone conversation between Mr. J. B. Little of the Bureau and Assistant Special Agent in Charge Donegan on January 11, 1943.

It was pointed out to Mr. Donegan that Sava Kosanovich, George Clark and Kenneth Swezey may have committed a burglary violation by entering Tesla's rooms after his death and particularly by using a locksmith to get into a safe containing some of Tesla's valuable papers. Mr. Donegan was advised this matter should be discreetly discussed with the State's Attorney, New York City, with a view to locating Kosanovich and apprehending him on a burglary charge, in order to ascertain the nature of the material taken from the safe of Nikola Tesla. It was also suggested that the New York Office contact the Surrogate Court, in order that Tesla's effects, as well as the contents of his safety deposit boxes, might not be entered without the presence of an Agent, in order that the secrecy of any plans or items essential to the conduct of the war or national security might be preserved. It was stated that Kosanovich might possibly make certain material available to the enemy.

A review of the Bureau files reveals considerable information concerning Nikola Tesla and his inventions and it should be noted that one Nicola Tesla, who might have been identical with Nikola Tesla, made a speech at the Grange Hall, Springfield, Massachusetts, on June 4, 1922, under the auspices of the Friends of Soviet Russia.

It further appears that Sava Kosanovich may be identical with an individual of the same name, who is a member of the Yugoslavian Government in exile. An examination of the files reveals that one Sava Kosanovich, described as the Minister of Supply, arrived with other Yugoslavian Government officials at Norfolk, Virginia, on September 4, 1941, on the SS City of Exeter, a British ship, from Cape Town en route to the United Kingdom via Washington and Canada.

In another instance the name of Sava N. Kosanovich appears on the stationery of the Central and Eastern European Planning Board (Czechoslovakia,

Mr. Tolson
Mr. E. A. Tamm
Mr. Clegg
Mr. Glavin
Mr. Ladd
Mr. Nichols
Mr. Rosen
Mr. Tracy
Mr. Carson
Mr. Coffey
Mr. Hendon
Mr. Kramer
Mr. McGuire
Harbo
Quinn Tamm
Nease
Gandy

SAC, New York   - 2 -

Greece, Poland, Yugoslavia). On this letterhead Kosanovich is described as Chairman of the Board and Minister of State for Yugoslavia. It is stated that this Board is interested in "planning for postwar Europe". (100-99042)

In still another file it is disclosed that Sava Kosanovich, a Serbian, was a member of one of the Yugoslavian minority parties and when an emergency government to overthrow an alliance with the Axis was formed, he was included as an official. He is alleged to be a Communist and is said to receive $1,250 a month salary from the exiled Yugoslavian Government. He and other exiled government officials are stated to use these large salaries to finance every Serbian paper in the United States except "Srbobran" published at Pittsburgh. (97-1340-18)

No record of Kenneth Swezey could be located in the Bureau files from the information available.

The foregoing information is being furnished for possible future reference in connection with this case and it is desired that the Bureau be kept promptly and currently informed of all developments in this case.

Very truly yours,

John Edgar Hoover
Director

Freedom of Information Release

On

Subject: Nikola Tesla

Cross References
Pages Reviewed - 127
Pages Released - 127

Federal Bureau of Investigation

Federal Bureau of Investigation
United States Department of Justice
New York, New York

EBC:PM
65-12290

March 19, 1943

Director, FBI

Re: UNKNOWN SUBJECTS; SAVA KOSANOVICH;
EXPERIMENTS AND RESEARCH OF NIKOLA TESLA
(Deceased);
ESPIONAGE, MISCELLANEOUS

Dear Sir:

Reference is made to the Bureau letter in the above-captioned matter dated January 21, 1943, in which it is stated that it is desired that the Bureau be kept promptly and currently informed of all developments in this case.

In view of a telephone call from Mr. Little of the Bureau to Mr. T. J. Donegan, Assistant Special Agent in Charge of the New York Office, dated January 14, 1943, in which Mr. Little stated that the above-captioned matter was now being handled as an Alien Enemy Custodial Detention matter and therefore no further action should be taken in the matter by the New York Field Division, this case is being considered closed in this Office, unless advised to the contrary by the Bureau at some future time.

Very truly yours,

E. E. Conroy
E. E. CONROY
Special Agent in Charge

ALL INFORMATION CONTAINED
HEREIN IS UNCLASSIFIED
DATE 4-18-89 BY SP4A

COPIES DESTROYED
148 OCT 26 1960

RECORDED & INDEXED

65-47953-3

FEDERAL BUREAU OF INVESTIGATION

Form No. 1 THIS CASE ORIGINATED AT	NEW YORK CITY, N.Y.		FILE NO. 100-8189	
REPORT MADE AT	DATE WHEN MADE	PERIOD FOR WHICH MADE	REPORT MADE BY	
BALTIMORE, MARYLAND	3-29-43	3-6-43	CHARLES J. FOSTER :MHR	
TITLE			CHARACTER OF CASE	
SAVA M. KOSANOVICH, with alias Sava M. Cosonovitch			INTERNAL SECURITY G. CUSTODIAL DETENTION	

SYNOPSIS OF FACTS:

Subject SAVA M. KOSANOVICH, Secretary of State to Yugoslavian Government in exile. Resides Navaro Hotel, NYC. Reported to have turned over patents and effects to Alien Property Custodian, NYC, for NICK TESLA. ABE SPANEL advised subject for United Nations and desires to become U.S. citizen.

- R U C -

ALL INFORMATION CONTAINED
HEREIN IS UNCLASSIFIED
DATE 4-7-15 BY SP/ADM

REFERENCE: Letter from New York Field Division dated 2-22-43.

DETAILS: AT DOVER, DELAWARE

It is to be noted that subject's correct name is SAVA M. KOSANOVICH and not COSONOVITCH as carried in reference letter.

Mr. ABE SPANEL, President of the International Latex Corporation, advised that the subject is presently the Secretary of State to the Yugoslavian Government in exile and that he resides at the Navaro Hotel, New York City. He stated that he had been a very good friend of NICK TESLA who has died recently and that he believes that the subject is a third or fourth cousin of TESLA and that when TESLA died, the subject was his only close relative in this country and TESLA's effects came into his possession.

SPANEL related that the subject had recently turned over to the government the majority of the patents of NICK TESLA. SPANEL described TESLA as being one of the greatest inventors that has ever lived. He stated he had more than

COPIES DESTROYED
148 OCT 26 1960

COPIES OF THIS REPORT
5 - Bureau
4 - NYC (2 G-2)
2 - Baltimore

65-147953
APR 22 1943

100-8189

900 inventions and patents. SPANEL stated that at one time TESLA had an invention in which he was able to direct electrical current without the means of a conductor. He felt that this type of an invention would be of invaluable assistance to any country at war and for this reason felt that TESLA's inventions and patents should be put into the hands of proper Government officials, where they might be put to the best advantage for the United States. He does not believe the subject is engaged in any un-American activities and stated that he was more than willing to turn these patents and inventions over to the proper Government agency. He asserted that before TESLA died, he had spoken to the subject regarding his becoming a United States citizen and SPANEL believes that he is now taking the proper steps to achieve that end.

SPANEL also stated that the subject had handed all of the effects of the deceased TESLA to the Alien Property Custodian in New York City.

SPANEL advised that the day before TESLA died he had tried to get in touch with War Department officials in Washington in order that he might make available to them patents and inventions that he had developed. However, he was not able to get in touch with the proper authorities and he died the following day.

SPANEL advised that the Yugoslavian Government had been sending TESLA approximately $600.00 per month for sometime prior to his death and this was described as being a sort of pension.

SPANEL stated further that he has previously turned over information regarding the subject to Special Agent FRED B. CORNELL of the New York Field Division. He also advised that WALDEMER KEMPFERT, Science Editor, New York Times and BILL LAURENZ, Science Feature Writer, New York Times and the Science Editor of the Herald Tribune would be able to elaborate on some of the accomplishments of NICK TESLA and that the June 1900 issue of the Century Magazine also contained an article relating to the inventions of TESLA.

SPANEL also stated that he believed BLOYCE FITZGERALD, Pierpont Hotel, Brooklyn, New York, Secretary to TESLA, has been contacted by Special Agent CORNELL and that if the New York Office wishes to contact SPANEL he may be reached at his home

b7C
o/s

- REFERRED UPON COMPLETION TO THE OFFICE OF ORIGIN -

JOHN EDGAR HOOVER
DIRECTOR

CC-287

Federal Bureau of Investigation
United States Department of Justice
Washington, D. C.

FLR:lem
2:45 p.m.

July 17, 1943

Mr. Tolson	
Mr. E. A. Tamm	
Mr. Clegg	
Mr. Glavin	
Mr. Ladd	
Mr. Nichols	
Mr. Rosen	
Mr. Tracy	
Mr. Carson	
Mr. Coffey	
Mr. Hendon	
Mr. Kramer	
Mr. McGuire	
Mr. Harbo	
Mr. Quinn Tamm	
Tele. Room	
Mr. Nease	
Miss Beahm	
Miss Gandy	

MEMORANDUM FOR Mr. E. A. LADD

RE: SAVA KOSANOVICH
INTERNAL SECURITY (G)
CUSTODIAL DETENTION

At this time SA John Parker of the New York office telephoned, stating on the previous afternoon ▓▓▓▓ telephoned that office through the assistance of ▓▓▓▓ a well known lecturer, author and traveler. ▓▓▓▓ stated that she would like to be interviewed concerning certain information she possessed relative to Yugoslavian activities and, in particular, data which she has concerning a man by the name of Kosanovich, whom she believes to be an enemy agent. ▓▓▓▓ stated she was preparing statements of fact which she intends to turn over to the State Department concerning Kosanovich. She advised she was proceeding to her home at ▓▓▓▓ and can be reached at her address, which is ▓▓▓▓

Agent Parker stated ▓▓▓▓ is apparently referring to Sava Kosanovich and added this individual is mentioned in two teletypes which the New York office forwarded to the Bureau under dates of January 9 and 12, 1943, in the case entitled UNKNOWN SUBJECTS, EQUIPMENT, EXPERIMENTS AND RESEARCH OF NICOLA TESLA, DECEASED, ESPIONAGE M (Bureau file 100-2237). Briefly, the information contained in these teletypes is that shortly after Nicola Tesla, one of the world's outstanding scientists in the electrical field, died in his hotel room at New York City on January 8, 1943, Sava Kosanovich, a distant relative, and other individuals entered his room and opened a safe, examining certain materials which he possessed. On January 8, Mr. L. M. C. Smith of the Department advised Mr. Tamm that he was concerned about the possibility of enemy agents confiscating some of the trunks of Tesla and that apparently the Alien Property Custodian was taking some action in this matter. Inasmuch as the matter was being handled by the Alien Property Custodian's office, the Bureau did not conduct any inquiries into this situation.

It is also noted that on July 19, Mr. James Sharpe of the Special War Policies Unit of the Department forwarded to Mr. ▓▓▓▓ a letter reported ▓▓▓▓ who was described as the Ex-Minister of the Yugoslav Government in Exile by one ▓▓▓▓. This letter, which Sharpe understood ▓▓▓▓ April 7, 1943, was of a threatening nature.

COPIES DESTROYED
148 OCT 26 1960

ALL INFORMATION CONTAINED
HEREIN IS UNCLASSIFIED
DATE 4-18-89 BY ▓▓▓▓

Mr. Ladd - 2 -

A newspaper article which Mr. Sharpe also exhibited revealed that ▬▬▬▬ was arraigned in local court in New York City on ▬▬▬▬ after having been charged with sending a threatening letter through the mail to Kosanovich. In connection with this trial, Agent Parker stated that the case has been postponed for six months. In the letter which ▬▬▬▬ wrote Kosanovich, he makes reference to ▬▬▬▬ and instructs that Kosanovich discontinue his attacks on her.

At the time Mr. Sharpe called at the Bureau, he pointed out the strong animosity and dissension which exists between the various nationalist groups in this country, because of their conflicting opinions as to the type of postwar government which should be set up in the smaller countries in Europe and mentioned that Kosanovich and ▬▬▬▬ have opposite political theories. He also mentioned that ▬▬▬▬ is one of the greatest contributors to dissension between the Serbs in this country and has been active in publicizing her views concerning postwar Serbia.

b7C Recently the Bureau instructed the Pittsburgh office to interview ▬▬▬▬ concerning certain statements which she has been making relative to the Bureau and to date, this interview has not been consummated.

ACTION:

Inasmuch as Miss ▬▬▬▬ indicated to the New York office she had certain information she desired to make available and that she believes Kosanovich is an enemy agent, it is believed that an interview with her should be had. It is felt that this interview should be carried out as soon as possible by the well-qualified Agents of the Washington Field Office, because of her prominence and political views.

There is attached for your approval a letter directed to the Washington Field Office requesting that this interview be conducted and also instructing that she be interrogated concerning the other matter referred to above, inasmuch as the Pittsburgh office has not as yet covered this interview.

Respectfully,

F. L. Welch

10/17/1945 — FBI–ESPIONAGE

Federal Bureau of Investigation
United States Department of Justice
New York 7, New York

IN REPLY, PLEASE REFER TO
FILE NO. 65-12290
HER:mhm

CONFIDENTIAL

October 17, 1945

Director, FBI

Re: UNKNOWN SUBJECTS;
SAVA KOSANOVICH;
Experiments and research of NIKOLA TESLA (deceased)
ESPIONAGE - M

Dear Sir:

Reference is made to the Bureau letter dated January 21, 1943, which bore a caption similiar to that mentioned above.

The referenced letter dealt with the death, on January 7, 1943, of the famous inventor, NIKOLA TESLA, who as well as being the inventor of Alternating Current, perfected many electrical devices. He is also credited with having developed the so called "death ray" which would safeguard any country from attack by air.

On June 9, 1945, a ▇▇▇▇▇▇▇ of New York City furnished information of a nonspecific nature indicating that it was his belief that persons sympathetic to Russia were making an effort to secure the effects of NIKOLA TESLA in order to salvage therefrom any models or designs of possible military value. ▇▇▇▇▇ claimed that he heard that ABRAHAM N. SPANEL, President of the NATIONAL LATEX CORPORATION, of Dover, Delaware was the motivating influence behind this attempt to obtain TESLA'S papers which are presently held in storage at the MANHATTAN STORAGE WAREHOUSE in New York City. ▇▇▇▇▇ promised to return to the New York Field Division shortly after his initial visit and furnish further and more specific information to support his claims.

ENCLOSURE ATTACHED

He was not heard from again, however, until September 27, 1945, at which time he furnished the following additional information:

He said that a boyhood chum of his from Wichita, Kansas, BLOYCE FITZGERALD, had been TESLA'S protege and one of the inventors few confidents. According to ▇▇▇▇▇ FITZGERALD who is now an Army Private stationed at Wright Field, Dayton, Ohio, is a brilliant 29 year old scientist who spent endless hours with TESLA prior to the latters death, during which time TESLA explained to him most secret experiments. ▇▇▇▇▇ stated that FITZGERALD met TESLA in November 1942, but he had been corresponding with the latter since 1935. According to the informant, FITZGERALD had developed some sort of anti-tank gun, the details of which he presented to TESLA who made certain corrections in design and specifications to further perfect the weapon.

▇▇▇▇▇ related that sometime in December 1942, when FITZGERALD was attending a meeting of the AMERICAN SOCIETY OF MECHANICAL ENGINEERS, he made the acquaintance of ABRAHAM SPANEL who became interested in FITZGERALD'S

RETURN TO
INDEXING DESK

Letter, DIRECTOR,
NY 65-12290   r 17, 1945

gun. SPANEL offered financial aid to FITZGERALD and the two were in the closest contact with each other for a considerable period of time. ▇▇▇▇ said that FITZGERALD had lined up a deal for the purchase of the gun by the REMINGTON ARMS COMPANY, but for some reason SPANEL blocked this deal by reaching top men in the REMINGTON COMPANY. SPANEL is then reported as having obtained a job for FITZGERALD with the HIGGENS SHIP BUILDING COMPANY in New Orleans and negotiated a contract with FITZGERALD for the purchase and manufacture of the gun in a manner which would return 80% of the profits derived to SPANEL.

▇▇▇▇ stated that in November of 1943, for some unknown reason but which he believes to be attributable to SPANEL, FITZGERALD was fired by the HIGGENS COMPANY. In September of 1944, FITZGERALD was inducted into the Army and for a considerable period of time was located at an ordinance experimental station at Elgin Field, Florida. ▇▇▇▇ stated that at the present time FITZGERALD is engaged in a highly secret experimental project at Wright Field in Dayton, Ohio. In spite of his rank of Private, FITZGERALD actually is the director of this research and is working with many top young scientists who were inducted into Army from leading industrial posts.

According to ▇▇▇▇ FITZGERALD is presently working on the perfection of TESLA'S "death ray" which in FITZGERALD'S opinion is the only possible defense against offensive use by another nation of the Atomic Bomb. In this connection, it is noted that the New York Times of September 22, 1940 in an article entitled "SCIENCE IN THE NEWS" by WILLIAM A. LAURENCE, Science Editor states that TESLA divulged to LAURENCE the fact that he had developed a "death ray" or "teleforce" which TESLA claimed would melt airplane motors at a distance of 250 miles, so that actually an invisible Chinese Wall would be built around a country against attack by an enemy air force.

According to the article in the TIMES, this electrical device would operate by the generation of power from a plant, a number of which might be located strategically along our coast lines and the beam from which would melt any engine within a radius of 250 miles.

▇▇▇▇ stated that during FITZGERALD'S acquaintance with SPANEL, FITZGERALD had told SPANEL of his associations with TESLA and had apparently described to SPANEL some of TESLA'S most secret work. ▇▇▇▇ believes that SPANEL, who he claims is definitely pro-Russian in attitude, is now attempting through legal procedure to secure custody of TESLA'S effects which are now held by TESLA'S only heir, one SAVA KOSANOVICH, who is presently in Yugoslavia occupying some governmental post.

It will be recalled that in an article published on March 15, 1945, by the KING FEATURE SYNDICATE INCORPORATED, WESTBROOK PEGLER charged SPANEL with spreading pro-communist and pro-Russian propaganda through his full page advertisement in the newspapers, which SPANEL characterized as being published for the INTERNATIONAL LATEX CORPORATION, as a public service feature. It is also interesting to observe that in the New York Times of October 2, 1945, an article appears which states that SPANEL is suing the KING FEATURE SYNDICATE INCORPORATED for six million dollars alleging the column by PEGLER to have been libelous.

Letter- Director, FBI
NY 65-12290   October 17, 1945

███████████ stated that through FITZGERALD he too had met SPANEL
and from this personal acquaintance he formed the opinion that SPANEL was
definitely a communist and is probably one of the financial supporters of
the Communist Party in this country. ███████████ stated that SPANEL was
born in Russia, but is now an American citizen. He also charged that SPANEL
exerted tremendous political influence in Washington, D. C., and said that
one of SPANEL'S closest political friends was HENRY WALLACE.

███████████ advised that two agents from Army Intelligence contacted
and stated that in an investigation to determine the qualifications of
FITZGERALD for a commission, they had developed information indicating that
SPANEL was definitely endeavoring to secure possession of TESLA'S effects.
███████████ indicated that Army Intelligence was pursuing an investigation
along these lines in an attempt to ascertain the complete story in this
regard.

For the Bureau's information, ███████████ was born on
at ███████ is ███████ and ███ family resides in ███████
He is a graduate of ███████ and ███████ had been
████ of ███████ from ███████
had been ███████████████████████████████████
and was in charge of ███████████████████ of the
███████ at present is ███████, however, he appears to have ample
funds since he travels all over the country and resides in reputable hotels.
Just recently he stated that he had ███████████████████ from
Washington to the West Coast as ███████████████████
He advised that it is his desire to cooperate with FITZGERALD in securing
legal possession of TESLA'S effects in order that a memorial foundation may
be established for the protection of TESLA'S experiments and for the preservation of the inventors memory.

███████████ stated that FITZGERALD had interested a group of young
Army scientists now working with him at Wright Field in this foundation, and
their ultimate goal is to secure the support of a wealthy backer in order that
a foundation might be established and that a sort of "idea factory" might
result. He said that they intended to contact HENRY FORD, SR., to solicit
his aid in this regard.

███████████ related that probably the greatest idea of TESLA'S was
that involving the wireless transmission of electrical power. He claimed
that TESLA had performed a successful experiment many years ago at Pikes
Peak, at which time he harnessed local current from the sun's rays which he
built up into a huge potential of electrical energy ███████████ said that
according to FITZGERALD, if this idea could be furthered, all electrical
energy to operate the world's machinery might be gotten absolutely free rather
than by the costly method with which electrical power is presently generated.
He said that his idea was to conduct further experiments along this line
in China where the need for electrical power is very great.

Inquiry was made at the MANHATTAN STORAGE WAREHOUSE in New York City,
and it was determined that the effects of NIKOLA TESLA are contained in some

-3-

Letter, Director,
65-12290
er 17, 1945

75 packing cases and trunks and are presently under seal by the New York State Department of Taxation. It was learned that the rental for this storage, which approximates $15 per month, is being paid by one CHARLOTTE MUZAR, 134 East 63rd Street, New York, New York, who is listed as the agent for SAVA KOSANOVICH.

Inquiry was also made at the office of the Alien Property Custodian in New York City, concerning an investigation conducted by this office at the time of TESLA'S death, and at which time the latter's property was placed under seal by the United States Government. Mr. WALTER GORSUCH, Chief Investigator for the Alien Property Custodian, provided a cover letter and a summary of materials owned by TESLA at the time of his death which was examined by JOHN G. TRUMP, of the office of SCIENTIFIC RESEARCH & DEVELOPMENT. Mr. GORSUCH also stated that his file in this matter reflected that on the night TESLA died his safe was forced open by a representative of the SHORE & WALKER SAFE COMPANY. It was Mr. GORSUCH'S belief that a Mr. SWEEZEY who is believed to be one of the editors of the POPULAR SCIENCE MAGAZINE was present in TESLA'S room shortly after the safe was opened. These individuals were WILLIS GEORGE, EDWARD PALMER, and JOHN J. CORBETT.

There are enclosed herewith two typewritten copies of the report by Mr. TRUMP of the ALIEN PROPERTY CUSTODIAN reflecting the findings of Mr. TRUMP, following his examination of TESLA'S effects. There is also enclosed herewith a photostatic copy of a list of persons associated with NIKOLA TESLA. This latter item was furnished by ▇▇▇▇▇▇▇▇▇▇▇▇ b7C

The above information is furnished for the Bureau's information, and no investigation is being conducted by this office.

Very truly yours,

E. E. CONROY, SAC

3 Enclosures

Address writer at:

Mass. Inst. of Tech.,
Cambridge, Mass.
January 30, 1943.

13810

Mr. Walter Gorsuch,
Alien Property Custodian,
120 Broadway,
New York, New York.

Dear Sir:

At your request and that of Mr. Joseph T. King of the Washington office of the Alien Property Custodian, I have examined the private papers, writings, and other property of the late Dr. Nikola Tesla with the view to determining both their possible usefulness to this country in its war effort and the possible hazard attendant on their falling into unfriendly hands.

This examination was made at the Manhattan Warehouse, 52nd Street, New York City, on January 26-27, and included all of the notes and material in Dr. Tesla's immediate possession at the time of his death and now in the custody of your office. For reasons indicated below, no investigation was made of material in trunks which had remained untouched in the basement of the New Yorker Hotel for ten years prior to Dr. Tesla's death.

As a result of this examination, it is my considered opinion that there exist among Dr. Tesla's papers and possessions no scientific notes, descriptions of hitherto unrevealed methods or devices, or actual apparatus which could be of significant value to this country or which would constitute a hazard in unfriendly hands. I can therefore see no technical or military reason why further custody of the property should be retained.

For your records, there has been removed to your office a file of various written material by Dr. Tesla which covers typically and fairly completely the ideas with which he was concerned during his later years. These documents are enumerated and briefly abstracted in the attachment to this letter.

COPIES DESTROYED
148   OCT 26 1966

000005

WG   -2-   January 30, 1943.

It should be no discredit to this distinguished engineer and scientist whose solid contributions to the electrical art were made at the beginning of the present century to report that his thoughts and efforts during at least the past fifteen years were primarily of a speculative, philosophical, and somewhat promotional character—often concerned with the production and wireless transmission of power—but did not include new sound, workable principles or methods for realising such results.

                         Very truly yours,

                                   JOHN G. TRUMP,
                                   Technical Aide,
                                   Division 14, NDRC.

Enclosure.

JGT/G

ABSTRACTS OF DR. NIKOLA TESLA'S WRITINGS
RETAINED AS EXHIBITS
FOR THE ALIEN PROPERTY CUSTODIAN

1.

On January 26 and 27, 1943, an examination was made of the technical papers of Dr. Nikola Tesla which, after his decease, had been stored in the Manhattan Warehouse in New York City. This examination was made for the purpose of determining if any ideas of significant value in the present United States war effort could be found among his possessions. Participating in this examination were Mr. John C. Newington, New York Office of the Alien Property Custodian; Mr. Charles J. Hedetniemi, Washington Office of the Alien Property Custodian; Dr. John G. Trump, Office of Scientific Research and Development, Massachusetts Institute of Technology, Cambridge, Massachusetts; Willis George, Office of Naval Intelligence, Third Naval District; Edward Palmer, Chief Yeoman, USNR; John J. Corbett, Chief Yeoman, USNR.

2.

The following papers, which are regarded as typical of Nikola Tesla's writings and thoughts in the period of 1925 to 1942, were removed for the purpose of record and are listed below in the random order in which they were found, together with a brief individual abstract.

Exhibit A

"Possibilities of Electrostatic Generators" - an undated article probably written about 1934 discussing the possibilities, as a source of high-voltage D-C power, of the Van de Graaff type of electrostatic belt generator. The article states correctly the electrostatic principles employed in this device and points out that such generators are not suitable for commercial high-power applications, though of undoubted scientific value. Tesla's wireless tower, erected in 1902 on Long Island, is stated in this memorandum to have been charged to 30 million volts.

Exhibit B

"Reactive Forces of Glycerine and Dynamite" - an undated memorandum involving some calculations of the explosive power of certain compounds and then deviating to a discussion of the possibility of transmitting power by mechanical vibrations along the earth's crust.

000007

Exhibit C

"Process of De-Gassifying, Refining, and Purifying Metals" - a 41-page memorandum probably written about 1930 dealing with the above subject and proposing new theories of capillarity and surface tension. This correspondence indicated that this had been submitted to various industrial companies.

Exhibit D

"Reply to Amtorg re 'the generation of high-voltage and the acceleration of charged particles'" - This document, dated November 8, 1935, answers questions raised by Soviet engineers and scientists regarding Tesla's proposal of May 16, 1935. From this answer, it is deduced that the proposal concerned the generation of high voltages by electrostatic means. These means consisted of a high-voltage terminal presumably supported on an insulating column and charged by a gaseous charge conveying medium passing between ground and terminal. The ideas contained in this memorandum are fairly similar to the belt-conveyor electrostatic generator methods proposed by Van de Graaff and do not appear to offer any unusual features.

Exhibit E

"Art of Telegeodynamics, or Art of Producing Terrestrial Motions at Distance" - This document, in the form of a letter dated June 12, 1940, to the Westinghouse Electric & Manufacturing Company, proposes a method for the transmission of large amounts of power over vast distances by means of mechanical vibrations of the earth's crust. The source of power is a mechanical or electromechanical device bolted to some rocky protuberance and imparting power at a resonance frequency of the earth's crust. The proposed scheme appears to be completely visionary and unworkable. Westinghouse's reply indicates their polite rejection of this idea.

Exhibit F

"New Art of Projecting Concentrated Non-Dispersive Energy through Natural Media" - This undated document by Tesla describes an electrostatic method of producing very high voltages and capable of very great power. This generator is used to accelerate charged particles, presumably electrons. Such a beam of high-energy electrons passing through air is the "concentrated non-dispersive" means by which energy is transmitted through natural media. As a component of this apparatus there is described an open-ended vacuum tube within which the electrons are first accelerated.

000008

Exhibit F (cont.)

The proposed scheme bears some relation to present means for producing high-energy cathode rays by the cooperative use of a high-voltage electrostatic generator and an evacuated electron acceleration tube. It is well known, however, that such devices, while of scientific and medical interest, are incapable of the transmission of large amounts of power in non-dispersed beams over long distances. Tesla's disclosures in this memorandum would not enable the construction of workable combinations of generator and tube even of limited power, though the general elements of such a combination are succinctly described.

Exhibit G

A circular by Carol Bird, dated September 10, 1938, entitled "Tremendous New Power Soon to Be Unleashed". This describes in popular style some biographical information concerning Nikola Tesla and some ideas for the transmission of power on which he is stated to be working. It appears that the method of transmission is by the mechanical resonance method outlined in Exhibit F, above.

Exhibit H

This exhibit consists of a series of letters to representatives of the British Government dated August 28, 1936; October 26, 1937; December 15, 1937; and April 5, 1938. It includes a reply dated January 7, 1938, from the British Government. These letters offer to the British Government, for a fee, the disclosure of a means for accelerating to high energies minute particles. Such beams would constitute a death ray capable of the protection of Great Britain from air attack.

The method proposed is essentially that described in Exhibit F above. Following the initial letter dated August 28, 1936, the subsequent letters attempt to clear up the "misunderstandings" of the British representatives and to expedite their acceptance of the Tesla proposal. The British reply dated January 7 is a polite expression of disinterest in the proposal.

Exhibit I

An undated memorandum written after Tesla's 79th birthday describing several discoveries which he believed he had made. The first related to a dynamic theory of gravity which is described as not yet completed. The second stated as a physical truth the belief that "there is no energy in matter other than that received from the environment". This second statement, which is discussed at length in this and other writings of Tesla, indicates his disbelief in the existence of atomic or nuclear energy.

Exhibit J

"A Method of Producing Powerful Radiations" - an undated memorandum in Tesla's handwriting describing "a new process of generating powerful rays or radiations". The memorandum reviews the works of Lenard and Crookes, describes Tesla's work on the production of high voltages, and finally in the last paragraph gives the only description of the invention contained in the memorandum. This description is as follows: "Briefly stated, my new simplified process of generating powerful rays consists in creating through the medium of a high-speed jet of suitable fluid a vacuous space around a terminal of a circuit and supplying the same with currents of the required tension and volume".

Exhibit K

A letter to prospective licensees on telegeodynamics dated December 27, 1941. This is a single-page letter with the typewritten signature of Dr. Nikola Tesla, in which he addresses himself to the prospective licensees of telegeodynamics, states that over a half million dollars was spent on this development with funds contributed by the Morgans, Crawford, J. J. Astor, and Fish, as well as commercial organizations, and states this to be a new art with which "unbelievable wonders can be achieved".

Exhibit L

Tesla's "New System of Fluid Propulsion". This is an undated memorandum of about 20 typewritten pages describing a system of fluid propulsion in which the conversion from hydraulic to rotary mechanical power is achieved by passing the fluid between flat circular disks, shaft-mounted and enclosed in a casing.

This memorandum written about 1925 describes in general terms a kind of hydraulic turbine which seems practical. There is copious evidence among the other of Tesla's papers that this idea was generally disclosed to appropriate individuals and that it received favorable comment and possibly some use. Some of these comments are contained on the last page of the exhibit.

Exhibit M

"The Power of the Future" - a memorandum apparently written by Tesla and probably in response to a request from some popular science group for an opinion as to the source of future power. This memorandum reviews the gradual evolution of power sources. It discusses in some detail the possibility of atomic power and states as his opinion that atomic power is not feasible. The discussion of atomic energy is apparently confused to some extent

000010

Exhibit M (cont.)

with planetary energy. The article further discusses the subject of wind, tides, lightning, and water power as a source of commercial energy. The last sentence of this memorandum states: "With my wireless system, it is practicable to transmit electrical energy at a distance of twelve thousand miles with a loss not exceeding 5 per cent. I can conceive of no advances which would be more desirable at this time and more beneficial to the further progress of mankind." This memorandum constitutes an interesting generalized discussion of the various sources of power. It is qualitatively correct for the most part except probably in that portion which deals with atomic power.

Exhibit N

"The Transmission of Electric Energy Without Wires" - an article by N. Tesla in the Electric World, March 5, 1904, pages 429-431. A general, somewhat biographical article on Tesla's early work with some speculation on the possibility of long-distance wireless transmission of large amounts of energy.

Exhibit O

"World System of Wireless Transmission of Energy" - an article by N. Tesla in Telegraph and Telephone Age, October 16, 1927, pages 457 and 460. An article which traces the early work on the production and transmission of electromagnetic radiations, describes Tesla's efforts to increase the amount of power which can be transmitted without wires and concludes with a proposed "World System" for the wireless transmission of both power and communications. No workable disclosure of a means for accomplishing this is included, and such generalities as suggest the approach which Tesla had in mind do not seem capable of accomplishing the desired result.

Exhibit P

"Interview with Dr. Nikola Tesla" by Alden P. Armagnac for Popular Science Monthly, May 24, 1928. An 11-page memorandum written in popular conversational style describing an interview with Dr. Tesla and reporting his present work. This report includes statements on a new airplane, on rocket ships, on the wireless transmission of power, on a world system plan for the transmission of speech and television, on the impracticability of harnessing atomic energy, on radio activity, and on the acceleration of charged particles, such as cathode rays, by high voltages.

Exhibit Q

An agreement dated April 20, 1935, between Nikola Tesla and the Amtorg Trading Corporation, in which Tesla agreed to supply plans, specifications, and complete information on a method and apparatus for producing high voltages up to fifty million volts, for producing very small particles in a tube open to air, for increasing the charge of the particles to the full voltage of the high potential terminal, and for projecting the particles to distances of a hundred miles or more. The maximum speed of the particles was specified as not less than 350 miles per second. The receipt of $25,000 fee for this disclosure was acknowledged in this agreement, which was signed by Nikola Tesla and by A. Bartanian of the Amtorg Trading Corporation. The method referred to in this agreement is apparently that described in Exhibit F, above. It is probable that Exhibit D, above, is an effort by Tesla to clear up the questions raised by Soviet engineers after the subject disclosure had been made. There is no evidence that the inventions and information referred to in this agreement are other than those described in a number of Tesla's papers and published articles. It should therefore be expected, and it is substantiated by Exhibit D, that this disclosure subsequently proved unworkable.

3. An examination of several items of scientific apparatus among the Tesla efforts at the Manhattan Warehouse and in a deposit box at the Governor Clinton Hotel showed those to be standard electrical measuring instruments in common use several decades ago.

JOHN G. TRUMP,
Technical Aide,
Division 14, NDRC.

Mass. Inst. of Tech.,
Cambridge, Mass.,
January 30, 1943.

JGT/G

LIST OF PERSONS ASSOCIATED WITH NIKOLA TESLA

Kerrigan, William - 89 Logan St., Brooklyn, N. Y.
Employed as building supt. Washington Market, Brooklyn. Mr. Kerrigan was the messenger boy for Postal Telegraph some years prior to Jan. 1943. At Mr. Tesla's request, he continued his services as special messenger when convenient. He had called upon Tesla the week prior to his death and has much valuable data and information concerning Tesla's contacts. I first met Mr. Kerrigan at the Frank Campbell funeral church.

Baumgarten, Charles - Room 1203, Municipal Bldg., Budget Bureau, N.Y.C.
Mr. Baumgarten was met at the funeral and Mr. William Lawrence of the New York Times and myself had lunch with him. Mr. Baumgarten knew Tesla and his connections with the Queensboro Bridge and many of his developments of Civic interest.

Skerritt, Miss Dorothy F. - Office, Biddle Purchasing Company, 107 Chambers Street, N.Y.C. - Wo. 2-5500.
Residence: Hasbrook Heights, New Jersey
Miss Skerritt was secretary to Doctor Tesla from 1912 until 1922. She is familiar with the Marconi patent suit, many of Tesla's scientific theories; knows the names of some of his friends; has witnessed demonstrations in his laboratory, then at 8 W. 40th St. N.Y.C. Miss Skerritt also knows that between 1916 and 1918, Doctor Tesla was at the Blackstone Hotel, Chicago and may have material there. She can give account of many of his deals with various firms.

Merrington, Marguerite - 46 W. 97th Street, N.Y.C. - Riverside 9-9186
Miss Merrington has known Doctor Tesla since 1893 and has been a guest of his on several occasions at the old Waldorf Hotel and at his laboratory in 1894 on Houston Street. Miss Merrington recalls the lighting effects without filaments and his radio controlled boat demonstrations. She also recalls statements regarding communication without wires by means of a small instrument. She has witnessed many laboratory experiments including power transmission without wires over short distances in the laboratory and also metallic plate suspension. He had also talked about communication with mars to her.

Holden, Mrs. Agnes, J - 327 E. 52 St. N.Y.C. - Plaza 3-2341
Mrs. Holden is the daughter of Robert U. Johnson (deceased) (1936) who was a close friend of Tesla for many years. Mrs. Holden first met Mr. Tesla at her father's home when she was about 12 years old. The Johnsons were connected with the Century Magazine which published many articles regarding Tesla. Mr. Johnson wrote several poems about Tesla, one of which appeared in the April, 1895 issue of the

Century Magazine and the others appeared in "Poems of 50 years, 1880-1930 by Robert Underwood Johnson. Mrs. Holden has been in close contact with Doctor Tesla and has witnessed many of his demonstrations including that of the oscillator of 1899. She recalls the near destruction of the laboratory. Since "World II", she has talked with Doctor Tesla with regard to instruments of war and he told her in response to her inquiry regarding tanks recently that he could stop them or the war. She recalls his discussions with her and her father regarding transmissions of power and Mars, etc. She says that she knows that Tesla has things for our Government only. Mrs. Holden witnessed many of the experiments and was present at the radio-controlled boat demonstration many years ago.

Lowenstein, Fritz (Deceased) Brother, Emil Lowenstein - 182 Bennett Ave. N.Y.C. - Wa-7-4519. Business (Artist) 420 Lexington Ave. N.Y.C. - Mu-5-8065.
Mr. Fritz Lowenstein was the assistant to Dr. Tesla during his historic laboratory experiments in Colorado Springs in 1899. He was also to have appeared as a defense witness for Tesla in his Marconi patent suits during 1915, but for some reason failed to testify. The brother, Emil, address above, knows of the relatives of Mr. Fritz Lowenstein who have documents pertaining to the 1899 experiments. (Mr. G.H. Clark provided information re documents and Lowenstein) (Mr. Czito mentioned Lowenstein). Mr. Emil Lowenstein is not on friendly terms with the entire Lowenstein family and a Mr. Massey, 52 Vanderbilt Ave. can furnish additional information re Lowenstein.

Shirk, A.J. - Inventor's Model Shop, 70 West 100th St. N.Y.C. Ac-2-9466.
Mr. Shirk has met Tesla on 3 occasions and appears to know quite a bit about his model work and laboratory developments, particularly within recent years. His exact status can only be determined by another call or exact-status interview. He is attempting to determine the address of a Laboratory that existed at about 57th and 3rd Ave. and with whom a certain Dr. Walker was connected.

Arbus, Muriel, Miss - Res: 600 W. 13th St. Tel: Vanderbilt 4-9816, Bus: WPB, Chanin Building, N.Y.C.
Miss Arbus has several photographs of Tesla and was a secretary to him before Miss Dorothy Skerritt, i.e. before 1912. She has not been interviewed except by phone.

-8-

Berg, Seigurd (or Sigmund) - Copenhagen, Denmark. Business: Paris, France. He has not been interviewed. See Mr. E. Fiensen of the International Latex Corp., Dover, Del. for information. Mrs Berg was a close friend of Tesla in Europe and mentioned other members of his family; Mr. Ernest and Mr. Esko Berg are found in correspondence from Mrs. B.A. Behrend to Mr. Kenneth Sweezy in 1935 and 1934.

Behrend, Bernard, A. Mrs. - Rond Point, Aiken, S.C. Phone 135. Mr. Behrend and Mrs. Heaviside were very close friends of Dr. Tesla. Mrs. Behrend has many notes and technical data concerning Tesla's work either stored near Boston, Mass or at Aiken, S.C. Mr. Behrend was Chief Engineer for Westinghouse and supervised the construction of a great number of Tesla's motors and generators. He is author of "The Induction Motor" pub. 1921 in which a considerable portion is devoted to Tesla's work.

Boskan, Slavko, Mr. Engineer and author, Belgrade, Yugoslavia. Mr. Boskan published a book in Dresden, Germany entitled "Nikola und His Werk" in 1932 (Approx) Mr. Boskan was a close friend of Mr. Tesla and has considerable engineering data in his possession according to Mr. Sweezy.

Denton, Clifford, Mr. - Science Reporter.. New York Daily News, 220 E. 42nd St. N.Y.C. Mu-2-1234 Ext. 557 Mr. Denton has been present at many of Dr. Tesla's press releases and has many notes regarding the conferences. He said that he gave most of his data to Mr. Wm. Lawrence of the New York Times.

Brown Brothers (Mr. Arthur Brown) 220 W. 42 St. Bryant 9-4742. N.Y.C. Brown Brothers are photographers and have a large number of photos of Tesla and his laboratory equipment from which may be deduced mechanical construction details.

Curtis, Thomas Stanley - Address: unknown. Author "Experiments with High Frequencyes currents" It is important to locate Mr. Curtis because he discussed many of Tesla's problems and appears to have technical data regarding his work.

Cramps, Shipbuilding Co. Philadelphia, Pa. Mr. Crosby, former Sec. of Commerce, and Mr. Cramps became interested in the radio controlled boat of Dr. Tesla about 35 years ago. Negotiations were carried on between Dr. Tesla and the above executives. This information was furnished by Mr. Kerr.

It may be well to contact Mr. Crosby's relatives or Mr. Cramps.

Czito, Julius - 4629 193rd St. Flushing, Long Island. Tel: Flushing 7-4711.
Mr. Czito was mentioned to me first by Mr. Kosenovich and later Mr. Spanel had received his name from Mr. Wm. Lawrence. Mr. Czito is a machinest by trade and worked for Dr. Tesla as such from 1915 to 1929. He was particularly concerned with the construction of a turbin, and a fountain developed for a Mr. Hatmaker. Among other things, he worked on an extractor for sulpher from sea water and mechanical device for measuring the resistance of a ball bearing. He has little data left of Dr. Tesla's work but has a very good memory. He mentioned the Boston gear works, Mr. Bradley, Mr. Miller, the Zumbach Machinery Co. and Mr. Barney Levi. Mr. Czito's father also worked for Dr. Tesla in 1894 and was with him at his Houston St. laboratory. Mr. Czito, Sr. accompanied Dr. Tesla to Colorado Springs in 1899. Mr. Czito has a very good memory and can furnish additional information. He has discovered a photograph showing all of the employees of the old Tesla laboratory. He worked for Dr. Tesla on the development of a speedometer for the Waltham Watch Co. (This information from interview).

Clark, Mr. Geo. H. - Res: 349 E. 49th St. Tel: El-5-1603. Bus: RCA Mfg. Co. (Library) 25 Beaver St. N.Y.C. Room 314 A, Tel: Hanover 2-1829. Ext 123.
Mr. G.H. Clark was contacted by virtue of a call placed in December to Mr. Oran Dunlap of the RCA Corp. Mr. Clark has a very large collection of personal data pertaining to radio pioneers, particularly Marconi. His business has been to collect such data in order to assist the prosecution of a suit of infringment against the Marconi patents. He has never met Dr. Tesla but he knows of his work and is interested in collecting historical data for preservation. Mr. Clark is a friend of Mr. Sweezy.

Crosby, Former Sec. of Commerce, Washington, D.C.(address unknown)
See Cramps and Kerr

Wetzel, Tailors - 2 E. 44th St. Murry Hill 2-6757. N.Y.C.
This firm was tailor for Dr. Tesla throughout most of his life and may have information with regard to his friends, not otherwise listed.

French, Shriner, and Urner— Shoe Shops. 250 Madison Ave. Murry Hill 2-0319.
N.Y.C.
Dr. Tesla purchased most all of his shoes from this firm for the past 50 years and data may be gathered from their records such as mailing addresses, etc.

Cornels, Fredrick C. F.B.I. Office Federal Court House Bldg. 12th Floor.
Regent 2-2315
Mr. Cornels was informed of the possible value of Dr. Tesla's data immediately following his death. So far as known, no action was taken.

Commercial Photostat Company, 11th Floor, Woolworth Bldg. N.Y.C.
Firm which made photostats of Tesla patents for Kerr.

Cramm, Ernest R. to contact call Mr. Clark of RCA.
Mr. Cramm knows a great deal about Dr. Tesla's relations with the RCA Company. Mr. Cramm was a former employee of RCA.

Gilder, Rodman – 108 E. 82nd St. N.Y.C. Butterfield 8-7397.
Son of Richard Watson Gilder, former Pub. of Century Magazine. Mr. Gilder knows of some old Tesla manuscripts and what has happened to his files of the Century Magazine at its dissolution. This name was received from Merrington.

Denmark, Lt. 1270 6th Ave. Room 811, Circle 6-1484 (restricted number)
N.Y.C. U.S. Army Int. G2.
Lt. Denmark and his superiors were notified by Mr. Spanel and Washington with regard to Tesla devices. Lt. Denmark was interviewed personally with a group of 4 other officers including Mr. Ritchen.

Kirsch, Leon – a former draftsman for Tesla – name from Miss Dorothy Skerritt.
This party should be located because he had a lot of confidential data of Tesla's and made many drawings according to Miss Skerritt.

Drews, Lillian Married to an Austrian by name of DePrec about 1914.
Miss Drews was Secretary to Dr. Tesla prior to 1912. Her present address is unknown and she was not in good favor with Dr. Tesla, according to Miss Skerritt, the informant.

DosPassos, John – Attorney, and very good friend of Dr. Tesla. Address unknown. Wanted Tesla to stop the Spanish American War. Formerly lived in New York. The Gentleman was expensively dressed and wore frocked coat similar to Tesla with bright checkered vest.

-6-

Had office in vicinity of 200 Broadway, as late as 1920. Mr. DosPassos is believed to have engineering data of Tesla's according to Thomas Byrne.

DeForrest, Dr. Lee- 6190 Hollywood Blvd. Los Angeles, Calif. - Dr. DeForrest is still alive and was a friend of Dr. Tesla in the late 90 and early 1900's. There is a possibility that he may be able to assist in interpreting Tesla's works.

Dubilier, William - President of Cornell Dubilier Co., Manufacturers of CCondensers. Mr. G.H. Clark informs that Mr. Dubilier has in his possession some of the original notes of the 1899 experiments in Colorado Springs.

Fradenburg, A.E. A reporter for the Brooklyn Eagle during 1930 who had numerous contacts with Tesla with regard to Power Transmission. His present address is unknown but he formerly resided in Brooklyn until 1934.

Fitzgerald, Francis, A. - Niagara Power Commission, Buffalo, N. Y. Mr. Fitzgerald, according to a personal interview with Dr. Tesla, was a friend of his on the A.C. power proposition for the development of Niagara. He also told me that Mr. Fitzgerald attempted to influence the Canadian Power Commission in 1927 for a project to transmit power without wires. There is a possibility that he may have some data.

Gernsback, Hugo p Publisher, Res; 230 West End Ave. Sohhler 4-2130 Bus: 25 W. Broadway, Tel: Rector 2-9690. A friend of Tesla for about 35 years. Published many articles about Tesla during 1919 in the "Electrical Experimenter and later in Science and Invention." Has many of Tesla's original manuscripts and photos. Believes in all of Tesla's theories and has a working knowledge of them. This party was contacted several weeks prior to Dr. Tesla's death. Mr. Gernsback attempted to assist Dr. Tesla personally and appealed to Westinghouse for funds in 1933.

Hammond, John Hayes, Jr. Glochester, Mass. Tel. 2080 Mr. Hammond, Sr., financed some of Dr. Tesla's boat experiments and only 10 years ago John Hayes Hammond, Jr. operated one of Tesla's original models. The family has one of the boats in their possession now. Much technical data can be gathered from this source.

Hassell, Eugene Floyd - Res: Belport, Long Island
Machinest, Sperry Gyroscope Company, Garden City, L.I. Employee Number 5470, Phone Vigilent 4-5400 (Restricted number) Ext. 211. Use any New York Phone. Name from Czito. This party knows of Tesla's laboratory on Long Island through the laundry driver named Tommy Wallen.

Hobbs, Octavious - Springfield Gardens, Long Island.
(Has not been contacted)

Hatmaker, (no initials) party who financed fountain built by Czito. Has not been contacted, but he lived in the St. Regis Hotel in 1920.

Kosonovich, Sava - Navarro Hotel, apt. 17B. 112 Central park south, N.Y.C.
Tel: Circle 7-7900, Office- Regent 7-4662. President of the Central European Powers Association and former Minister of Yugoslavia to the U.S. Mr. K. is one of the two living nephews of Dr. Nikola Tesla (see Nikola Trbjevich) Mr. K. was present in the Hotel New Yorker on the morning following Dr. Tesla's death. Others present were K.K. Sweezy, G.H. Clark. Mr. K. knows of many blue prints that were in the rooms and a black notebook with several hundred pages containing the last notes of Dr. Tesla. Mr. K. says that some of the papers were marked "Government" and that Dr. Tesla had told him he had valuable information. Mr. K. is of the opinion that it may have been for the Yugoslav Gov't. He says that no will was found. His attorney is Mr. Wittenberg. He was appointed heir by the Surrogates Court of New York County. He said that the other nephew waived any interest. Mr. K. is not in accord with Mr. Fotich, present Ambassador of Yugloslavia to U.S., now in Washington. There is a bit of political unrest in the Yugoslav organization.

Kerr, John - Attorney, 233 Broadway, N.Y.C. Cooper Kerr Dunham (att. at Law)
Courtland 7-9334 - also associated by Byrns. This firm was the patent attorney for 112 of the Tesla patents. They also instituted the proceedings of the infringement suits for the Westinghouse Company. Mr. Kerr knew Tesla very well and can give considerable data. Mr. Cooper, now deceased, was however, the main instigator of the patents for Tesla. Mr. Cooper left this firm some time ago and Tesla apparently took some of his business

to the new Cooper associates. Many of the old patents of Tesla in his own handwriting are available at this office. Mr. Byrne has additional information. I am of the opinion that this firm still has a connection with Westinghouse.

Byrne, Thomas, J works for Cooper Kerr and Dunham (see John Kerr above). Mr. Byrne knew Tesla very well and also knows of the connections with the Union Sulpher Company and the turbine for which see Czito. There is a wealth of information in the office of this company regarding the system of Power Transmission and any patents on file which were never issued. Mr. Kerr and Mr. Byrne were contacted before Mr. Tesla's death.

Kostich (first name unknown) New York, Official photographer for the Yugoslav group. Office believed to be 235 E. 72nd St. and Residence in Long Island City. He may be reached through Regent 7-4662. He is a friend of Mr. Kosonovich.

Kulishich, Prof. Kosta Res: Belgrad, Yugoslovia at the Tesla Institute. He was a school mate of Tesla in Grotz. See the N.Y. Sun of August 27, 1931.

Gage, E. G. 111 Nassau St. N.Y.C. Engineer, works for Leon Ottinger, Courtland 7-5500.
He was a friend of Mr. J.S. Leach (deceased) formerly of Redbank, N. Y. who made electrical parts for Tesla's laboratory. He says that he can get information regarding Leach's relatives and perhaps drawings.

Levi, Bernard - Machinest, Zumbach Machinery Co. 134 W. 54 St. N.Y.C. Circle 7-1444
Received this name from Czito who said that Levi knew of other work by machinests on Tesla's equipment.

Lucan, John - address unknown - presumed to be in Manhattan. A former Western Union Messenger boy during June of 1937 who has other data regarding recent contacts by Tesla during his services as a messenger. He has not been located.

Lynch, Arthur. Lived in England. Believed to be near London, now deceased. Family had considerable correspondence with Tesla regarding transmission of power without wires.

Lawrence, William. Science Writer, New York Times. 229 W. 43 St. N.Y.C. Lackawanna 4-1000. Res: 541 E. 72nd St. Rhinelander 4-5588.

-9-

A friend of Tesla's for about 25 years. Has much old data regarding Tesla and has talked to him on many occasions regarding power transmission and the war effort. Has Assisted greatly in providing information for gathering material, etc. This party was contacted before Dr. Tesla's death.

Lassie, M.C. 62 Vanderbilt Ave. N.Y.C.

Maier, Ruth N. The Yugo Slow Society, 565 5th Ave. Room 807. Pl-8-0256
This is the information center and serves as the publicity agent for the group.
Miss E. Oppa also works there and has many names of Tesla's friends.

Martin, Octavo. Employee of Hotel New Yorker and friend of Tesla.

Matthews, Grenville (deceased) wife was Gana Walker, Met. Star sponsored by McCormick. The family lived in England until his eath and his wife now resides in New York. Mr. Matthews was refered to in Tesla's articles for the Telephone and Telegraph Age for Oct. 1927. Mr. Matthews had correspondence with Tesla on the so-called "Death-Ray". Gana Walker has all of her husband's data.

Mott, C. Jordan, Jr. 620 E. 90th St. N.Y.C. Bus: 6 E. 45th St.
Tel: Vanderbilt 6-0345.
The Mott family financed Tesla in various ventures. They may have some of this data.

Gossett, W. O. Ford Museum, Detroit, Mich.
Mr. Gossett is associated with a Mr. Black while he is on leave of absence to the Army. Mr. Black may be reached regarding some models of Tesla's which are understood to be on display at the Ford Museum.

Nathan, Thoma, A. 25 E. 83rd St. N.Y.C.
We do not know what connection this party had with Tesla but his name was secured.

O'Neill, John, J. Res: 209 N. Long Beach Ave. Freeport, Long Island.
Tel: Freeport 2-493.
Science editor of the New York Herald Tribune, 230 W. 41 St. N.Y.C. Pennsylvania 6-4000.
Mr. O'Neill has known Dr. Tesla for 40 years. He has had many discussions with him regarding his equipment and scientific ventures. He interested Dr. Tesla in 1934 and 1935 to present the matter of national protection devices to the U.S. Govt. Mr. O'Neill made

-10-

a few contacts and the matter was dropped. Mr. O'Neill has notes of 1938 and 1939 wherein Dr. Tesla declared he had been approached by the British Govt. through Stanley Baldwin and Neville Chamerlain to negotiate for one of his devices. Mr. O'Neill thought that the sum offered was for 30 millions of dollars. In the interview, Dr. Tesla stated that his device would operate over a range of 200-250 miles. Mr. O'Neill is of the opinion that Tesla had unusual powers. Mr. Lawrence is of the opinion that he does not know what he is talking about. O'Neill can furnish much additional information.

Pickard, Dr. Greenlief Whittier.. 59 Dalton St. Newton Center, Mass.
Dr. Pickard was a very good friend of Dr. Tesla. Dr. Pickard developed the vertical antenna system and has correspondence with Tesla concerning "wave propagation". This information should be valuable.

Sarony, Inc. Photographers, 362 5th Ave. N.Y.C. Wis 7-1713
They have photos of the old Tesla Laboratory and pictures of Tesla to 1914.

Page, Parker W. Attorney. Present address unknown, however he resided in Manhattan for about 40 years and was formerly associated with Cooper Kerr and Durham. He was last known to be associated with an attorney by the name of Bean in Manhattan. He worked out many of Tesla's details concerning Power Transmission and Tesla gave him many notes according to Mr. Kerr.

Radosavljevich, Paul, R. New York University, Professor, Education Dept.
Tel: Spring 7- 2000.
A friend of Tesla for 35 years and knows much of his work with regard to the retina and bile chemistry.

Ritchen, (first name unknown) Anti-Trust Division, Custodian of Alien Property, 18th Floor, 120 Broadway, N.Y.C. Regent 2-3582 (restricted number). Mr. Ritchen supervised the various agents who were responsible for the sealing of the property in the Manhattan warehouse and various hotels. On Saturday eve., January 10, 1943. This office worked with Lt. Denmark.

Astor, Mrs. John Jacob (Lady Ribblesdale) now living in the U.S.
420 Park Ave., Plaza 9-6646
Lady Ribblesdale is the Mother of Vincent Astor who financed many of Tesla's developments about 1910 and their family may have data of importance.

-11-

Secor, Harry. Island Road, Ramsey, N. J. Res. Business: Model Craftsman Publication. Ramsey, New Jersey. Tel: Ramsey 519. This party knew Dr. Tesla very well and I talked to him several weeks prior to Tesla's death. He has some plans of Tesla equipment.

Sweezy, Kenneth, M. 163 Milton St. Brooklyn, N. Y. Evergreen 9-5809
Mr. Sweezy has known Dr. Tesla for approximately 15 years. He became a close confident of his on many things and did a very notable work in 1935 when he arranged for a collection of 100 letters from various scientific authorities commemorating Tesla's 75th birthday. Mr. Sweezy wrote many articles about Dr. Tesla and has some old clippings and miscellaneous data including several books detailing Tesla's work. Mr. Sweezy corresponded with Mr. Boskan and Mrs. Behrand. He is a friend of Mr. Clark. Mr. Sweezy would like to write a book of Tesla's life and had spoken to with Dr. Tesla regarding it. I contacted Mr. Sweezy several weeks before Dr. Tesla's death. (Much information can be obtained here).

Scott, Prof. Charles F. Instructor of Electrical Engineering, Yale University, New Haven, Conn.
Prof. Scott was a friend of Tesla for about 43 years. He worked as an electrician with Tesla in the early days and knows a great deal about his work. Prof. Scott and Tesla did not enjoy close friendship during recent years because Prof. Scott could not understand in full, all of Tesla's work. More information can be obtained here.

Scherff, George, Mrs. 219 Grant Terrace, Maroneck, N. Y.
Mrs. Scherff was the auditor for Tesla for many years and has much information to give. She has information concerning Tesla's personal things and technical data and can provide much of value, including old documents.

Skerrett, John. Author- believed to be from Philadelphia, Pa. who witnessed many of Tesla's demonstrations. Miss Dorothy Skerrett can furnish additional information regarding him.

CC-247

Mr. Tolson	
Mr. Clegg	
Mr. Glavin	
Mr. Ladd	
Mr. Nichols	
Mr. Rosen	
Mr. Tracy	
Mr. Egan	
Mr. Gurnea	
Mr. Harbo	
Mr. Mohr	
Mr. Pennington	
Mr. Quinn Tamm	
Mr. Nease	
Miss Gandy	

June 8, 1949

MEMORANDUM FOR MR. WHITSON

RE: SAVA N. KOSANOVIC
     YUGOSLAV AMBASSADOR TO THE US
     INTERNAL SECURITY - R
     (Bureau file 65-47953)

ALL INFORMATION CONTAINED
HEREIN IS UNCLASSIFIED
DATE 4-15-89 BY SP1NK6 cm

PURPOSE

This memorandum is submitted to incorporate all the pertinent references in the Bureau files concerning the entitled individual who is the Yugoslav Ambassador to the United States.

A case was opened on this individual when information was received that Kosanovic had taken possession of the scientific papers of his uncle, Nikola Tesla, the internationally known inventor. Subsequent investigation determined that Kosanovic had turned over the possession of these scientific papers to the Alien Enemy Custodian in New York City.
(65-47953-X1 & Serial 3 & 4)

Sava N. Kosanovic was interviewed in either April or May, 1948, for the purpose of ascertaining whether or not the Serbian National Federation should be required to register under the Foreign Agents Registration Act.
(97-1340-178, pg.5)

Pertinent information concerning this individual has been properly forwarded to the State Department by separate letters.

The main file on Kosanovic contains only two reports, one of which was sent to the Attorney General by letter dated December 13, 1943, (other report not pertinent). This case is currently in a pending status.

C. J. Myrtle

65-47953-21X

cc - Mr. Ladd
cc - Mr. Fletcher
cc - Whitson
cc - Mr. Myrtle

CJM:jpa

THIS MEMORANDUM IS FOR ADMINISTRATIVE PURPOSES TO BE DESTROYED AFTER ACTION IS TAKEN AND NOT SENT TO FILES

Office Memorandum • UNITED STATES GOVERNMENT

TO : The Director
FROM : D. M. Ladd
SUBJECT: SAVA N. KOSANOVIC
INTERNAL SECURITY - YU
Bureau File 65-47953

DATE: April 3, 1950

ALL INFORMATION CONTAINED
HEREIN IS UNCLASSIFIED
DATE 4-18-89 BY SP/AGLC
291860

Reference is made to my memorandum dated March 29, 1950, relating to the telephone inquiry by the Yugoslav Ambassador Sava N. Kosanovic as to the possibility of obtaining a copy of a microfilm copy of the technical papers of the late Nikola Tesla, world-famous scientist who died in New York in 1943.

Kosanovic claims to have been a nephew of Tesla and is known to have tried to obtain these papers at the time of Tesla's death. However, they were taken over at that time by the Alien Property Custodian. If any copies were made of these papers, they were made by the Office of the Alien Property Custodian which took possession of Tesla's papers in 1943 or the Department of the Army which was interested in copying Tesla's notes in 1945. The Army's interest apparently was developed by a young scientist named Bloyce Fitzgerald who had been a protege of Tesla and one of his few confidants. Fitzgerald, who knew that Tesla had been endeavoring to perfect the wireless transmission of electrical current, one of the basic concepts involved in the production of a "Death Ray" had subsequently entered the Army, and in October, 1945, appeared at our New York Office, together with three other members of the United States Army, to request our assistance in obtaining access to Tesla's papers which were stored in a warehouse of the Manhattan Storage Company. Fitzgerald and his associates were referred, at that time, to the Alien Property Custodian which was reported to have made an investigation of Tesla's belongings following the latter's death.

Although the Office of Alien Property or the Department of the Army might be able to furnish a copy of Tesla's papers to Kosanovic, it is not believed that the FBI should facilitate his search for this material, which although possibly of no present value from a National Defense standpoint, could still conceivably be of assistance to the Yugoslav Government.

COPIES DESTROYED
148 OCT 26 1960

65-47953-25

RECOMMENDATIONS:

1. That the attached letter explaining that we have never had such a copy as he requests, be sent to Mr. Kosanovic.

2. That the attached memo to the New York Office, instructing them to make further inquiry at the Manhattan Storage Company and advising that firm that we have no copy of Tesla's papers as they allegedly claim, be forwarded.

Freedom of Information Release

On

Subject: Nikola Tesla

Cross References
Pages Reviewed - 127
Pages Released - 127

Federal Bureau of Investigation

MEMORANDUM—TESLA ESTATE

4/17/1950

STANDARD FORM NO. 64

Office Memorandum • UNITED STATES GOVERNMENT

TO : Director, FBI

FROM : SAC, New York

DATE: April 17, 1950

SUBJECT: SAVA N. KOSANOVIC
INTERNAL SECURITY-YU
(Bufile 65-47953)

ALL INFORMATION CONTAINED
HEREIN IS UNCLASSIFIED
DATE 2-3-80 BY ___

Rebulet dated April 3 last.

On April 7, 1950 agents of this office interviewed Mr. J.V. POTTS, Vice President of the Manhattan Warehouse and Storage Company, 52nd Street & 7th Avenue, New York City, and at that time MR. POTTS advised that the rules of his firm required that all persons gaining access to goods stored by Manhattan first had to fill out an appropriate form setting forth their names, date of visit, and reason for requesting access to the goods.

In a review of the file pertaining to the storage of the effects of NIKOLA TESLA, MR. POTTS revealed that only one such visit had been made by persons outside of the management of Manhattan Storage itself. This one occasion took place on January 26 and 27, 1943, at which time representatives of the Alien Property Custodian made a thorough review of the entire effects of the TESLA estate.

The TESLA effects are stored in rooms 5J and 5L of Manhattan Storage's warehouse at 52nd Street & 7th Avenue, New York City. MR. MICHAEL KING, who stated he had been Floor Supervisor for approximately 10 years on the floor in question, stated that he could recall only one occasion in early 1943 when an examination was made of the TESLA effects. He stated that at that time numerous photographs were taken by the examiners. His description of the equipment used would tend to show that a microfilm reproduction was made of some of the papers of the deceased scientist. MR. KING added that several of the group making the examination wore U.S. Navy uniforms, and during the two days required to complete the examination the civilian assistants in the group were identified to him only as "FEDERAL AUTHORITIES". According to Mr. KING, no other instance of microfilming of the records of the TESLA estate has taken place since that time.

It should be noted that the Bureau was informed of the examination mentioned above by New York letter (with attachments) dated October 17, 1945, entitled UNKNOWN SUBJECT; SAVA KOSANOVICH; Experiments & Research of NIKOLA TESLA (Deceased), Espionage-M.

cc: 65-12290

RECORDED - 38
INDEXED - 38

65-47953-27

APR 18 1950

37

Letter to Director, FBI
NY 105-1391

MR. POTTS stated that no inquiry had been received by Manhattan from SAVA N. KOSANOVICH, nor had Manhattan informed him, in any way, that an examination of the TESLA effects had been made by anyone. In fact, added MR. POTTS, the only correspondence relating to the TESLA estate has been in the form of bills for storage.

MR. POTTS stated that any personal inquires regarding the estate would of necessity be directed to him, and to date no such inquiries have been made.

Interviewing agents explained to MR. POTTS that the examination made, as mentioned above, was not instigated by the Bureau, nor had the Bureau taken part in that examination.

Unless advised to the contrary, this investigation is being placed in a closed status, and no further investigative action is contemplated by this office. CLOSED.

Letter to Director, FBI
NY 105-1391

MR. POTTS stated that no inquiry had been received by Manhattan from SAVA N. KOSANOVICH, nor had Manhattan informed him, in any way, that an examination of the TESLA effects had been made by anyone. In fact, added MR. POTTS, the only correspondence relating to the TESLA estate has been in the form of bills for storage.

MR. POTTS stated that any personal inquires regarding the estate would of necessity be directed to him, and to date no such inquiries have been made.

Interviewing agents explained to MR. POTTS that the examination made, as mentioned above, was not instigated by the Bureau, nor had the Bureau taken part in that examination.

Unless advised to the contrary, this investigation is being placed in a closed status, and no further investigative action is contemplated by this office. CLOSED.

ACTIVITIES OF CONSULATE EMPLOYEES

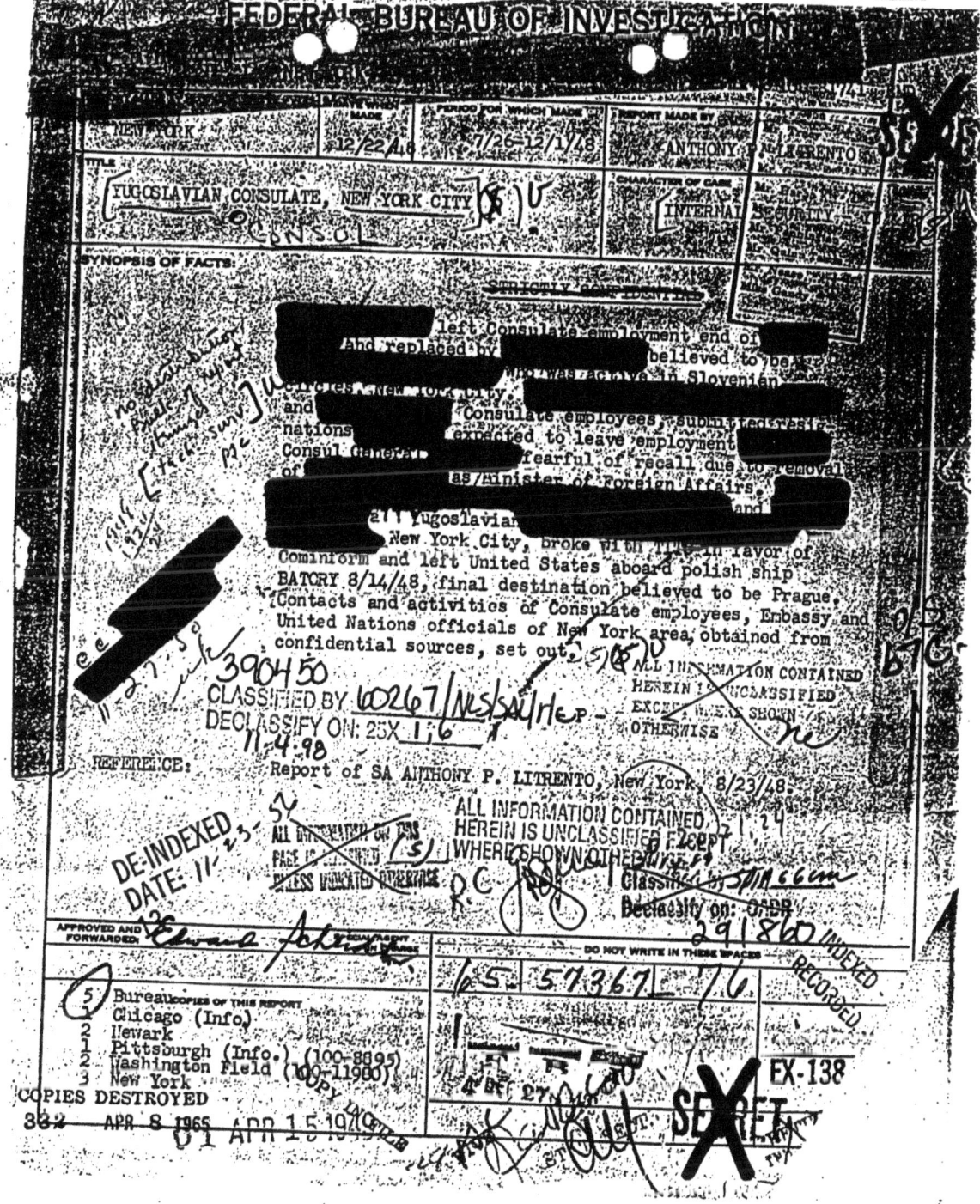

NY 100-81741

█████ also mentioned that █████ would be at the Delegation Home at 7:30 that evening.

On October 11, 1947 █████ made an appointment to meet █████ (phonetic) at 1870 Third Avenue the following Monday after 7:00 p.m.

On October 14, 1947, █████ contacted █████ and said "we have things to talk over so that we know how things stand." They made an appointment to see each other the next morning at 11:00 o'clock.

On October 16, 1947, an unidentified man asked █████ about a Macedonian, █████ (phonetic). █████ requested that the man be sent over to see him.

On October 20, 1947, one █████ advised █████ that he had received a phone call from Pittsburgh, requesting that he contact Ambassador KOSANOVICH. He is to ask KOSANOVICH to prepare a talk on NIKOLA TESLA, the great Yugoslav inventor, which is to be delivered over a Pittsburgh radio station the following Sunday at 2:30 p.m. █████ stated that █████ told him to contact █████ about these arrangements. He also requested that █████ appear at the meeting of the Congress. █████ declined, stating that he had too much work to do.

b7C
b7D

On October 22, 1947, a █████ asked █████ about a visa for a █████ an export-import man who desired to go to Yugoslavia. █████ answered that he would contact the Embassy to see if a passport could be obtained.

On October 23, 1947, an unidentified man advised █████ that he had two Bulgarians who needed visas to go to Montreal via the RADNIK. █████ told the man to come over to the Consulate with them.

On October 30, 1947, one █████ (phonetic) asked █████ about insuring 140,000 pounds of aircraft and radio accessories, with a

- 10 -

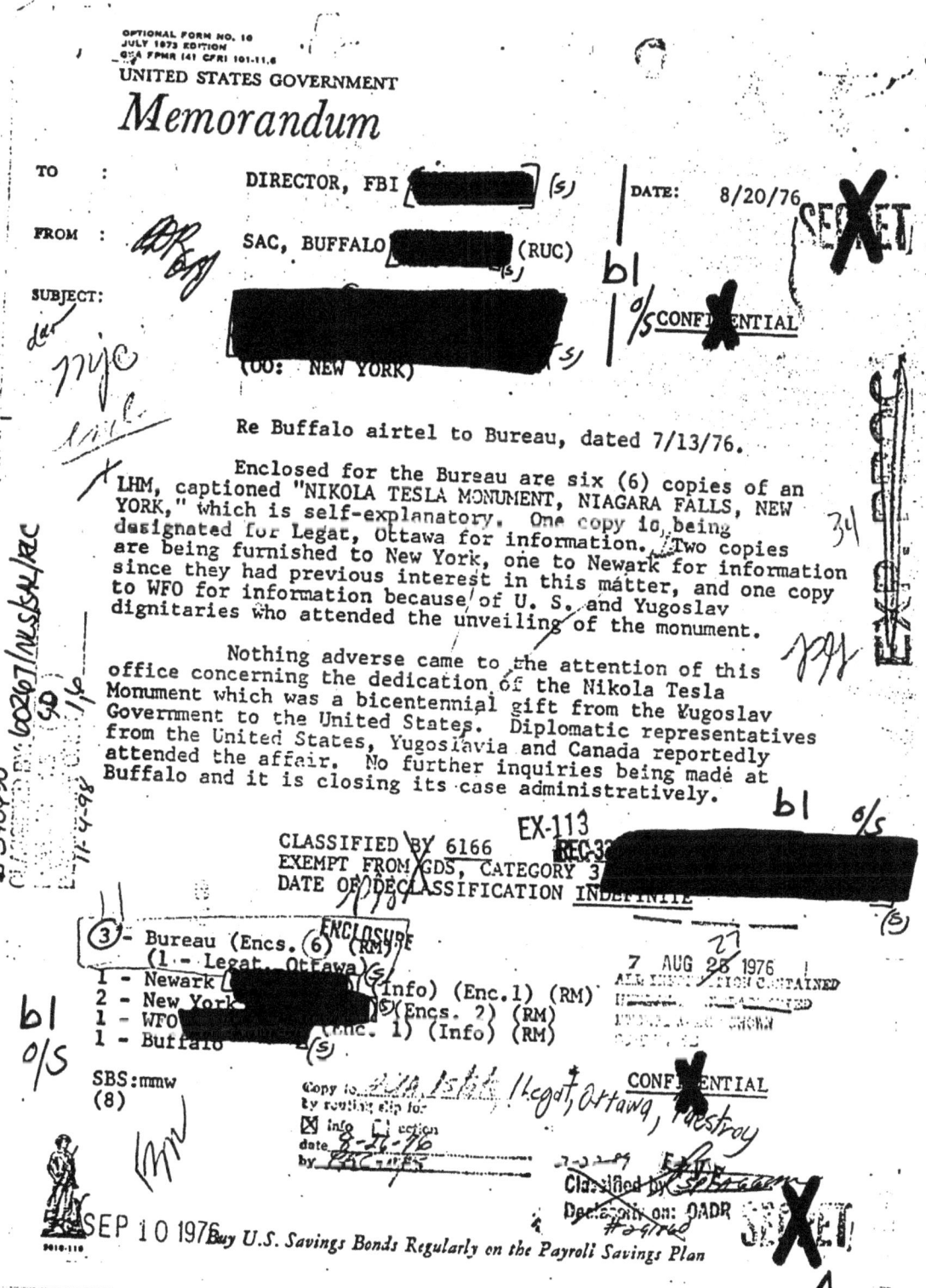

UNITED STATES DEPARTMENT OF JUSTICE

FEDERAL BUREAU OF INVESTIGATION
Buffalo, New York
August 20, 1976

In Reply, Please Refer to
File No.

NIKOLA TESLA MONUMENT / NIAGARA FALLS, NEW YORK

An article appeared in the "Buffalo Evening News," a daily newspaper published in Buffalo, New York, on July 24, 1976, which in part contained the following information:

The article was captioned "Dignitaries Unveil Statue of 'Genius' Tesla."

The article contained information that NIKOLA TESLA was the inventor of the alternating current and the first man to successfully transmit electric power. The background of TESLA set out in the article revealed that he arrived in New York City in 1884 with four cents in his pocket and plans for an airplane and a book of poetry. In 1888, he invented a system to make the transmission of alternating current practical, at 37 was a millionaire but died at the age of 88 in New York City alone and penniless.

The statue, approximately nine feet high, was erected on Goat Island, a site which is located on the property of the New York State Park and Recreation Department.

The article revealed that more than a thousand people listened to FRANK G. ZARB, Federal Energy Administration, representing President FORD, and Dr. IVO MARGAN, President of the Socialist Union of Croatia, representing Yugoslavian President TITO, as both pulled the cord unveiling the nine foot high statue of TESLA.

NIKOLA TESLA
MONUMENT
NIAGARA FALLS, NEW YORK

The sculpture was created by Yugoslavian FRANO KRSINIC and was the bicentennial gift of the Yugoslavian people to the United States. Both of the above men read official greetings from their presidents and exchanged pledges to continue good will and friendship between the two countries.

The article stated that following the unveiling, a reception-luncheon was held for several hundred persons at the Parkway-Ramada Inn, Niagara Falls, New York. Mr. ZARB toasted the Yugoslavian delegation which was answered by that country's Ambassador to the United States, DIMCE BELOVSKI.

According to the article, there was a bit of diplomatic byplay between Mr. ZARB and Ambassador BELOVSKI during the ceremonies. In his remarks at the statue unveiling, Mr. ZARB included an appeal to Yugoslavia to stop all harassment of Americans visiting that country.

In responding to Mr. ZARB's toast at the luncheon, the Ambassador gave assurance that his country wants American visitors and will welcome them.

According to the article, some observers thought that the Yugoslav release of an American held for the past seven months was timed to coincide with the unveiling of the statue.

The tribute to TESLA was sponsored by several Yugoslavian groups in cooperation with the Niagara Mohawk Power Corporation, Westinghouse, and the New York State Park and Recreation Commission.

An article appearing in the "Niagara Falls Gazette," a daily newspaper published in Niagara Falls, New York, captioned "Zarb Calls for Energy Independence for U. S." the article dealt with the unveiling of the Nikola Tesla Monument and stated that accompanying the Yugoslavian Ambassador to the ceremonies on July 23, 1976, were Dr. PAVLE SAVIC, President of the Academy of Science of Serbia,

NIKOLA TESLA
MONUMENT
NIAGARA FALLS, NEW YORK

and VASA VESKOVIC, Yugoslavian Consulate General in New York City.

An article appeared in the "Niagara Gazette" on July 24, 1976, captioned "Aide Almost Missed Event." The article in part indicated that friendship and cooperation between the United States and Yugoslavia was the theme of the day as that nation dedicated a statue of NIKOLA TESLA on July 23, 1976.

The friendship was personalized when a Yugoslavian tried to cross the border from Canada to the United States to attend the dedication without a visa.

The individual was GOJKO SEKULOVSKI, who was in Montreal, Quebec, Canada, as the Chairman of the Olympic Commission of Yugoslavia. He also happens to be the Assistant Secretary of State for Foreign Affairs in that country.

He did not have an American visa and almost missed the unveiling of the statue.

Fast thinking on the part of representatives of the Niagara Frontier State Park and Recreation Commission sent an official car to take the dignitary across the border, which saved the day.

In the "Niagara Falls Gazette" on July 24, 1976, there appeared an article concerning the unveiling of the statue which indicated that Dr. BOGDAN MAGLICH was Chairman of the Yugoslavian-American Bicentennial Committee and was a speaker at the affair. Dr. MAGLICH also serves as President of the Fusion Energy Corporation, Princeton, New Jersey. Dr. MAGLICH eulogized the inventor TESLA and stated "only America could have taken a giant of Tesla's stature, embraced him and provided him the means he needed to bring his talent to its best use of humanity."

- 3 -

NIKOLA TESLA
MONUMENT
NIAGARA FALLS, NEW YORK

Established sources, who have furnished reliable information in the past and were in a position to observe the commemoration of the Tesla Monument, stated that no adverse information came to their attention concerning the dedication of the statue on July 23, 1976.

SAC, Chicago (100-18406)   February 19, 1953
Director, FBI (65-58528)-183

YUGOSLAV CONSULATE GENERAL, CHICAGO, ILLINOIS
INTERNAL SECURITY - YU

REGISTERED MAIL

    Attached is the translation which you requested by letter dated January 22, 1953.

    The contents thereof, where pertinent, must be reported under appropriate captions and afforded whatever investigative attention is necessary.

    Disposition of the foreign language material submitted in this connection is set forth below:

    Returned herewith.

Enclosure
MO:pab

TRANSLATION FROM SERBO-CROATIAN AND SLOVENE

Item No. 1:

This announcement by the American Yugoslav Committee invites all Americans of Yugoslav descent in the Chicago area to attend a commemoration affair to be held at Kordovan Hall, 1802 South Racine Avenue, Chicago, Illinois, on November 16, 1952, at 3 P.M., in observance of the 9th anniversary of the founding of the Yugoslav Republic. Representatives of the FPRY, continues the announcement, will speak at this affair. The Tamburica orchestra "Jadran" (Adriatic) will furnish the music and the Slovene Singing Society "France Preseren" will appear on the program.

The following paragraph in the announcement appears in bold face type:

"It is our old desire to have the friendship between our new homeland and our old homeland - Yugoslavia - deepened and strengthened still more, because this will be to the benefit of the peoples of both countries. It is our duty as Americans of Yugoslav descent to help as much as we can in this sense. Our celebration of the Day of the Republic is dedicated precisely to this end."

GERTRUDE RAJACIC, secretary
MATTJA MARKOVIC, president.

Item No. 2:

This mutilated letter is datelined Chicago, December 10, 1952, and is addressed by Consul YOZE MORAVEC to the Slovene Emigration Society (Slovenska Iseljeniska Matica) in Ljubljana, Slovenia, and reads in substance as follows:

MORAVEC advises that he was on a visit to Cleveland several weeks ago and that on this occasion he spoke to several members of the Central Committee for a Slovene Concert Tour (Slovene Octet). Although the preparatory work is going along fine, continues MORAVEC, there are certain difficulties stemming from the (Slovene Emigration) Society which directly hamper this work and which can easily bring about the failure of the octet or even bring into question the octet's arrival in the US. Most of the difficulties MORAVEC attributes to a lack of understanding on the part of the above-named Slovene Society of the "American situation."

"In the first place," says MORAVEC, "it is necessary to emphasize that this tour by the octet IS NOT being organized by SANS, but rather by the Central Committee in Cleveland, which is a completely separate body from SANS and works independently. This committee is neutral; it belongs to no political movement and an attempt has been

TRANSLATED BY:
MIKI OLIVICH:pab
February 5, 1953

DECLASSIFIED BY SPS/PC
ON 5/25/00

but must rather return them and consequently the entire procedure, from the local people's committee right up to the Ministry of Interior, has to be repeated. In the reports concerning the Consular Service we constantly made reference to this problem and begged the Ministry of Interior to verify the accuracy of documents (at least the crude errors which anyone can detect); the situation has now improved somewhat, but the problem of slowness still remains in sending documents so that in urgent cases we are forced to expedite the matter by telegram.

4. Apropos of the conversation with the ambassador we sent the proposal to the Personnel Section of the Ministry of Interior asking for authorization to hire ▓▓▓▓▓ as a second female clerk at the Consulate (she was born in the U.S. while her parents come from Hercegovina; she is now visiting the ▓▓▓▓▓ In her present position she earned ▓▓▓ a month for a 5-day week; consequently, she can be authorized a starting salary of at least this much. Before (approaching) ▓▓▓▓▓ who talked to five other female clerks - some because they earned more money in their present positions than we can give them, some for other reasons, turned down the offer. The present female clerk we shall be able to release only after another one is hired and broken in and after we find another female clerk to replace the present one. We remind you that the Consulate had less work in past years and yet had, in addition to ▓▓▓▓▓ still another male clerk (former ▓▓▓▓▓ while during 1951 it was ▓▓▓▓▓

5. The problem of purchasing a house for the Consulate comes up from before. We are now paying $400 a month for the Consulate and $200 for the residence of the Consul General, a total of $600, which means $7200 a year. We took an interest in various houses be able to which were for sale and ascertained that for $50,000 to $80,000 would get a building for the Chancery, the residence of the Consul General and one or two small rooms in addition. If the offer for purchasing a house were to be accepted, we would forward concrete proposals for your consideration. We remind you that the present premises of the Consulate are small (we need at least one more room) and consequently this too would be settled by the purchase of a house.

Item No. 12:

A routine memo concerning the personal correspondence of the late NIKOLA TESLA and the possibility of purchasing the same from unidentified owner (name illegible). There is also a notation to the effect that PALANDACIC has only receipts of the money which he sent TESLA as aid."

Item No. 13:

The first page of item no. 13 is insufficiently legible to render intelligible translation.

July 7, 1975

[redacted]
b7C
San Jose, California 95117

Dear [redacted]

This will acknowledge your letter of June 9th.

In response to your inquiry, the papers of Dr. Nikola Tesla were impounded, after his death, by the Office of Alien Property of the Department of Justice.

U.S.A.

Sincerely yours,

C. M. Kelley

Clarence M. Kelley
Director

~~1 - The Deputy Attorney General - Enclosure~~
~~Attention: Susan M. Hauser~~ REC 22 77-32591-20

NOTE: Bufile 100-2237 indicates that Dr. Tesla was a world famous electrical inventor, and at the time of his death his personal papers and effects were impounded by Office of Alien Property for national security reasons. Since Tesla's death in 1943 the Bureau has received numerous inquiries about the disposition of his technical papers. The above reply is forwarded in answer to these inquiries. Bufiles contain no information identifiable with requesters.

JUL 8 1975

dbb:cgg (4)

MAILED 7
JUL 7 1975
FBI

5 b JUL 29 1975

ENGINEERING MANAGEMENT SOCIETY   6/27/1983

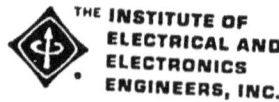

THE INSTITUTE OF ELECTRICAL AND ELECTRONICS ENGINEERS, INC.

ENGINEERING MANAGEMENT SOCIETY

JUN 27 1983

[OUTSIDE SOURCE b6]

Please address reply to:
ENGINEER CONSULTANT
WASHINGTON, D.C. 20015

MF

Director, Federal Bureau of Investigation
Washington, D.C. 20535

Dear Sir,

Research Matters

As a member of the IEEE I receive and read a considerable volume of Institute material. The current issue of our Engineering Management Society Newsletter carries a reprint of an article from another society newsletter entitled: "Nikola Tesla: The Greatest Inventor of all Time?". In my opinion (having some knowledge of electrical engineering history) it is overly lauditory, but worse than that it implies suppression of his electro-technical work by our government.

The third from last paragraph states: "At his death, in 1943, what papers he did have were confiscated by the FBI. These papers remain sealed from the general public to this date. Their contents are totally unknown, nor has it been revealed whether the U.S. Government has made use of them."

Personally, I do not believe this and I would like to refute the statement. Please let me know whether the statement is true and if so what disposition has been made of the papers. The quotation does not say what type papers were confiscated. I am not concerned here with his ideological views (I don't know what they were), only with those relating to electricity.

Thank you.

DE70 94-5-90140

Yours very truly,

b6

Life Senior Member, IEEE

83 JUL 29 1983

Ack. 7/25/83
BHM:kmf
4 AUG 1 1983

July 25, 1983

[OUTSIDE SOURCE]

~~Engineer Consultant~~
~~Washington, D. C. 20015~~

Research Matters

Dear Mr. Ellenberger:

Your June 27th letter to the FBI requesting information concerning Dr. Nikola Tesla was referred to me for reply.

On January 26 and 27, 1943, Federal authorities made a thorough review of the effects of Dr. Tesla to determine if any ideas of significant value to the United States war effort could be found. His effects were examined at the Manhattan Warehouse and Storage Company at 52nd and 7th Avenue, New York, New York, where they apparently were taken after his death. Participating in this examination were representatives from the New York and Washington Offices of the Alien Property Custodian, the Office of Scientific Research and Development at the Massachusetts Institute of Technology, the Office of Naval Intelligence, and United States Naval Research. The FBI did not participate in this examination.

It was the considered opinion of a spokesman of those examiners "that there exist among Dr. Tesla's papers and possessions no scientific notes, descriptions of hitherto unrevealed methods or devices, or actual apparatus which could be of significant value to this country or which would constitute a hazard in unfriendly hands." There was thought to be no technical or military reason why further custody of the property should be retained, and in February, 1943, the papers apparently were released to Mr. Sava N. Kosanovic, Dr. Tesla's nephew and the administrator of his estate. Mr. Kosanovic's address at that time was 112 Central Park South, New York, New York.

BHM:kmf (4)

AUG 11 1983

Mr. ▆▆▆▆▆▆▆▆▆▆ b6

Our files do not reveal any pertinent information on the Tesla materials since the 1940s, and their current whereabouts or condition is unknown.

Sincerely,

[S]

Roger S. Young
Assistant Director in Charge
Office of Congressional
   and Public Affairs

b6

1 - Mr. ▆▆▆▆▆▆▆▆▆ - Enclosure

NOTE: Reply discussed with ▆▆▆▆▆▆▆ FOIPA, RMD, who has handled similar requests for information in our files concerning Dr. Tesla. In numerous previous responses, we have said that the Office of Alien Property of the Department of Justice impounded Dr. Tesla's papers after his death. However, the Office of Foreign Litigation, Civil Division, indicated that Dr. Tesla's papers are not in their possession and may, in fact, have been turned over to Tesla's nephew and the administrator of his estate, Sava N. Kosanovic, in February, 1943.

CURRENT BIOGRAPHY

Published monthly by The H. W. Wilson Company
950 University Avenue   New York

Editor: Maxine Block   Managing Editor: E. Mary Trow

Copyright, 1942, The H. W. Wilson Company. Reasonable quotation from this publication is permitted provided due credit is given to CURRENT BIOGRAPHY

Vol. 4   February 1943   No. 2

Explanations

Authorities for forms of names are the Library of Congress and the Wilson Company bibliographical indexes. Exception is made to the authorized form when the shortened form of a name is better known: e.g., Monty Woolley instead of Edgar Montillion Woolley. If the full name is not given in the heading it will be found in the sketch itself.

After the name, pronunciation is given if the name is difficult, and then the date of birth as fully as possible. The date of death is given for those who have died. The occupation of the subject follows. Next comes the sketch itself, followed by a list of references for further study. These include magazine and newspaper references (in one alphabet) and books. If the person is not living, references are made to obituaries in newspapers and magazines. Only books of an autobiographical or biographical nature are listed, including such well known reference works as *Who's Who*, *Who's Who in America*, etc.

The magazine articles listed under *References* are in abbreviated form (see list "Periodical and Newspaper Abbreviations" for complete title). The form of entry is as follows: Sat Eve Post 56:78-9 S '39 por. This means that an article supplementing our sketch will be found in *Saturday Evening Post*, volume 56, pages 78-9, in the September 1939 number. The abbreviation *por* means that the article is accompanied by a portrait. In the case of newspapers, the name of the paper is followed by paging and date.

When a name in a sketch is followed by '⁴⁰' a biography of that person may be found in the 1940 *Current Biography* Yearbook published in December 1940; for a name followed by '⁴¹' see the 1941 *Current Biography* Yearbook; for a '⁴²' name see index in the December 1942 *Current Biography*.

Photographs not credited to various studios and not obtained from the individuals themselves are obtained from Press Association, Inc., Rockefeller Plaza, New York City.

SMITH, IDA B. WISE—*Continued*

References

Christian-Evangelist p423-4 Ap 16 '42 por
Lit Digest 121:33 Je 13 '36 por
N Y Times IV p2 Ag 31 '41 por
Newsweek 16:40 Ag 19 '40 por
Time 29:55 Mr 1 '37 por; 39:51 Mr 2 '42 por; 39:12 Je 15 '42
Who's Who in America 1942-43

STAUSS, EMIL GEORG VON (shtous fŏn) Oct. 6, 1877—Dec.(?) 1942

German state councilor and a Vice-President of the Reichstag; former director of the Deutsche Bank in charge of its oil interests.

Obituary

N Y Times p17 D 12 '42

SYKES, CHARLES H(ENRY) Nov. 12, 1882—Dec. 19, 1942

Nationally known as the newspaper cartoonist, "Bill" Sykes; drew famous war cartoons for the First and Second World Wars; editorial cartoonist of the *Evening Public Ledger* of Philadelphia from its founding in 1914 until its suspension in January 1942.

Obituary

N Y Times p44 D 20 '42

TESLA, NIKOLA (tes'lä) July 9, 1856—Jan. 7, 1943

One of the world's greatest electrical inventors and designers; American citizen of Greek origin; worked with Edison; credited with many "epic making" inventions since he came to the United States in 1884; in his old age claimed to have invented a "death beam" powerful enough to destroy 10,000 airplanes at a distance of 250 miles and to annihilate an army of 1,000,000 soldiers instantaneously.

Obituary

N Y Times p19 Ja 8 '43 por

TINNEY, CAL(VIN L.) Feb. 2, 1908-

Radio commentator

Address: b. c/o Mutual Broadcasting System, 1440 Broadway, New York City

Since August 1941 Cal Tinney's slow Texas drawl and homespun humor, with intimate, folksy interpolations, have been heard over the Mutual network in *Sizing up the News* each Monday and Wednesday evening from 8:00 to 8:15 p.m. Tinney's colloquialisms, which the folks "back home" chuckle over—his "just-between-you-and-me, ain't it the truth?" "it shore is" method—has captured many a listener bored with the formal, polished, or cut and dried comments of other newscasters.

But there has been more to Tinney than his mannerisms. Speaking usually as a representative of what the "common man" thinks about affairs at home and abroad, he has taken more than one direct and shrewd pot shot, left of center, at stuffed shirt policy, the doings of Big Business, politicians who coddle Fascism at the expense of democracy under high-sounding terms of Americanism, etc. It is not surprising that the sandy-haired young man from the West has occasionally found himself in hot water. Objections have at times been made to the FCC on the "character of the broadcaster's utterances." But Tinney has apparently survived the allegations against him, since he currently continues his bi-weekly talks.

The outspoken homespun philosopher, who has become a kind of Will Rogers columnist of the air, was born February 2, 1908 on a ranch in Pontotoc County, Oklahoma. His family, however, originally came from Texas, where his grandfather, a rugged individualist, had strange politics for those parts. "My grandfather was a Texas Republican," Tinney says sadly, "and they shot him. Seems he exploited his sentiments one Saturday night in a bar room. Ever since then my Pop has been a Democrat." So has the son and, judging by his broadcasts, a fervent New Deal-supporting one.

After attending the Oklahoma public schools Tinney enrolled at the Murray State School of Agriculture in Tishomingo, Oklahoma. There, however, his education lasted only two weeks. "I never did stay there long enough to find out whether it was a high school or college," he says. Young Tinney apparently decided he could get a better schooling by traveling and seeing the world at first hand. For some years he tramped around, often as an ordinary seaman aboard freighters off for foreign ports. He was a newspaperman of sorts, also, and found jobs in Shanghai and Paris. His work in the pre-War French capital was rewriting material found in English-printed newspapers. "It was easy," Tinney explains. "All you had to do was change words like lift to elevator, and caretaker to janitor."

After getting his education by travel, Cal Tinney settled down in Oklahoma to edit a country paper, and began to advertise it over Station KVOO at Tulsa. That was in 1932. His humorous, drawling voice soon became more popular than his gazette. So he gave up his job as an editor, but since 1934 he has written a weekly feature, "Man of the Week," for the McNaught Syndicate. He is the author, also, of a book called *Is It True What They Say about Landon? a Non-Partisan Portrait* (1936). When Tinney turned to radio for a living, his voice was heard, successively, on the *March of Time* (1932), the *Voice of America* (1933), and the *Maxwell House Show Boat* program (1934). From 1937 to 1939 he was on the *Vanity Fair* feature, and from 1939 to 1940 on *Youth vs. Age*. That year he originated, but did not appear on, *Stop Me If You Heard This One*.

Tinney is married to Mary Maxine Noble. The couple have two sons, David N. and Scott.

It was in 1940 that Tinney hit on the idea of a folksy newscast and tried it out in Tulsa, Oklahoma. Farm listeners chuckled, appreciated a commentator who spoke their own

Office Memorandum — UNITED STATES GOVERNMENT

DATE: March 12, 1948

TO: Director, FBI

FROM: SAC, New York

SUBJECT: "PLAIN TALK"
INFORMATION CONCERNING
Bureau file #94-36511

Transmitted herewith for the information of the Bureau is the March 1948 issue of "Plain Talk."

Enc. (1)

NOL ATTACHED

JTM:MTH
62-8845

RED AMBASSADORS
Sava Kosanovich of Yugoslavia

By BOGDAN RADITSA

This is the first in a series of profiles of the Red Ambassadors who represent the several Soviet satellite governments in Washington. Others will follow shortly.

FAMILIAR as they are with the blasts of Vishinsky and Molotov, most Americans are not aware that some of the most fervid tirades against "U.S. imperialism" delivered in this country come from an officially accredited ambassador. Sava Kosanovich, a wiry, reddish-haired man in his early fifties, represents Tito in Washington and in the United Nations. He travels all over this country making speeches in praise of the "new progressive democracy" in the Balkans, denouncing "Anglo-American reaction" and helping to form front groups for Tito. Incidentally, the American ambassador in Yugoslavia cannot even move around Belgrade without special permits and a guard of secret police agents.

From Kosanovich's speeches at Lake Success and elsewhere, it would appear that everything in Yugoslavia before Tito came to power was reactionary or Fascist. Yet, when he was touring America during the war, he used to introduce himself as a "member of the democratic government of His Majesty King Peter the Second."

Kosanovich is a restless man—his face and hands seem to be always agitated and moving. He is a cultured man with a long background in liberal, democratic movements. But he is a man of strong ambitions, who was willing to betray his own past and his closest friends for those ambitions.

In an Embassy which is more of a propaganda bureau than a diplomatic office, Kosanovich is only the front man for the Cominform's schemes in America. The real power in the Embassy is held by members of the Communist Party and the secret police, OZNA, just as its real policy is directed from Moscow through Belgrade. Though Kosanovich repeats the Moscow line, he is not yet one of the inner circle.

I first met Kosanovich in the fall of 1941 in the United States, where he had come with some members of the exiled Royal Yugoslav Government, representing Croatia, Serbia and Slovenia. The tragicomic adventures of that royal mission in America centered around the battle between those who wanted Yugoslavia, after its liberation from the Nazis, to become a democratic federal union, and those who demanded a Yugoslavia which would be a Greater Serbia administered on the old prewar pattern. The grim outcome was that Tito succeeded in charming American public opinion with his sweeping promises of democracy and federation, while the exiles were quarreling among themselves—mostly for personal, rather than ideological, reasons.

KOSANOVICH dreamed for a good many years of becoming Yugoslav ambassador to Washington. His uncle, Nikola Tesla, was an important scientist in America. He himself is descended from a long line of Serbian Orthodox ministers. His friends in politics used to tease him about his shyness toward women, his hatred of smoking and drinking. A strong and dynamic political leader, they said, should be a lady-killer, a hard drinker and a chain smoker.

In prewar Yugoslavia, Kosanovich always attached himself to some popular political leader. (It seemed to give him the feeling that he was running things himself.) In the beginning of his career he followed the tide of Svetozar Pribichevich, the leader of the Democratic Party, who sought a highly centralized Yugoslav state and drove the Communists underground through his secret police. That policy helped to reinforce communism for the present job.

Next, Kosanovich was attracted by the leaders of the Croatian peasants, Stevan Radich and Dr. Vladimir Machek, now in exile in Washington. He considered that he was Machek's "brain." Machek, however, did not always welcome the attentions of his satellite: several times he told me that he was tired of Kosanovich's "old maidish suggestions and tearful interventions." For when he is arguing any involved issue, Kosanovich's voice takes on a querulous tone which makes him sound like an adolescent.

During the war, Kosanovich defended Mihailovich and a united Yugoslavia. He took an active part in Allied meetings and the affairs of American Yugoslavs. His name often appeared in the "Letters to the Editor" column of *The New York Times*. He was a chairman of the Southeastern European Planning Board—a movement not popular with Stalin, as it threatened to block his plans for regional agreements and the artificial building up of buffer states. And he was active, with his friends Louis Adamic and the violinist, Zlatko Balokovic, in the formation and promotion of the United Committee of South Slavic Americans, subsequently metamorphosed into an important part of the Kremlin's Pan-Slavic front.

In his speeches Kosanovich has been one of the principal promoters of an idea first advanced by Adamic—that America is a nation of nations. As such, she is not only Anglo-Saxon, but German, Italian, Negro or Slav. The Slavs of America should unite in the name of brotherhood to carry on their glorious traditions, to show other Americans the heritage they have brought to this country, and to keep in touch with their motherlands. On the surface this idea seems harmless enough, but it is the banner of Stalin's movement to divide the United States. Russia and her satellites carry the idea farther in their controlled press by openly maintaining that America cannot be progressive until it is transformed into a series of "people's republics" on the Soviet pattern, giving their national sovereignty to all the racial groups that compose the population. Behind that scheme is the desire to Balkanize the United States—to divide it into conflicting clans so that a revolution may be centralized through the only uniting force, the Communist Party.

FIORELLO LA GUARDIA was Kosanovich's greatest acquisition. He led the New York Mayor through the same political zig-zag he himself followed—first to Mihailovich, then to Tito. The speech of greeting to King Peter that La Guardia read in Serbo-Croatian on July 8, 1942, was written by Kosanovich. The Mayor read:

"Drazha Mihailovich and Vladimir Machek are the expression of the Yugoslav spirit of resistance—from Triglav to Vardar. They will go down in history. . . ."

In his own speeches Kosanovich often compared Mihailovich with MacArthur, Chiang Kai-shek and Timoshenko. For example, at a meeting of the anti-Nazi League in New York, June 8, 1942, he spoke of "the epic struggle which my people are making under the man whose name already symbolizes to mankind indomitable spiritual and physical resistance—Drazha Mihailovich."

Mihailovich was killed by a government of which Kosanovich was a member. Machek fled the country to escape the fate of Petkov, Maniu and other peasant leaders. Immediately after he became Tito's ambassador, Kosanovich quoted Count Ciano to prove that Machek had been willing to sell out Croatia for a relatively small amount of money. The former follower of Machek admitted intimately to a friend that he did not believe the accusation, but that Tito had asked him to make it.

On July 6, 1942, at a reception held in the Yugoslav delegation's mansion on New York's Fifth Avenue, Kosanovich introduced Mirko Markovich, editor of the Serbian Communist newspaper, *Slobodna Rec*, and now professor at Belgrade University. Markovich offered King Peter a check of one thousand dollars for "the Chetniks and regular army of General Mihailovich."

A week later orders arrived from Moscow that Mihailovich should be considered a traitor and Tito accepted as leader of the war for liberation. Markovich and his Serbian equivalent of the *Daily Worker* suddenly switched to attacking Mihailovich. Kosanovich did not—but his defense of the Chetniks' leader grew weaker. Shortly before he went to London in March, 1944, Kosanovich in a *New York Post* interview was quoted as follows: "Mihailovich is in the position of a General Lee. Tito is some kind of a Lincoln out to save the Union. Mihailovich was an army officer. I think he is sincere but he is surrounded by a very bad political entourage. The entourage was catastrophic. The Government, diplomats abroad, working in his name, are even more catastrophic."

Curiously, Kosanovich himself was a member of that same "catastrophic" government. When he joined the Yugoslav government-in-exile in London in the spring of 1944, it had already dismissed Mihailovich and sought an agreement with Tito's National Liberation Movement.

KING PETER was in London. Heading his government-in-exile was Dr. Ivan Subasich, the viceroy of Croatia. The group was more or less agreed that Yugoslavia should be restored on the basis of a federal union.

Kosanovich asked for a government representing all political parties, which would be strong enough to fight the Communists. He was a frequent visitor to King Peter and his mother. And when an agreement was drawn up between Subasich and Tito, Kosanovich was terribly dissatisfied with its terms. (I suspect that was because he had not taken an active part in it; he was inclined to think that everything in Yugoslav politics needed his guiding hand.)

Tito was in Belgrade. The Red Army was crossing the Danube in its push toward Vienna. On January 18, 1945, Tito's emissary, General Velebit, visited Kosanovich in Kingston House, London. Kosanovich left the interview pale and nervous. For the first time he realized that dealing with the Communists demanded fortitude.

A few days later, on January 23, King

Peter dismissed Subasich's cabinet and reappointed its members only after all of them—including Kosanovich—had agreed in writing that, on their return to Yugoslavia, they would defend certain obligations the king had made concerning the Tito-Subasich agreement. The chief obligation was that the new united Yugoslav Government to be formed under Tito should guarantee all fundamental political and civil rights and freedoms to the Yugoslav people. Kosanovich took a prominent part in drafting this public statement announcing the reappointment of the previous cabinet and the obligations its members assumed. As the king's most intimate adviser, he drafted Peter's act of consent to the Regency. Before Kosanovich left London, the young king kissed him, and received his formal promises that he would defend the interests of the monarchy.

In the spring of 1945, Yugoslavia was "liberated" and the members of its London government-in-exile came back to join Tito's government with the blessing of Churchill, Roosevelt and Stalin. It was at that time that the Communists characterized Kosanovich as a "useful innocent" (*koristna budala*). In a meeting held in a swanky Belgrade apartment house—still the headquarters of the Communist Party of Yugoslavia—the ex-schoolteacher, Edward Kardelj, the Montenegrin, Milovan Gjilas, and other top Communist leaders were talking over the political characteristics of their new partners.

Gjilas said, according to a witness who reported the meeting to me: "The Anglo-Americans dream that they may influence us through someone who is not a Communist. Therefore Ivan Subasich is best fitted for the job of foreign minister. Though he sometimes wavers, he defended the agreement with Tito stubbornly in London and Washington. Milan Grol (the vice-premier and leader of the Serbian democrats) will serve as a Trojan Horse for the West. He is a reactionary politician who backed Mihailovich. If Grol declares that the Serbian people have to abandon Mihailovich, they will accept the idea. As for Kosanovich—he is not an important personality nor a politician. But he is a useful innocent, who may be of help in the United States where he is considered to be a Western-type democrat."

The only member of that London government who still survives politically is the "useful innocent." Subasich, after having been Tito's prime minister and foreign minister, is now a prisoner in Zagreb. Franty Snoj, after participating in the Communist government of Slovenia, was recently sentenced to seven years of slave labor for "espionage in favor of the Western democracies." The liberal Dr. B. Markovich of Serbia died in New York. I arrived there in time to see him before his death. After I had told him the grim story of what Yugoslavia looked like under the Communists, he said very sadly:

"How is it possible that Savitsa (the diminutive of Kosanovich's first name) could stay in such an outrageous government?"

Tito soon began to ignore all the obligations assumed in his agreement with Subasich. Even before the elections he declared that the king was never to come back. Milan Grol and others immediately left Tito's government. Everybody in Yugoslavia expected Kosanovich to do the same. But he began to yield to the Communists.

Subasich had just come back from a trip around Yugoslavia. He had seen that the people did not want communism; they wanted quick action by the democrats. And he had the courage to tell this to Tito. Although he was foreign minister, he was arrested.

I was with Kosanovich in his room in Belgrade's Hotel Majestic when Mrs. Subasich telephoned and asked for immediate help. Her husband was arrested and ill. Kosanovich tried to reassure her. He telephoned Lt. General Rankovich, OZNA's chief trigger-man. The Communist hangman answered coldly that nothing would happen to the foreign minister. Precautions were merely being taken to defend him from any attempt of the "Western reactionaries" upon his life.

We had just been reading Dante there in the hotel room—the part where Count Ugolino hungrily devours the brain of Archbishop Ruggieri, describing the merciless end of all traitors. The blood and turmoil of ancient fratricidal war rose before us: it seemed very near to our own Yugoslav tragedy.

Only a little later Kosanovich entered the new People's Front against the will of the Independent Democratic Party, of which he was Secretary-General. His party issued a clandestine communiqué describing his defection. Soon after that the chairman of the party, Dr. D. Boshkovich, was terribly beaten for three hours by a Communist youth mob. He was lying in a hospital the same night that Kosanovich was flying to the London conference of the Big Four, accompanying the Communist Kardelj as a "liberal and democrat." Before he left, Kosanovich had published an article in the Communist official organ, *Borba*, in which he attacked Subasich and the leadership of the party with whom he had worked closely for twenty years. The Communists wanted a proof of "betrayal." And the price was paid. From London, Kosanovich went to the Paris Peace Conference, and from there to Washington—to attack American democracy, which he had formerly praised.

I CANNOT BELIEVE Kosanovich is a happy man, though he has attained his ambition. Those who once opposed fascism and are now serving communism have lost all faith in themselves and in mankind. There are no more miserable people than the intelligentsia who know better—but who have been afraid to resist in the last battle for man's liberty.

Kosanovich once asked for a synthesis between political and economic democracy for the good of the people, and he is now defending the complete subjugation—economic, political and moral—of Yugoslavia to the Communists. Kosanovich once wanted Yugoslavia to be free of the influence of any big power, and he is now ambassador of a puppet state in Stalin's empire.

THE SOLUTION FOR PALESTINE

A comprehensive and authoritative discussion of the Hoover Plan (pages 32-33) and of the Lowdermilk Plan (*Palestine—Land of Promise*), offering an engineering rather than a political solution for the crisis in the Near East, will be presented in the next issue of PLAIN TALK.

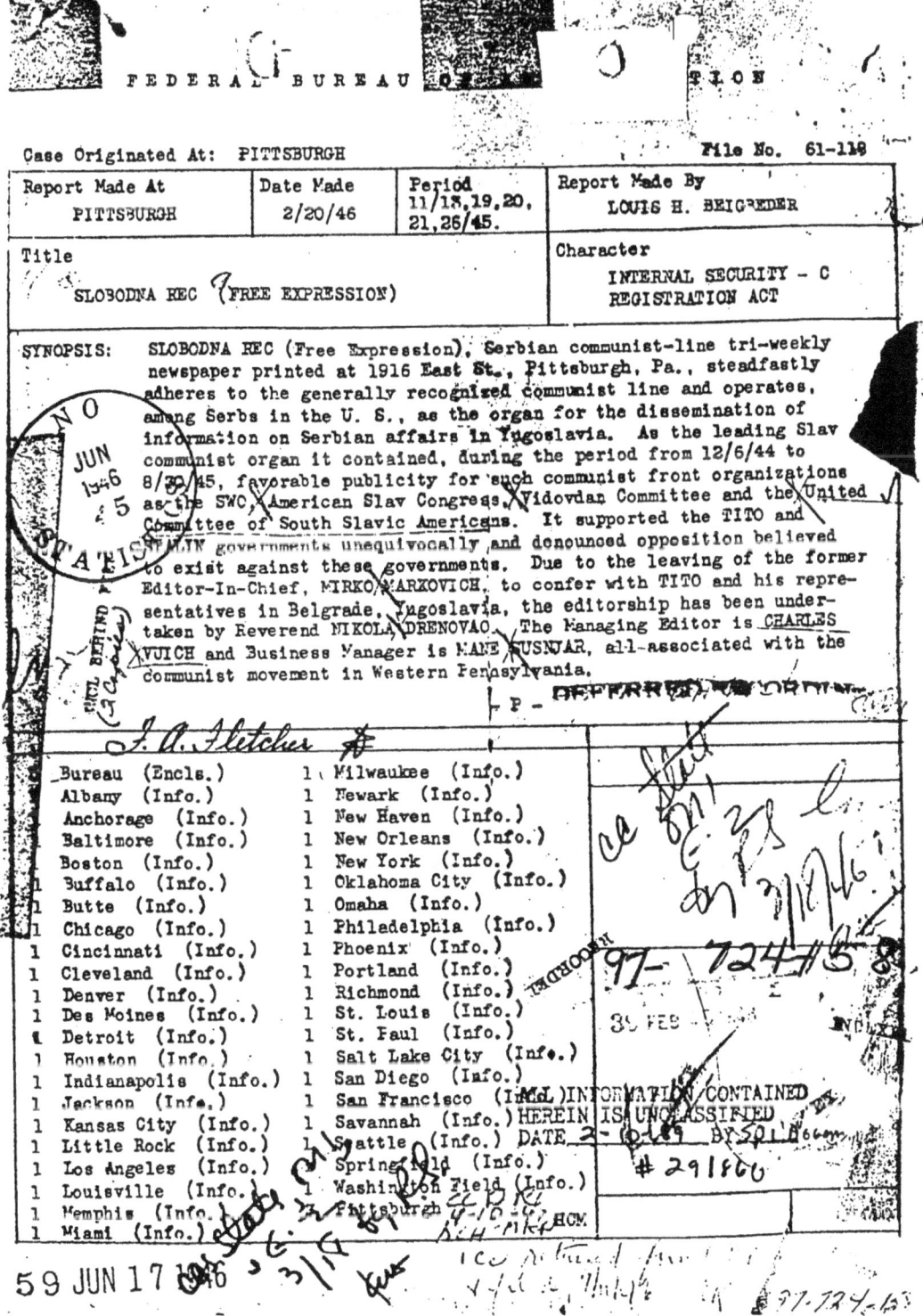

Pgh. Field Division
61-118

MARKOVICH's lack of complete coordination with the Communist Party movement in the United States may best be indicated by his individual editorial policy in SLOBODNA REC. Unlike other foreign language communist organs, as will be shown in Section III of this report, SLOBODNA REC did not pursue a predominate loyalty to the American Communist Party, but rather concentrated its efforts on foreign news, policy and information.

The administration of SLOBODNA REC during the period covered by this report may be seen to pursue a more cautious line or policy regarding the printing of sources of news items and other information in the newspaper. Many items appear in the translations of this newspaper which of necessity must have been derived from a foreign source. One such source may be pointed out in that during the early part of 1945 MARKOVICH had installed in his home a Hamerlin model short-wave radio receiver with a special short-wave antenna and with logging for radio Belgrade.

Translations of SLOBODNA REC as contained in this report were made at the Pittsburgh Field Office by ▇▇▇▇▇▇▇ Serbo-Croatian translator, and ▇▇▇▇▇ Slavonic translator.

II

ORGANIZATIONAL STRUCTURE

1 - OFFICERS

In the "Statement Of The Ownership, Management, Circulation, Etc., Required By The Acts Of Congress Of August 24, 1912, and March 3, 1933," regarding newspapers utilizing the mails as a means of transmission, furnished the Pittsburgh Office by ▇▇▇▇▇▇▇ Foreman, Pittsburgh Post Office, the following are given as officers of SLOBODNA REC:

Publisher	J. KRSTOVICH
Editor	CHARLES VUICK
Managing Editor	None
Business Manager	MANE SHUSHNAR
Owner	JOHN KRSTOVICH

This statement was filed at the Pittsburgh Post Office by MANE SHUSHNAR on October 2, 1945.

Pgh. Field Division
61-118

"2. It is true that this year's calendars were printed too late, but we have inspite of this sold a sufficient number of calendars and some of the sellers have not sent in their money. In addition to the excellent success in advertisements for the calendar and besides the fact that the calendar was excellent, the work of the sale of the calendars is not satisfactory. Our activists should have paid more attention to this then than before selling the calendars.

"3. Soon we shall have received several hundred copies of the new book 'Guns For Tito.' We ought to do our best to sell these books as soon as possible. The book was compiled by an American Major who organized a shipment of weapons to TITO's Army and met TITO personally several times. The price of the book is $2.75.

"4. We must finish the sale of the book of NIKOLA TESLA. We should particularly interest the American engineers and unionists in it.

"5. Soon a book of MIRKO MARKOVICH will be off the press: 'That We May Understand Each Other.' Therefore it will be necessary to organize the sale of the same. The book contains 350 pages and the price of the same is $2.50.

"The working committee decided that by the end of the month of March or in April, MIRKO MARKOVICH should start for the Pacific Coast, to California, to work in the strengthening of our movement and newspaper and in building up of clubs and the apparatus. This will be discussed in detail at the meeting of the Supreme Board in Cleveland."

August 14, 1945   "Reorganization Of Leadership Of Serbian Progressive Movement In City Of Akron Carried Out." This article, which is quoted below, indicates the then policy of SLOBODNA REC in its leadership in the Serbian Progressive Movement in the United States.

"Akron, August 10 - Last week, on Thursday evening, there was here held a special meeting of the Serbian political progressive club, which was attended by the editor-in-chief of SLOBODNA REC, MIRKO MARKOVICH, and the manager of the paper, MANE SHUSHNAR.

Office Memorandum • UNITED STATES GOVERNMENT

TO : Director, FBI

FROM : SAC, Pittsburgh

SUBJECT: SLOBODNA REC
INTERNAL SECURITY - C
REGISTRATION ACT

DATE: November 7, 1947

The following article which appeared in the November 1, 1947, issue of the above captioned Communist line newspaper published at 1916 East Street, Pittsburgh, Pa., is furnished for your information:

Address of Ambassador KOSANOVICH at Banquet of 2nd Serbian Congress, October 26 in Pittsburgh, Pa.

Brothers and Sisters:

I come among you to extend you the greetings of the peoples and the government of the Federated People's Republic of Yugoslavia, headed by Marshal Tito and to thank you for the considerable aid which you have given your brothers in the old homeland.

By coincidence, I found myself in the period of 1941-44 in this great country where I did my best to defend the truth and contribute to the best of my ability to the thwarting of spreading untruths on the part of the official representatives of the then Yugoslav government in exile and of all those who wanted to convince public opinion of America and its official circles of the impossibility of restoring Yugoslavia. I recall your valuable help of that time. I remember a dear friend in the person of the late Rev. KRAJNOVICH and his constant struggle, as well as of so many others of that period.

You Americans of Serbian descent were hit the hardest. You were exposed to the greatest trials and the heaviest attacks. You had to exercise the greatest self-denial and perspective correctly to see the course of events because every effort was made to confuse you. The idea was that when Serbian Americans follow the wrong path, when chauvinism and national hatred get possession of them, when hatred toward the Croats and Slovenes and toward Yugoslav unity is aroused in them, then it will be easy for the same attitudes to work among Croatians and Slovenes as regards Yugoslav unity, giving chauvinism full sway and thus contributing to the weakening of the war effort in American and rendering impossible the struggle for the salvation and restoration of Yugoslavia and the Balkans.

In a letter of thanks for an honor which was shown me in February, 1944, by a great number of you who are now assembled at this Serbian

RECORDED
INDEXED 97-724-175

To: Director, FBI
Re: SLOBODNA REC
IS - C; REGISTRATION ACT

November 7, 1947

Congress when I was elected an honorary president of the Vidovdan Congress I said:

"In an extraordinary difficult period of mankind you have with sacrifice and self-denial done your duty also toward your people from whom you sprang and toward America of which you are good citizens, and toward mankind. Since my arrival in America in 1941, in an official capacity, I found among you the best understanding and best cooperation for an ever greater unification of national forces in the struggle against all manifestations of fascism. Together we tried to be as serbs - bearers of Serbo-Croato-Sloveno-Macedonian harmony and unity at a time when the enemy banked his entire hope on disharmony and hatred. Working thus we have contributed to the correct understanding of the national-liberation struggle beset with so many obstacles and bedevilled with so much gossip. Time and events have borne out the truth thereof."

And when taking leave of Serbs in America in a letter of July 24, 1944, among other things I wrote:

"We have here been those who have defended the purity of the Serbian name at a time when it was being most degraded by the ignorant. History will show that we were right and that by our defending the unity of Serbs, Croats, Slovenes, and Macedonians we have best represented the true national Serbian interests and thus represented the interests not only of Yugoslavia but also of America and all United Nations. We have by common sacrifices of a liberation war achieved great successes in the country, but there still are great trials. Enemies will particularly seek to confuse the Serbs and destroy them with false defense of Serbian interests. I ask all my good friends to make every effort to promote harmony and unity. I ask all those who were being deceived in returning to Serbian tradition and enter the great circle of national harmony . . . I ask friends who have had the opportunity and bravery of seeing the right path from the very outset, that they forgive those who haven't seen it because they were deceived by those who thought they must be believed. The true national champion is known by his setting the errant ones on the right path. Responsible culprits who misused their positions and misused the credulity of the ignorant will answer to the people for their misdeeds. The more you will promote harmony, the better it will be for Serbdom, for Yugoslavia, and for America - toward which you have the greatest obligation."

To: Director, FBI
Re: SLOBODNA REC
IS - C; REGISTRATION ACT

November 7, 1947

That was the path to which you were called until his last days by our great countryman NIKOLA TESLA.

And you, by your moderation, have contributed to the interest of the democratic struggle of the world. You have contributed to the unification of all national forces in America in the organization of the war effort. And at the same time, as Americans of Serbian descent together with other Yugoslav Americans, you have shown your American fellow-citizens that your brothers in the old homeland are with united efforts resisting fascism and struggling for freedom and the restoration of their independent state, Yugoslavia.

In this you were able to be the best spokesmen. You and your predecessors have come to this country in search of freedom and better economic conditions.

Most of you and those before you have fled from Hapsburg serfdom because you were being oppressed both nationally and economically. You and your predecessors made valuable contributions to the development of the New World. You with your brother Slovenes and Croatians have sweated, shed blood, worn your bones, expended brains, and whatnot for the progress of this country. Long is the chain of miners, farmers, scientists, and soldiers who gave their best for the general progress and prosperity of the American Union. You have conscientiously been doing your duty and you have become good citizens of this great land. Who of us is not proud of the work, life and nobleness of NIKOLA TESLA without whose work and mind electricity would not be what it now is in the world; whose motor has harnessed the Niagara and the Dnieper, turning the wheels of industry wherever there is electricity? In every spark of electricity, shines his name. America is the greatest beneficiary of TESLA's genius. He asked for no riches.

And so, brothers and sisters, when during the war you have raised your voice for your brethren in the Balkans struggling not only for their life but also for a better and more secure existence of mankind, your voice thus had significance and importance. You were able to be the authorized spokesmen of the struggle which was going on over there.

- 3 -

FEDERAL BUREAU OF INVESTIGATION

Form No. 1
THIS CASE ORIGINATED AT PITTSBURGH, PENNSYLVANIA   FILE NO. 100-2225

REPORT MADE AT	DATE WHEN MADE	PERIOD FOR WHICH MADE	REPORT MADE BY	
MILWAUKEE, WISCONSIN	5/4/45	4/6,7/45	ELMER A. WATSON, JR.	EAW/fh

TITLE	CHARACTER OF CASE
NARODNI GLASNIK (The National Herald)	INTERNAL SECURITY – C

SYNOPSIS OF FACTS: The 37th Anniversary Celebration of the existence of NARODNI GLASNIK held in Milwaukee, Wis. 2/18/45. Known CPA members and sympathizers present at meeting. ███████ CPA sympathizer, ███████ all known Party members, present. ███████ in charge of general arrangements for meeting. Chief speaker MRS. MARY MRNJAC of Chicago, Ill., officer of the Supreme Committee of Croatian Fraternal Union. Work of NARODNI GLASNIK in connection with present War effort and particularly in support of Marshal TITO set forth by various speakers.

– R U C –

ALL INFORMATION CONTAINED HEREIN IS UNCLASSIFIED
DATE 2-22-69 BY SP1A6...

REFERENCE: Letter from Pittsburgh to Milwaukee dated 1/16/45.

Report of Special Agent HARRY MORRISON dated 4/28/41 at Pittsburgh, Pa.

DETAILS: Confidential Informant ███ advised that under date of February 18, 1945, he was in attendance at the 37th Anniversary Celebration of NARODNI GLASNIK (The National Herald), a Croatian language newspaper, which celebration was held in Harmony Hall located at 939 South Sixth Street, Milwaukee, Wisconsin.

APPROVED AND FORWARDED: J K Johnson, SPECIAL AGENT IN CHARGE

COPIES DESTROYED 5/15/9 716
COPIES OF THIS REPORT:
5 – Bureau
4 – Pittsburgh
1 – Chicago (info)
2 – Milwaukee

100-10123-124

EX-23

Mi 100-2225

The next speaker introduced by Chairman JUROVICH was a MR. CHRIST MIKALACHI who spoke on the need of funds for the continued support of the paper NARODNI GLASNIK.

Following this, was a speech by Mr. FRANK PETRAK, who also praised the NARODNI GLASNIK for its wonderful work.

At the conclusion of these various speeches, JUROVICH acting as Chairman, again discussed the need of funds for NARODNI GLASNIK and requested a collection from the audience. He told them that the amount collected was $586.10.

According to ▮▮▮ the celebration closed at approximately 9:15 P.M. ▮▮▮ said that during the course of the afternoon he was contacted by ▮▮▮, known CPA member, who gave him a pamphlet entitled "The Bulletin of the United Committee of South-Slavic Americans" dated November, 1944. ▮▮▮ made reference to an article in this pamphlet which was written by LOUIS ADAMIC, formerly President of the AMERICAN SLAV CONGRESS and President of the UNITED COMMITTEE OF SOUTH-SLAVIC AMERICANS. ▮▮▮ then attempted to sell ▮▮▮ a book entitled "The Prodigal Genius", which was the life story of NIKOLA TESLA written by JOHN J. O'NEIL. He also showed ▮▮▮ a calendar with a picture of Marshal TITO and the inscription "Death to Fascism, Freedom for the People". He explained that these calendars were being printed in Canada and he was taking orders for them.

Confidential Informant ▮▮▮ advised that he had previously made arrangements with ▮▮▮ for announcing the proposed banquet and celebration over Radio Station W-E-J-W on the Croatian Radio Hour.

▮▮▮ was also present at the 37th Anniversary Celebration and confirmed the information set forth by Confidential Informant ▮▮▮.

The following individuals were listed by ▮▮▮ as being present at this meeting:

b2
b7C
b7D

- 3 -

Mi 100-2225

KEY SHEET

Confidential Informant

b2
b7C
b7D

Confidential Informant

(was designated as a Confidential Informant at own request.)

FBI—INTERNAL SECURITY REGISTRATION ACT — *5/8/1945*

STANDARD FORM NO. 64

Office Memorandum · UNITED STATES GOVERNMENT

TO : Director, FBI
FROM : SAC, Pittsburgh
SUBJECT: ▓▓▓▓▓▓▓▓
INTERNAL SECURITY - R

DATE: 5/8/45

▓▓▓▓▓▓▓▓▓▓▓▓▓▓▓▓▓▓▓▓▓▓▓▓▓▓▓▓▓▓ Pittsburgh, ▓. S., Pa., would-be radio repair man, advised this office that on April 29, 1945 he installed at the home of captioned subject, ▓▓▓▓▓▓▓▓, a "Hammerlund H.Q. Receiver #120X". ▓▓▓▓▓▓▓▓ stated that since this type receiving set is of a kind which is generally used by amateur radio experts or professionals and since the radio set itself was in such condition as to indicate that it had been purchased under a very high priority, he inquired of the subject how he happened to be in possession of such a radio set. ▓▓▓▓▓▓▓▓ according to ▓▓▓▓▓▓▓▓ was vague as to where he got it, saying that it had belonged at one time to NIKOLA TESLA'S son and was purchased before the war in New York City. ▓▓▓▓▓▓▓▓ did not make any notation of the serial number of this radio but advised that under pretext he can review the operation of this set in the apartment of the subject and at that time get the serial number.

Pursuant to request by the subject, the set was installed and a short wave aerial was put up. After the set had been tuned by ▓▓▓▓▓▓▓▓ he was requested to locate the radio station at Belgrade, Yugoslavia. ▓▓▓▓▓▓▓▓ told him that he wished to get direct reports from Belgrade in order that they might be ▓▓▓▓▓▓▓▓▓▓▓▓▓▓▓▓▓▓▓▓▓▓▓▓.

Inasmuch as investigation may subsequently develop a censorship violation on the part of the newspaper, SLOBODNA REC, Serbian Communist line tri-weekly newspaper, printed at Pittsburgh, and in order that the Bureau might be immediately advised on the developments in this case, the above information has been set forth.

Translations of SLOBODNA REC at the Pittsburgh Field Office made currently by ▓▓▓▓▓▓▓▓ Slavonic Translator, are at this time and continue to be reviewed for any releases which appear to emanate from a foreign rather than from any source approved by the Office of War Information or like agencies.

It should be noted that during this week since the radio has been installed at the home of ▓▓▓▓▓▓▓▓ several articles have appeared ▓▓▓▓▓▓▓▓ which appear to have emanated from foreign radio broadcasts.

COPIES DESTROYED

ALL INFORMATION CONTAINED HEREIN IS UNCLASSIFIED
DATE 4-7-89 BY ▓▓▓▓▓▓▓▓

8/30/1946 — YUGOSLAVIAN ACTIVITIES IN THE US

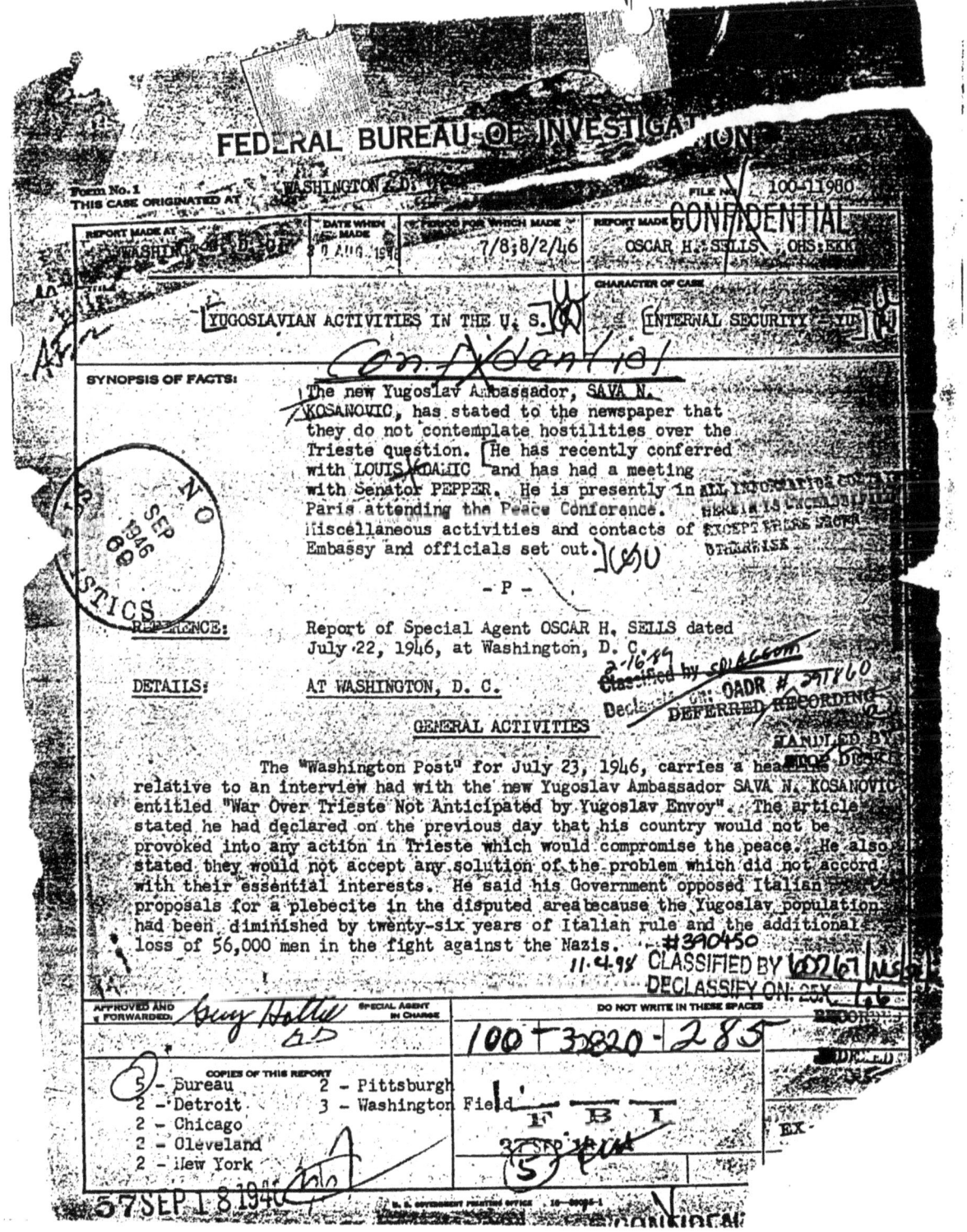

FEDERAL BUREAU OF INVESTIGATION

Form No. 1
THIS CASE ORIGINATED AT WASHINGTON, D.C.   FILE NO. 100-11980

REPORT MADE AT	DATE WHEN MADE	PERIOD FOR WHICH MADE	REPORT MADE BY
WASHINGTON, D.C.	30 AUG 1946	7/8;8/2/46	OSCAR H. SELLS OHS:EKK

CONFIDENTIAL

TITLE: YUGOSLAVIAN ACTIVITIES IN THE U.S.
CHARACTER OF CASE: INTERNAL SECURITY — Y

SYNOPSIS OF FACTS:

The new Yugoslav Ambassador, SAVA N. KOSANOVIC, has stated to the newspaper that they do not contemplate hostilities over the Trieste question. He has recently conferred with LOUIS ADAMIC and has had a meeting with Senator PEPPER. He is presently in Paris attending the Peace Conference. Miscellaneous activities and contacts of Embassy and officials set out.

– P –

REFERENCE: Report of Special Agent OSCAR H. SELLS dated July 22, 1946, at Washington, D.C.

DETAILS: AT WASHINGTON, D.C.

GENERAL ACTIVITIES

The "Washington Post" for July 23, 1946, carries a headline relative to an interview had with the new Yugoslav Ambassador SAVA N. KOSANOVIC entitled "War Over Trieste Not Anticipated by Yugoslav Envoy". The article stated he had declared on the previous day that his country would not be provoked into any action in Trieste which would compromise the peace. He also stated they would not accept any solution of the problem which did not accord with their essential interests. He said his Government opposed Italian proposals for a plebescite in the disputed area because the Yugoslav population had been diminished by twenty-six years of Italian rule and the additional loss of 56,000 men in the fight against the Nazis.

COPIES OF THIS REPORT:
- 5 - Bureau
- 2 - Detroit
- 2 - Chicago
- 2 - Cleveland
- 2 - New York
- 2 - Pittsburgh
- 3 - Washington Field

WFO 100-11980

Confidential Informant ▮▮▮▮ whose identity is known to the Bureau, learned on July 23, 1946, that ▮▮▮▮ conferred with Ambassador KOSANOVIC and told him that LOUIS ADAMIC had contacted her in order to find out definitely when KOSANOVIC was coming to New York City. It appears that ADAMIC planned to be in New York himself on the following Thursday and expressed a desire to have KOSANOVIC be there on Thursday night. KOSANOVIC told her he was leaving for Paris the following Sunday morning at 11:00 AM. He was told that ADAMIC would like to have dinner with him on Thursday night and on Friday morning for him to meet "this fellow that he has been talking about." KOSANOVIC said he knew it was something about publicity. KOSANOVIC stated he was not very happy about having to go to Paris. He said he hadn't "finished ending" and that it was very complicated. He indicated that ▮▮▮▮ would accompany him to Paris. They expressed amusement over the "Star's" account of KOSANOVIC's press conference the previous day.

The article in the "Evening Star" which was referred to above appeared July 23, 1946, and was entitled "New Envoy Disclaims Any Yugoslav Plans for Coup at Trieste." This article was written by NEWBOLD NOYES, JR. The article quotes the Ambassador as saying that Yugoslavia would not be "provoked into compromising the peace." The article stated that the Ambassador had indicated his country would boycott Trieste if they did not get it. The article stated that KOSANOVIC is a nephew of NICOLA TESLA, the Yugoslav-American inventor.

▮▮▮▮ learned on July 23, 1946, that ▮▮▮▮ conferred with ▮▮▮▮ relative to the newspaper coverage of the Ambassador's press conference the previous day. ▮▮▮▮ said there was a little on the first page of the "New York Herald Tribune" and ▮▮▮▮ said there was quite a bit in the "New York Times" also. ▮▮▮▮ told her that he expected more in the "Evening Star" than had appeared in the "Washington Post" because he had "one of their good people, who was very favorably impressed and said he would say so."

▮▮▮▮ learned on July 30, 1946, that ▮▮▮▮ contacted Senator TAYLOR's office and advised that the Ambassador would like to have lunch with Senator TAYLOR at the Senate dining room on Thursday at 1:00 P.M. along with some other members of the Senate.

Informant learned on the following day that ▮▮▮▮ made arrangements for Ambassador KOSANOVIC to have lunch with Senator PEPPER and probably Senator MAGNUSON in the Senate dining room.

Informant also learned on July 31, 1946, that Senator PEPPER had accepted the invitation to have lunch with the Ambassador at 1:00 P.M.

WFO 100-11980

[SAVA M. KOSANOVIC, Ambassador]

KOSANOVIC came as Yugoslav Ambassador in approximately July of 1946, presenting his credentials to the President on July 18, 1946. KOSANOVIC is generally considered not a Communist but an opportunist. He is a member of the Independent Democratic Party and previously served as a Minister under the Royal Government. He was born at Plaski, Croatia, May 29, 1894, was a nephew of the famous inventor, NIKOLA TESLA.

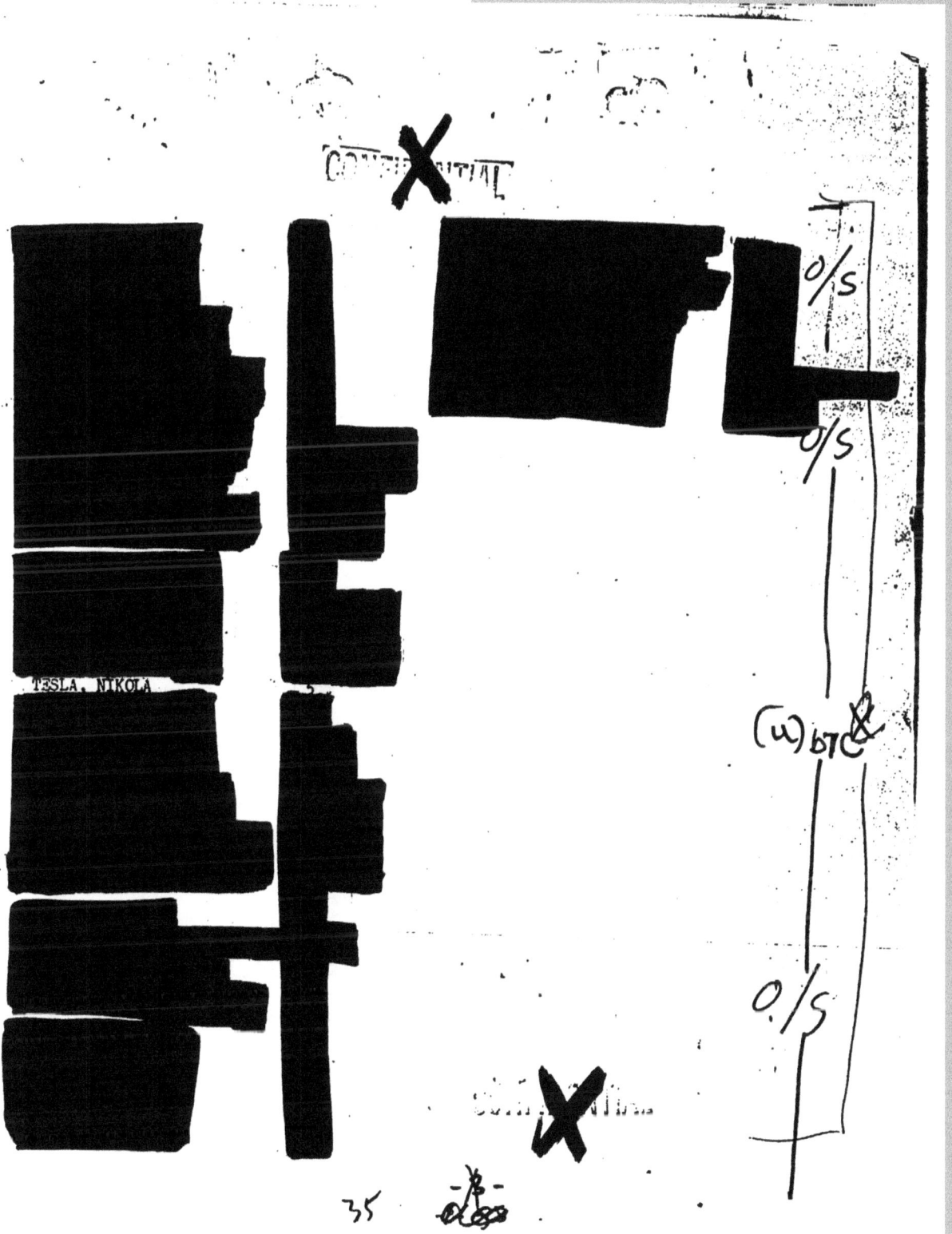

FBI–DELETED PAGE INFORMATION SHEET

UNDATED

4-750 (Rev. 9-29-95)

XXXXXX
XXXXXX
XXXXXX

FEDERAL BUREAU OF INVESTIGATION
FOIPA
DELETED PAGE INFORMATION SHEET

__4__ Page(s) withheld entirely at this location in the file. One or more of the following statements, where indicated, explain this deletion.

☑ Deletions were made pursuant to the exemptions indicated below with no segregable material available for release to you.

Section 552

- ☑ (b)(1)
- ☐ (b)(2)
- ☐ (b)(3)
- ☐ (b)(4)
- ☐ (b)(5)
- ☐ (b)(6)

- ☐ (b)(7)(A)
- ☐ (b)(7)(B)
- ☐ (b)(7)(C)
- ☐ (b)(7)(D)
- ☐ (b)(7)(E)
- ☐ (b)(7)(F)
- ☐ (b)(8)
- ☐ (b)(9)

Section 552a

- ☐ (d)(5)
- ☐ (j)(2)
- ☐ (k)(1)
- ☐ (k)(2)
- ☐ (k)(3)
- ☐ (k)(4)
- ☐ (k)(5)
- ☐ (k)(6)
- ☐ (k)(7)

☐ Information pertained only to a third party with no reference to the subject of your request or the subject of your request is listed in the title only.

☐ Documents originated with another Government agency(ies). These documents were referred to that agency(ies) for review and direct response to you.

_____ Pages contain information furnished by another Government agency(ies). You will be advised by the FBI as to the releasability of this information following our consultation with the other agency(ies).

_____ Page(s) withheld inasmuch as a final release determination has not been made. You will be advised as to the disposition at a later date.

_____ Pages were not considered for release as they are duplicative of _____

_____ Page(s) withheld for the following reason(s): **REFERENCE TO TESLA APPEARS IN 1 SENTENCE**

☑ The following number is to be used for reference regarding these pages.
100-32820-969

XXXXXXXXXXXXXX
X Deleted Page(s) X
X No Duplication Fee X
X for this page X
XXXXXXXXXXXXXX

XXXXXX
XXXXXX
XXXXXX

FBI/DOJ

Federal Bureau of Investigation
United States Department of Justice

Form No. 1
This Case Originated At INDIANAPOLIS, INDIANA   File No. 100-4006

Report Made At	Date	Period	Report Made By
Indianapolis, Indiana	11/18/42	10/29,30/42	CLARENCE E. CLAY CEC:NJO

Title
AMERICAN SLAV CONGRESS (ALL-SLAV CONGRESS)

Character of Case
INTERNAL SECURITY - C

Synopsis:

Information contained in bulletin entitled "News Flashes from Czechoslovakia under Nazi Domination" issued by Czechoslovak National Council of America, with reference to American Slav Congress, set forth herein. Includes information concerning the permanent committee set-up and a partial list of delegates to the American Slav Congress. Also set forth is a history of the All Slav Congress which was written by ▓▓▓▓▓ Information received that ▓▓▓▓▓ and ▓▓▓▓▓ Serbs of Gary, Indiana, and reported to be Communists, attended the All Slav Congress. ▓▓▓▓▓ attended All Slav Congress.

- P -

ALL INFORMATION CONTAINED
HEREIN IS UNCLASSIFIED
DATE 1-17-83 BY SPSRJG/PMC

Reference: Report of Special Agent CHARLES M. SOLOMON, dated May 12, 1942, at Detroit, Michigan.

Details: At Hammond, Indiana

From Confidential Informant ▓▓▓ has been obtained

Approved and Forwarded: Special Agent in Charge

Do Not Write in These Spaces
100-56674—42
RECORDED & INDEXED
15 NOV 21 1942

3 - Bureau
1 - New York (Inf.)
1 - Pittsburgh (Inf.)
1 - Newark (Inf.)
1 - Milwaukee (Inf.)
1 - Washington Field (Inf.)
1 - Chicago (Inf.)
1 - Philadelphia (Inf.)
1 - Cleveland (Inf.)
1 - Detroit
3 - Indianapolis

a copy of a bulletin entitled "News Flashes from Czechoslovakia under Nazi Domination", published by the Czechoslovak National Council of America, 4049 West Twenty-sixth Street, Chicago, Illinois, release no. 132, dated May 11, 1942.

This bulletin contains news concerning the American Slav Congress held at Detroit, Michigan, April 25 and 26, 1942. The article contains the permanent committee set-up of the Congress and a list of men of eminence among the delegates to the Congress.

This article is being quoted below:

"AMERICAN SLAV CONGRESS FOR GREATER WAR EFFORT"

The coordination activities of all groups of Slavic extraction in America for an intensified war effort moved a long step closer to reality as a result of the American Slav Congress held in Detroit April 25 and 26 and attended by more than 2300 delegates representing church, fraternal, labor, social and cultural groups from all parts of the country. Every substantial American Slav organization in the country was represented.

Permanent Committee Set Up

A permanent committee was elected with LEO KRZYCKI, Vice-president of the Amalgamated Clothing Workers for President; Prof. J. J. ZMRHAL, of the Czechoslovak National Council, Vice-president; STEPHEN ZEMAN, JR., of the Slovak Evangelical Union, Secretary; VINKO VUK, of the Croatin Fraternal Union, Treasurer; and BLAIR F. GUNTHER, member of the Educational Committee of the Polish National Alliance, Chairman of the Board of Directors.

Participating Slavic nationality groups elected vice-presidents to the Board of Directors. Vice-presidents for the respective nationality groups elected were: EDMUND POINC, Polish; W. J. MUZIK, Czech; V. S. PLATEK, Slovak; VASIL DICOFF, Bulgarian; SAMUEL WERLINICH, Serbian; JOHN BUTKOVICH, Croatian; VINCENT CAINKAR, Slovene; PETER RATICA, Carpatho-Russian; GEORGE PIRINSKY, Macedonien; HARRY LUBESHKOFF, Russian; MICHAEL TKATCH, Ukrainian.

The various nationality groups also elected members to the nationality committees of the Board of Directors. The National Committee of the congress held its first plenary session in Pittsburgh, May 10, to plan steps to translate the decisions of the congress into action.

Anti-Hitler Measures Adopted

Main decisions embodied in the resolutions of the congress were:

1. To make a direct appeal to American Slavs comprising more than half the workers in the war essential industries of the nation to intensify their production efforts to outproduce Hitler and the Axis.
2. To intensify vigilance against fifth-columnists operating within the various Slavic groups in this country aiming to sow division and disunity in the war effort.
3. To chart a plan to recruit 50,000 American Slav volunteers for a house-to-house campaign among American Slav families for raising the amount of war bond subscriptions to 10 per cent of income.
4. To take all measures to strengthen the bonds of solidarity among American Slav groups and between them and the Slav peoples of Europe for a concerted effort against HITLER.
5. To increase support of all war relief agencies, particularly the Russian, Yugoslavian, Polish, Czechoslovakian, British, Greek and Chinese.
6. To take steps to counteract the appeasers.
7. To set up a permanent organization to coordinate and assist in carrying out the decisions adopted by the Congress.

Response Exceeds Anticipations

The response to the first American Slav Congress ever held in America exceeded all anticipations. It revealed the depth of anti-Axis feeling that has seized hold of the Americans of Slav descent who came expressing desires to do their utmost to the end that the power of Hitlerism, arch-foe of the Slav peoples as of freedom-loving peoples everywhere shall be decisively smashed.

The delegates were mostly brawny men from coal mines, steel mills, machine shops—the men on whom the nation is counting for much of its war essential goods production and wholesome-looking women whose faces showed hardening lines of determination beneath war smiles.

Men of Eminence Among Delegates

Among the delegates were men and women of distinction in many fields of activity—scholars, writers and clergymen, among them Rev. VINCENT BORKOVICZ, who represented the Very Rev. Bishop STEFAN S. WOZNICKI at the Congress and delivered the opening invocation; Metropolitan Bishop Benjamin, of the Russian Orthodox Church; Most Rev. JOHN KRAJNOVICH of Johnstown, Pennsylvania, and Rev. PAWLOWSKI, of Buffalo, New York.

Among others present were JOSEPH WATTRAS, director of the Polish National Alliance of Pittsburgh; CHESTER A. WOZDROJ, President of the Polish Central Citizens' Committee of Detroit; Judge N. GRONKOWSKI of Hamtramch; Captain W. HETMAN, Polish War Veterans, Chicago; Dr. W. T. OSOWSKI, chairman Michigan All Slav Committee, Detroit; Mrs. M. NESTEROWICZ, dean of Polish Journalists, Buffalo, New York; ZLATKO BALOKOVICH, famed Croatian violinist; FRANK GRIGORSKI, assistant district attorney of Milwaukee and president of the Pulaski Council there; VINCENT KLEIN, Secretary Chrysler Local No. 17 of UAW-CIO; Michigan State Senator, STANLEY NOWAK; Prof. J. J. ZMRHAL, President of the Czechoslovak National Council; JOSEPH MARTINEK, Executive Secretary of the Czechoslovak National Council, Chicago; KAREL PRCHAL, President of the American Sokol Union; ADOLF RACER, President of the Czech American National Alliance; VINCENT VRDSKY, Secretary of the Czech American National Alliance; Rev. JAN S. BRADAC, Honorary President of the Slovak National Alliance; Rev. ARNOST BIZKA of the Federation of American Czechoslovaks in Texas; NICOLA TESLA, Serbian American inventor; ETBIN KRISTAN, prominent Slovenian writer; Dr. D. K. YATICH, first vice-president Michigan All-Slav Committee; SAMUEL ERLINICH, President of the Serbian National Federation, Pittsburgh; Judge ANTHONY LUCAS, Pittsburgh; Ohio State Senator BOYD-BOICH; Judge GEORGE S. TENESY, Cleveland;

RAYMOND TRAVNIK, Slovenska Narodna Podporna Jednota; Rev. M. F. DENKO, Cleveland; W. TRUZIK, President of the Czechoslovak Society of America; and Mrs. MARIE KRAL of the Nat'l Alliance of Czech Catholics.

From the serious and restrained mood of the delegates it was visible they had come for the one purpose of agreeing on a common line of action to be taken to guarantee a speedy end of HITLER and the Axis. There was a notable absence of the usual convention hilarity and abandon.

An International Event

It was a wartime meeting dominated by a wartime grimness. That the deliberations of the congress would have international repercussions was evidenced in the more than thousand telegrams from all parts of the world that reached the congress during the sessions.

One of the wires greeting it was from a Czech group in Teheran, Persia; there were many from Slavic groups in Chile, Argentina, Canada, and throughout America. Soviet writers and scientists and members of the Yuglslav government in Kuibyshev wired the congress messages of greetings and good wishes.

The Congress was not only an event significant in the history of America's 15 million Slav-descended citizens but fraught with meaning for the destiny of the more than 200 millions of Slav peoples across the seas engaged in a life-and-death struggle against Nazi enslavers.

For the first time the peoples of the diverse Slavic groups in America were reaching a common understanding on a world-wide issue—a matter that gave delegates a feeling of considerable satisfaction.

Far beyond the brilliantly delivered keynote speeches and the iron note of resolve sounded in the resolutions—all of which raised the assembly to wild cheers of enthusiasm—was the vibrant sense of unity which, given expression by the congress carried to the Slav peoples throughout the world its message of redoubled efforts to crush HITLER and guarantee a democratic victory for the world.

Keynote--Production for Victory

Production and sacrifice were the keynote motifs of the main address of the congress delivered by LEO KRZYCKI. Reminding listeners that American Slavs occupy a key position in America's war industrial pattern, he called for greater efforts this year to turn the scales of victory in favor of the democracies.

How to safeguard American war production and American morale took up the following sessions which were addressed by Prof. J. J. ZMRHAL, President of the Czechoslovak National Council of America, on fifth-column activities and measures to be taken against them; FRANK ISBEY, chairman of the Michigan Defense Savings Program on national morale; ELI OLIVER, of the Labor Division of the War Production Board and GEORGE ADDES, Secretary-Treasurer of the Auto Workers Union on problems facing labor in the war industries. These subjects were treated in further detail in special panel discussions later.

10,000 Hear Hon. Paul V. McNutt

Two thousand plates were served at the banquet tendered the delegates and guests by the Michigan Committee of the American Slav Congress in the Masonic Temple on April 25.

But the climax of the congress was a victory rally in the Michigan State Fair Coliseum where 10,000 persons assembled to hear the Hon. PAUL V. McNUTT, Federal Security Administrator and U. S. Government representative to the Congress who greeted the delegates and drew thunderclaps of applause by his appeal for "more tanks for TIMOSHENKO". "In this first Slav Congress you have shown the world the miracle of American unity," he declared.

A message from President ROOSEVELT was received wishing the Congress success in its work."

- 6 -

INDEX TO INFORMANTS

The following is the Index to Informants mentioned in the report of Special Agent CLARENCE E. CLAY, dated November 18, 1942, at Indianapolis, Indiana, in the matter entitled, "AMERICAN SLAV CONGRESS (All-Slav Congress) INTERNAL SECURITY - C", Indianapolis file 100-4006:

b2
b7C
b7D
o/S

1.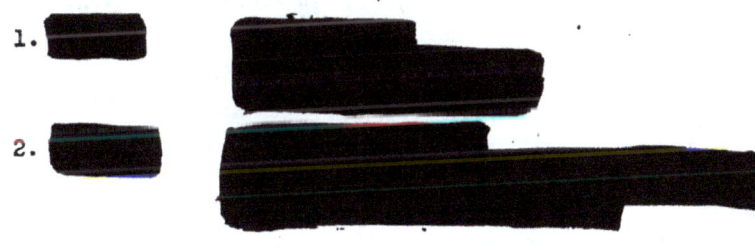

2.

P E N D I N G

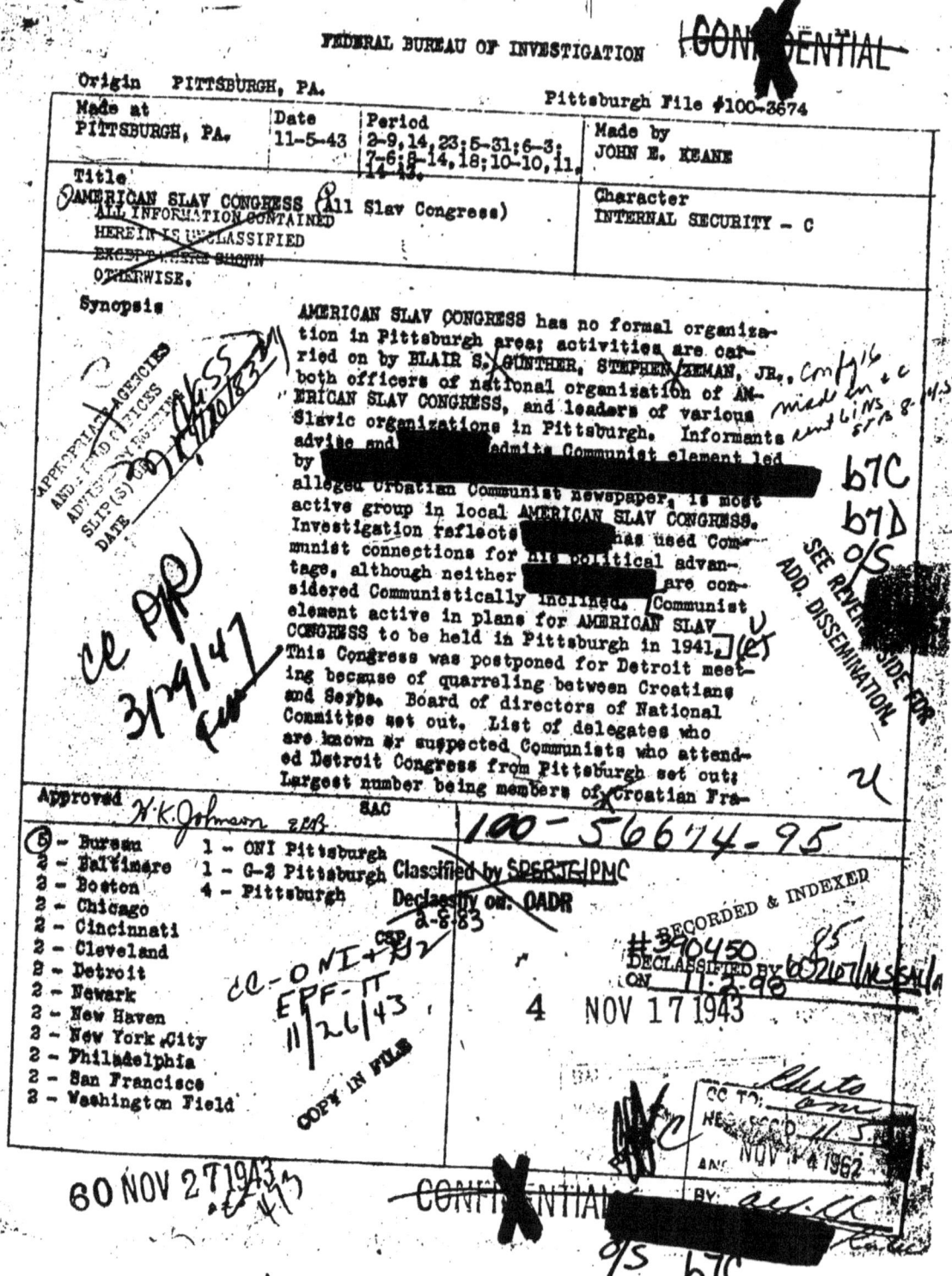

PG #100-3674

started calling him down for connecting his name with that of Communism.

▓▓▓▓▓▓▓▓▓▓ advised that he knew that ▓▓▓▓▓▓▓▓▓▓ was running the labor end of his campaign, and that if he didn't want his name linked with Communists he shouldn't associate with them. ▓▓▓▓ advised that during the ensuing conversation ▓▓▓▓ admitted that ▓▓▓▓ was running the labor end of his campaign, and that he had given support to ▓▓▓▓ on the occasion of his announcing his candidacy.

Confidential Informant ▓▓▓▓ was questioned regarding the infiltration of un-American elements into the AMERICAN SLAV CONGRESS, and corroborated the information furnished by ▓▓ and ▓▓▓▓

It should be noted that Confidential Informant ▓▓▓▓ advised that the national organization of the AMERICAN SLAV CONGRESS has no control with the various state organizations, such as the New York State and the Michigan State groups of the AMERICAN SLAV CONGRESS.

b2
b7C
b7D
O/S

▓▓▓▓ made available the current listing of officers of the AMERICAN SLAV CONGRESS. The national officers, and the national vice-presidents are not being set out here, inasmuch as the correct list is set out in referenced report of Special Agent A. ROBERT SWANSON, dated 3-16-43 at New York City.

The following are the names and addresses and organizational connections of the National Board of Directors of the AMERICAN SLAV CONGRESS:

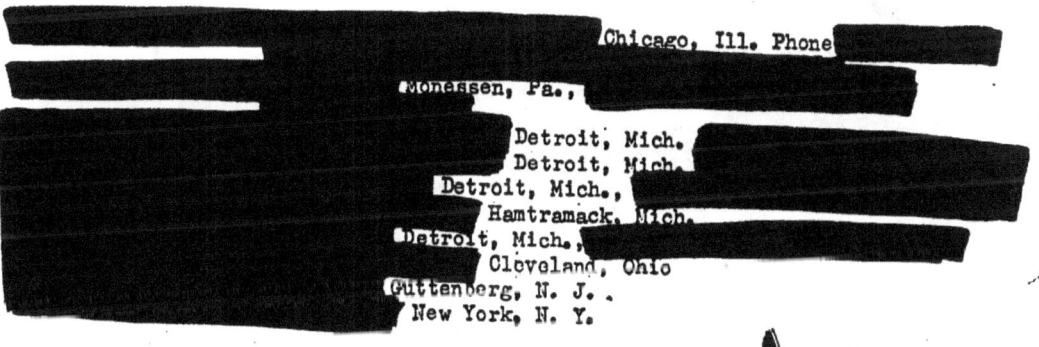

▓▓▓▓▓▓▓▓▓▓ Chicago, Ill. Phone ▓▓▓▓
▓▓▓▓▓▓▓▓▓▓ Monessen, Pa.,
▓▓▓▓▓▓▓▓▓▓ Detroit, Mich.
▓▓▓▓▓▓▓▓▓▓ Detroit, Mich.
▓▓▓▓▓▓▓▓▓▓ Detroit, Mich.,
▓▓▓▓▓▓▓▓▓▓ Hamtramack, Mich.
▓▓▓▓▓▓▓▓▓▓ Detroit, Mich.,
▓▓▓▓▓▓▓▓▓▓ Cleveland, Ohio
▓▓▓▓▓▓▓▓▓▓ Guttenberg, N. J.,
▓▓▓▓▓▓▓▓▓▓ New York, N. Y.

PG #100-3674

[redacted] Woodbridge, N. J.
[redacted] Whiting, Indiana
[redacted] Chicago, Ill.
[redacted] Cleveland, Ohio
Rev. KRAJNOVICH, (Deceased), Johnstown, Pa.
NIKOLA TESLA, New York City, N. Y.
[redacted] Detroit, Mich.
[redacted] Chicago, Ill.
[redacted] Berwyn, Ill.
[redacted] Detroit, Mich.
[redacted] address not known
[redacted] Chicago, Ill.
[redacted] St. Louis, Mo.
[redacted] Pittsburgh, Pa.
[redacted] Pittsburgh, Pa.
[redacted] N. S. Pittsburgh, Pa.
[redacted] Etna, Pa.
[redacted] Pittsburgh, Pa.
[redacted] Dearborn, Mich.
[redacted] Cleveland, Ohio
[redacted] Euclid, Ohio
[redacted] Detroit, Mich.
[redacted] Brooklyn, N. Y.
[redacted] New York, N. Y.
[redacted] Astoria Long Island, N. Y.
[redacted] Detroit, Mich.
[redacted] New York City, N. Y.
[redacted] Cleveland, Ohio
[redacted] Pittsburgh, Pa.
[redacted] Gary, Ind.
[redacted] address not known
[redacted] Scranton, Pa.

Confidential Informant [redacted] made available to the writer a listing of those persons from the Pittsburgh Field Division who attended the AMERICAN SLAV CONGRESS in Detroit on April 25 and 26, 1942. It is noted that this list totaled 198 names of persons who were representing 91 different organizations. The Croatian Fraternal Union with 35 representatives attending the Detroit Congress had the largest representation. Next in number of

PG #100-3674

The Newark Field Division will make a preliminary investigation of these officers by checking its indices, and interrogating Communist informants. If such preliminary check indicates Communist activity on the part of such officers, their activities as affects the AMERICAN SLAV CONGRESS, should be thoroughly investigated and reported herein.

THE NEW HAVEN FIELD DIVISION

* AT BRIDGEPORT, CONNECTICUT

Will ascertain the activities held on "All-Slav Sunday", June 21, 1942.

Will ascertain the extent of Communist control of the local offices of the AMERICAN SLAV CONGRESS, if such have been established, and in the organizations of which it is composed.

THE NEW YORK FIELD DIVISION

Will check the names of the delegates from New York to the Detroit Congress of April 25, 1942, with the indices, to ascertain if any of the delegates have previously been reported as Communists or as having been affiliated with Communist organizations.

Will keep in touch with confidential informants to ascertain further activities of Subject organization.

The following individuals are officers of the National Organization of the AMERICAN SLAV CONGRESS, residing in the New York Field Division:

NOKOLA TESLA

-22-

PG #100-3674

The New York Office will make a preliminary investigation as to such officers by checking the indices and interrogating Communist informants. If such preliminary check indicates Communist activity on the part of such officers, their activities as affects the AMERICAN SLAV CONGRESS should be thoroughly investigated and reported herein.

THE PHILADELPHIA FIELD DIVISION

* * AT PHILADELPHIA, PA.

Will ascertain the extent of Communist control in local offices of the AMERICAN SLAV CONGRESS and in organizations sending delegates to the AMERICAN SLAV CONGRESS.

THE SAN FRANCISCO FIELD DIVISION

* AT SAN FRANCISCO, CALIFORNIA

Through appropriate sources of information, will continue its contact with those All-Slav organizations in the San Francisco Bay Area which are known to subscribe to the platform of the Detroit Congress.

Through discreet investigation will endeavor to ascertain the activities of the All-Slavic Second Front Committee which was established in July of 1942.

Will continue its survey of organized Communist infiltration into the Slav community of Northern California.

THE WASHINGTON FIELD DIVISION

AT WASHINGTON, D. C.

Will establish connection between persons and organizations mentioned in the ████████████ with a view to determining Communist control thereof, and particularly to establish relation of the AMERICAN SLAV CONGRESS to the Russian government inspired ALL SLAV CONGRESS held in Moscow.

Will ascertain the extent of Communist control of the local offices of the AMERICAN SLAV CONGRESS, if such have been established, and in the organizations of which it is composed.

-23-

PG #100-3674

- CONFIDENTIAL INFORMANTS -

is ██
was vouched for by ██████████████ loyalty
set out in instant report.   whose identity is

is ██
████ located at ████████████████████████████
It is noted that all persons interviewed in
instant report advised that there is no question that
████ might be unloyal, and that he was not in any way
a Communist sympathizer.

It is also noted that prior to being interviewed in instant matter ████ was interviewed regarding another
case, at which time he voluntarily gave the name of an
individual ████████████████ whom he considered to
be a Communist.

is ████████████████ whose identity is known to the
Bureau, although not in connection with any symbol.

is ██
████████████████████████████████████ who has
previously been used by this office as a ████████ informant, and who is known to be reliable.

is the ██████████████████████████████████████

report of SA ████████████████████████████████
████ entitled ██████████████████████████████

is ██

b1
b2
b7C
b7D

- 25 -

SUBJECT: AMERICAN SLAV CONGRESS   CASE: INTERNAL SECURITY - C
S. A.: JOHN E. KEANE
DATE: 11/5/43

TABLE OF CONTENTS

AMERICAN-CARPATHIAN-RUSSIAN COUNCIL	2
AMERICAN SERBIAN PUBLISHING COMPANY	12
AMERICAN YUGOSLAV NATIONAL LEAGUE	3
	10
ARIA SINGING SOCIETY	10
	6
	10
	6
	16
	9
	9
	16
	9
	22
	19
	20
	9, 22
	10
	9
	10
	2, 4
CARPATHO-RUSSIAN SECTION	6, 7
	10
	7, 8
	6
	10
	10
CONFIDENTIAL INFORMANT	13, 14
CONFIDENTIAL INFORMANT	10, 13
CONFIDENTIAL INFORMANT	21
CONFIDENTIAL INFORMANT	12
CROATIAN FRATERNAL UNION	1, 3, 5, 9, 10, 11, 12, 14
CROATIAN NATIONAL CONGRESS	14
	14
	11
	14

-26-

IV

```
                                                              12   o/s
                                                          9,  20
                                                              12
                                                              19
                                                               6
                                                              22
TESLA, NIKOLA                                             8,  20   o/s
TESLA, NIKOLA                                                  9
                                                              22
                                                               9
                                                               9
TRI-STATE SLAV CONGRESS                                        2

UKRANIAN WORKING MEN'S ASSOCIATION                            11
UNITED AMERICAN SLAV COUNCIL                              16, 21
UNITED AMERICAN SLAVS                                         18
UNITED ELECTRICAL AND RADIO MACHINE WORKERS OF AMERICA    11, 12
UNITED MINE WORKERS                                           13
UNITED RUSSIAN WAR RELIEF COMMITTEE                            6
UNITED SLAV COUNCIL                                            6

VIDOVDEN COMMITTEE                                            11
                                                              12
                                                              12
                                                              12   o/s
                                                       2, 16, 17
                                                           3,  5
                                                               8
                                                              13

                                                              13
                                                              13
                                                           6,  9
                                                               6
                                                              14

                                                              13
                                                           8,  9
                                                           8, 22
                                                        1, 2,  5
                                                               9
                                                              21
                                                               7
```

b7C

-29-

FEDERAL BUREAU OF INVESTIGATION

FILE NO.				
OFFICE OF ORIGIN				
REPORT MADE AT	DATE WHEN MADE	PERIOD FOR WHICH MADE	REPORT MADE BY	
NEW YORK				
TITLE			CHARACTER OF CASE	
AMERICAN SLAV CONGRESS			INTERNAL SECURITY — C REGISTRATION ACT	

SYNOPSIS OF FACTS:

In radio broadcast 7/27/47 ASC official asserted that first ASC Congress held 4/25,26/42, Detroit, Michigan, grew out of Tri-State All Slav Congress meeting in Pittsburgh, Pa., 12/3/38; stressed role of ASC in uniting Slavic groups for "peace, economic security and progress". Present plans for expansion envision concentrated work through nationality panels. Recent activities include: National Committee Meeting, New York City, 10/11,12/47; testimonial banquet in honor of Senator CLAUDE PEPPER, NYC, 10/12/47; National Committee Meeting, Detroit, Michigan, 2/28,29/48. Views disseminated through quarterly magazine "The Slavic American", ASC Bulletins, leaflet "Keep America Free", published at Pittsburgh, and various releases. Attempts continue to expand activities of Slavic-American Youth Council. In spite of ██████████████████████ is extremely weak. ██████ recently replaced ██████ as Financial Secretary. Communist affiliation and connections of ██████████ reportedly known to Resident Board, summarized; ██████ has been in periodic contact with STEVE NELSON, Chairman, Nationality Groups Commission, CPUSA, who on 6/21/47 was reliably reported to have stated, "The American Slav Congress should be the Communist Party's top organization in the United States...." and who on 10/13/47 recruited ██████ Pittsburgh ASC leader, into ranks of CP, as possible successor to PIRINSKY. ASC follows

100 - 56674 - 1096

COPIES DESTROYED

ENCLOSURE BEHIND FILE

Copies:
- 6 - Bureau
- 2 - Chicago
- 2 - Cleveland
- 2 - Detroit
- 2 - Los Angeles
- 2 - Milwaukee
- 2 - Pittsburgh
- 2 - St. Louis
- 2 - San Francisco
- 1 - Washington Field
- 1 - Newark (Inf)
- 1 - Boston (Inf)
- 4 - New York

41824

NY 100-26200

▓▓▓ Confidential Informant ▓▓▓ supplied a circular letter
dated ▓▓▓ signed by ▓▓▓
▓▓▓ etc. ▓▓▓
planned. It has therefore become necessary to ▓▓▓

In the matter of finances it may be noted that according to
information supplied by Confidential Informant ▓▓▓
▓▓▓ reported that
the first edition of "The Slavic American" had been printed at a deficit
▓▓▓
▓▓▓ have been received, including
▓▓▓ from
▓▓▓ and that the remaining ▓▓▓ were scattered
throughout the United States.

The first two issues of "The Slavic American", furnished
by Confidential Informant ▓▓▓ contain the following articles:

Vol. 1, Fall 1947, No. 1

Articles

Henry Wallace, Champion of Peace	3	by Leo Krzycki
Poland's Western Boundaries	5	by Congressman G. Sadowski
Statement on the Truman Doctrine At Senate Foreign Relations Committee Hearings	6	By George Pirinsky
As a Veteran Sees It, First in a Series of Articles	9	by Captain George Pirinsky
Spotlight on the Balkans, Statements on Balkan-Greek Question at U.N. Security Council Hearings	20	by Warren R. Austin, U. S. Representative and Andrei A. Gromyko, U.S.S.R. Representative
The Real Bulgaria In Answer to Life Magazine	50	by Dr. Nissim Mevorah

CONFIDENTIAL

- 28 -

NY 100-26200

CONFIDENTIAL

41825

Features

Story of the American Slav Congress	10	The Record of an Organization
Leo Krzycki, Fifty Years a Servant of the People	18	............by Tabitha Petran
One World Flight, Stop-Over in Moscow	34	............by Norman Corwin
Czechoslovak Sokol in America	40	The Symbol of a People
We Felt the Heartbeat of New Yugoslavia; The Rebuilding of a Country	43	............by Zlatko Balokovic
Bright Passage, A Review of the new book on Czechoslovakia, by Maurice Hindus	47	
Savo Radulovich	48	............by Vsko Yugoslav Artist
Highlights of Slavic American News	52	Notes on Rallies and Conferences
Slavic American Youth Get Together	54	......Youth councils in action

Stories

My American Pilgrimage, Excerpts from the new novel	38	............by Stoyan Christowe
The Importance of Being Kobotchnick A story of a Man and His Dog	42	............by Louis Adamic

Vol. 1, Winter 1947, No. 2

Articles

Conspiracy Against Peace	5	............by Louis Adamic
Deportation Laws Hit Slavic Americans	13	............by Abner Green
Analysis of the Marshall Plan	22	............by George Pirinsky
Program and Activities of the American Slav Congress	29	............by George Pirinsky

- 29 -

CONFIDENTIAL

NY 0100-26200

Features

Nikola Tesla	3	by Pauline Kloptcka
Tribute to A Fighting Senator	9	ASC Testimonial Dinner
The World Youth Festival	10	by Ilona Vlahov
U.S.S.R. Thirty Years After Feudal-ism	14	by S. Aderbuzov
Summary of a Journey	24	by Ella Winter
The Story of Gee Milev	31	by Maria Vladimirova
Prague	32	Europe's New Film Capital
Slav Saga in Pennsylvania	33	by Lyla Y. Slocum
		Eugene Konecky
American Clergymen See the New Yugoslavia	38	Digest of their Report
Pages from an Artist's Notebook	42	by Alvent Bockar
Five Women	44	by Marie Seton

Fiction

Wedding Day	7	by Thomas Bell

2) <u>ASC Bulletins</u>

Confidential Informant ▬▬▬ furnished a copy of a circular letter dated February 12, 1948, addressed to members of the National Committee and to State and City Committees of the ASC, the opening paragraph of which letter reads as follows:

"This will introduce to you the ASC BULLETIN, a report on the activities of the National Office and the State and City Committees, which will be sent to you monthly. It will serve the dual purpose of keeping you informed of American Slav Congress doings around the country, and of supplying local ASC committees with helpful material for monthly meetings and general activities."

The six page ASC Bulletin itself, attached to the above mentioned letter, was dated January-February, 1948, and its contents were listed as follows:

NY 100-26200   41860

ENCLOSURES (5) TO BUREAU

        One copy of seating list of Testimonial Dinner in honor of Senator CLAUDE PEPPER, Pennsylvania Hotel, October 12, 1947, sponsored by American Slav Congress.

        One copy of press release dated October 12, 1947, entitled, "Excerpts from address of Senator CLAUDE PEPPER (D-Fla.) at Testimonial Dinner for him given by the American Slav Congress, New York City, October 12, 1947."

        One copy of nineteen page mimeographed brochure entitled, "Keep America Free! Help Prevent a New War! Excerpts from Report by GEORGE PIRINSKY, Executive Secretary of the American Slav Congress, delivered before the National Committee Meeting, October 11, 1947, Hotel Pennsylvania, New York. 1. Truman Doctrine; 2. Marshall Plan; 3. Loyalty Order; 4. Food Crisis; Inflation."

        Two copies of quarterly magazine "The Slavic American", Winter 1947 issue.

- P E N D I N G -

NY 100-26200

CONFIDENTIAL INFORMANTS

The Confidential Informants mentioned in the report of SA ELMER L. ROTH dated June 23, 1948 at New York are as follows:

- Confidential mailbox maintained by the New York Office.
- Confidential Informant ███████ whose identity is known to the Bureau.
- Confidential Informant ███████ whose identity is known to the Bureau.
- ████████████████████ (treated confidential at ███ request).
- Confidential Informant ███████ whose identity is known to the Bureau.
- ███████ who arranged to monitor the proceedings at the Hotel Pennsylvania, New York City, 10/12/47.
- SA ELMER L. ROTH, who, with SA LITTLE ███ above, arranged to monitor the proceedings at the Hotel Pennsylvania, New York City, 10/12/47.
- Confidential Informant ███████ whose identity is known to the Bureau.
- Confidential Informant ███████ whose identity is known to the Bureau.

- 69 -

THE SLAVIC AMERICAN

50¢

Louis Adamic
Thomas Bell
S. Garbuzov
Abner Green
E. Konecky
Alvena Seckar
Marie Seton
Lyla Y. Slocum
M. Vladimirova
Ilene Vlahov
Ella Winter

NIKOLA TESLA - Poet in Electricity

WINTER 1947

Nikola TESLA

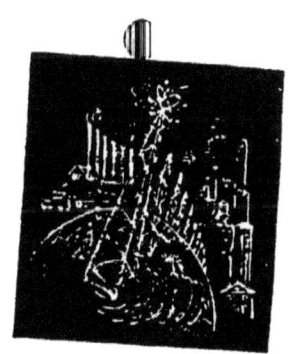

Whose daring imagination and concrete accomplishments are among the wonders of our age.

By PAULINE KLOPACKA

WHEN Nikola Tesla died in January of 1943 in comparative seclusion in a New York hotel, he owned no more than the few personal possessions that had become dear to him during the 86 years of his life. Yet his estate was so fabulous that its value can never be truly assessed. And his heirs were the men and women of all the world.

What price can be put on the work of a man who brought into being the electric power era? The industrial giant that the U. S. is today rests on the series of brilliant discoveries and inventions in the harnessing and transmission of electricity conceived by Nikola Tesla, who came to this country from the land of the South Slavs when he was 28 years of age.

It was at midnight between July 9 and 10 in 1856 that a son, Nikola, was born to the Rev. Milutin Tesla and Djouka, his wife, in the little Serbian village of Smiljan, in the province of Lika. Now a part of Yugoslavia, it was at that time under Austro-Hungarian rule.

Tesla's father, a Serb, was a priest of the Greek Church, and his mother of a distinguished Serbian family, came from a long line of inventors. Both father and mother gave to the child a valuable heritage and culture developed and passed on by ancestral families that had been community leaders for many generations.

It was at first planned that the son prepare for the priesthood but Nikola would have none of this. Physics and mathematics fascinated him. He would be a teacher of these favorite subjects. But then he switched to electrical engineering and at the age of 25 a graduate of Prague University—earlier training had been obtained at the Graz Polytechnic in Austria—he was set for his first job.

At that time the American Telephone System was brought to Europe and an installation set up in Budapest, where Tesla was a successful applicant for a position.

THREE years later, in 1884, he was U. S. bound. There were 4 cents in the young immigrant's pocket when he arrived in New York, but that did not disturb him. He had the names of friends. He would soon get to work.

His confidence was well founded, since within a few years he was counted among the ranking scientists of the country, his discoveries bringing in handsome royalties.

It is interesting to note the description of Tesla at this time by his biographer, J. J. O'Neill in the book, "Prodigal Genius": "Tesla was a

Drawings by Alvena Seckar

3

spectacular figure in New ...rk in 1891. A tall, dark, handsome, well-built individual with a flare for wearing clothes that gave him an air of magnificence, who spoke perfect English but carried an atmosphere of European culture. He was an outstanding personality to all who beheld him." One of his colleagues described him as "immaculately groomed, and of delightful courtesy and charm."

A review of Tesla's work is nothing short of amazing. To quote from J. J. O'Neill's book:

"It was Tesla's invention of the polyphase alternating current system that was directly responsible for harnessing Niagara Falls and opening the modern electric superpower era in which electricity is transported for hundreds of miles to operate the tens of thousands of mass production factories of our industrial system.

"Every one of the tall, Martian transmission lines that stalks across the earth and whose wires carry electricity to distant cities is a monument to Tesla, every dynamo and every motor that drives every machine in the country is a monument to him.

"He discovered the secret of transmitting electric power to the utmost ends of the earth without wires and demonstrated his system by which power could be drawn from the earth anywhere by making a connection to the ground; he set the entire earth in electrical vibration with a generator which sprouted lightning that rivaled the fiery artillery of the heavens. It was a minor portion of this discovery that he created the modern radio system. He planned our broadcasting methods of today 40 years ago when others saw in the wireless only the dot and dash message that might save ships in distress.

"Tesla was an inventor but he was much more than a producer of devices. He was a discoverer of new principles opening many new empires of knowledge which even today have been only partly explored. In a single burst of invention he created the world of power of today.

"He brought into being our electric power era, the rock bottom foundation on which the industrial system of the entire world is builded. He gave us our mass production system for without his motors and currents it could not exist.

"He gave us every essential of current radio. He invented radar 40 years before its use in World War II. He gave us our modern neon and other forms of gaseous tube lighting. He gave us fluorescent lighting. He gave us the high frequency currents which are performing their electronic wonders throughout the industrial and medical world. He gave us remote control by wireless."

Always proud of his national origin, Tesla spoke as follows during his visit to Belgrade in 1892 in answer to a speech of welcome by the city's mayor: "There is something in which is only perhaps illusory ... but if I were to be sufficiently fortunate to bring about at least some of my ideas it would be for the benefit of all humanity. If these hopes become one day a reality, my greatest joy would spring from the fact that this work would be the work of a Serb."

Tesla dedicated his life to peace, to lightening the burden of toil from the shoulders of his fellow man. As every scientist who so interprets his function in society, he was stricken when he saw the coming of World War II and his inventions being prepared for destructive purposes. He sought desperately to prevent the war and made available a device which he offered to the world, maintaining that it would make any country, no matter how small, safe within its boundaries. His offer was rejected.

But once the war was an accomplished fact, and when the people's armies rose in defense of their nations in what appeared to be an unequal fight, he did all he could to rally his countrymen to work to the limit in the war effort.

Shortly before his death he wrote as follows to his nephew, M. Sava Kosanovic, now Yugoslav Ambassador to the U. S.:

"President Roosevelt and Donald Nelson, Director of our War Production have repeatedly urged the American people, workers and employers, to meet as fully as possible the goals established for the production of war materials. ... For that reason, my dear brothers and sisters, as the oldest Serb, Yugoslav and American in the U. S., I am addressing this letter to you, asking you to answer the call of President Roosevelt.

"The achievements of our brothers in the old country are worthy of the spirit which permeates our folklore ... the fate of the Serbs, Croats and Slovenes is inseparable."

Tesla was not satisfied with his achievements in releasing the earth's energies so that men could work with less backbreaking effort and live more comfortably. The man who could draw up a design for a perfect motor was also concerned with drawing up a plan for a better world. When Tesla read the address of the then Vice-President, Henry A. Wallace, on The Future of the Common Man, he was fired with enthusiasm. The Yugoslav edition of the speech included a preface by Nikola Tesla written in October, 1942:

"Out of this war, the greatest since the beginning of history, a new world must be born, a world that would justify the sacrifices offered by humanity. This new world must be a world in which there shall be no exploitation of the weak by the strong, of the good by the evil; where there will be no humiliation of the poor by the violence of the rich; where the products of intellect, science and art will serve society for the betterment and beautification of life, and not individuals for the amassing of wealth. This new world shall not be a world of the downtrodden and humiliated, but of free men and free nations, equal in dignity and respect for man ..."

This man, whose work was so advanced of his time that much of it still remains unexplored could have amassed millions, but he was so little interested in personal gain that to save his friend, Mr. Westinghouse, from bankruptcy he tore up a contract which would have brought him $12 millions in royalties. Pressed for funds during the latter part of his life, many of his inventions are lost to the world.

But though he was often short of money he would walk over to Herald Square and feed the pigeons. It was almost a sacred trust, feeding the pigeons twice a day. They had been his personal responsibility through the years, and if he could not be there to do the feeding, a Western Union messenger boy would be hired to do the job in his stead. Often he would forget an important engagement so that he might keep his "date" on Herald Square. The pigeons were a way to relaxation, a note of warmth in an otherwise rigidly disciplined life. He had few friends and never married, since he felt a scientist must keep himself free of personal relationships that would be unduly demanding.

Restless and eager to unravel every possible unknown to the very end of

(Continued on page 49)

~ GEO MILEV

describes only from the standpo[int] of his art.... In his attitude to[war]d various events in the life around him, which impress him strongly, he does not take sides. He does not praise one and hurt the other; he merely describes everything he sees, describes it with the delicate, sweet colors of poetry.... ."

Geo was fined 20,000 leva and sentenced to one year in prison. He could not believe that the court could make such a decision. With joking reference to the dullness of "their Honors," he left the courtroom believing that the decision would never be carried out.

He was right. Unable to enforce their decision legally, the government resorted to illegal means.

Next day, May 15, 1925, Geo was kidnapped from his home and killed by underlings of Prime Minister Alexander Tzankoff.

The cultural world of Europe protested Geo's death. Henri Barbusse, of France, visited Bulgaria to investigate the case. In his book "The Murderers" he made reference to the circumstances of Geo's death. Max Reinhardt protested and "regretted the loss of a very gifted theater director." Oskar Kokoshka, in Vienna, recognized the loss of "a precious critic and learned connoisseur of modern art."

Many Bulgarian writers were silent. Fearing for their lives, they did not dare to speak a word for Geo Milev or express regret for his death. The more courageous of them stated that "talent such as Geo's is born only once in a hundred years," that "He was the most cultured Bulgarian," "The most honest and courageous."

THE youth and the common people deeply mourned for Geo. They knew they had lost a sincere friend and inspirer. Unable to use the Bulgarian printing presses, they copied his poem by hand and learned it by heart. Bulgarian students abroad printed it in Paris, and in Belgrade. In Prague it was translated into Czech and in Russia into Russian.

A few courageous young people in Bulgaria printed pamphlets about Geo. They were promptly tortured and imprisoned.

We, his family, searched for him for months, but we never learned exactly where and how he was killed. There were rumors that he had been shot in the mountains, that he had been burned in the furnace of "Public Safety." These measures were used by Bulgarian Fascists long before the world knew of Hitler. Both stories, however, avowed that his spirit was not crushed.

Geo's voice was silenced forever. The murderers triumphed, but they forgot that he who speaks for the freedom of a tormented and deprived people does not die. In today's New Bulgaria, Geo Milev is honored as one of her most cherished sons. Geo's poems are celebrated especially by the youth of today, the heirs of the September Revolution of 1944, which fulfilled his prediction of a decade before that "September will be May."

TESLA
(Continued from page 4)

his life, he read a paper on the occasion of his 80th birthday on the perfection of a tube for atom smashing. As if that were not enough, he also presented a system of interplanetary communication.

Thus the fragmentary story of the life and work of a Yugoslav immigrant who, like so many tens of thousands of his fellow countrymen, left their homeland rather than live as subjects within the Austro-Hungarian empire.

He made a unique contribution to his adopted land, so ideally suited to the full scope of his genius, "the like of which in all history could probably be counted on the fingers of one hand."

It is to be hoped that just as he brought electrification to the U. S. in the short span of ten years, his adopted country might assist in the full electrification of the Balkans, reversing its present policy toward New Yugoslavia.

THE AMERICAN SLAV COMMITTEE
of Canton, Ohio
welcomes the new magazine
THE SLAVIC AMERICAN
and projects best wishes for its success. This organ, we know, will be a great contribution to the enlightenment of the homes of American Slavs.

Greetings to the Second Issue
of
THE SLAVIC AMERICAN
and
Best Wishes for Continued Success
in the Coming Year
ALL SLAVIC COUNCIL OF
NORTHERN CALIFORNIA
739 Page Street, San Francisco, Calif.

GREETINGS FROM
JIM BALANOFF

Greetings from Lodge 3052
American-Russian Fraternal Society, IWO
1010 East Foss Avenue   Flint, Mich.

Greetings from
CLUB "YUGO-FORWARD"
Detroit, Mich.

THE STANLEY THEATRE
Presents
The Best Films from the U.S.S.R.
NOW! "THE GREAT GLINKA"
7th Ave. & 42nd St.   New York City

Best Wishes for Success to
THE SLAVIC AMERICAN
American Russian Fraternal Society
Lodge 3069
120 Glenmore Ave.   Brooklyn, N. Y.

Efficient Service Since 1919
LEON BENOFF
General Insurance Broker
391 East 149th St., New York
MElrose 5-0984
Insurance is cheaper to have than to need

49

Office Memorandum • UNITED STATES GOVERNMENT

TO : Director, FBI
DATE: April 11, 1949

FROM : SAC, New York

SUBJECT: AMERICAN SLAV CONGRESS;
INTERNAL SECURITY - C
(Bufile 100-56674)

Enclosed are two copies of the Fall, 1948 issue of "The Slavic American", a quarterly, published by the American Slav Congress.

These are being submitted for information only, not for evidence. One copy is being retained in the files of this office.

Encls. 2

AS:DC
100-26200

100-56674-1168

SLAVIC AMERICAN

a Quarterly

CONFIDENTIAL

The American Slav Congress

The Fourth American Slav Congress

Hysteria and Red-Baiting

Club Metro Dancers, Chicago

FALL 1948

Published by The American Slav Congress

The American Way of Life

by **LOUIS ADAMIC**

"Why Go to War to Keep Others From Having Their Way of Life," asks Adamic

THE opening lines of the Progressive Party's platform read: "Three years after the end of the Second World War the drums are beating for a third. Civil liberties are being destroyed. Millions cry out for relief from unbearably high prices. The American Way of Life is in danger."

The American Way of Life has been the issue in any American election ever since 1776. Every voter who goes to the polls, votes—intelligently or mistakenly; independently or under the spell of inveterate partisanship—for one or another concept of the American Way of Life.

Of course, various people, living in various circumstances, have various ideas of what constitutes the American Way of Life. I propose to state my ideas of it; also I shall presume to fit those ideas within the frame of the new Progressive Party which must continue to grow from its beginnings in 1948.

As I see the American Way of Life, its principles were born of the American Revolution. They were won in struggle; nothing as fundamental and deep-reaching comes easy. They are stated in the Declaration of Independence and the Constitution of the United States. Our job now is to perceive what policies and measures will safeguard the Way against decay and corruption, and will further its growth and evolution to meet successfully the problem of changing times and new conditions. The principles of 1776 are as valid as ever, but life is different today from what it was then. Fortunately growth and change are of the very essence of the American Way.

The first principle of the American Way of Life is the *right to life* itself; and this must be safeguarded against war on the one hand, and on the other against poverty, which in recent decades has taken a far heavier toll than any war in which this nation has ever so far been involved—though the "next war," if we permit it to be drummed up, will reverse the story.

The second principle of the American Way is *liberty* . . . it has always been our slogan and our pride. But we have long been cautioned that its price is eternal vigilance, and we know how to recognize those who have designs on it.

The third principle of our Way is *abundance*. When migrants from Europe first began to settle here, this was a land rich in the gifts of nature; and for all that those gifts have been abused by ignorance and irresponsibility, and particularly by exploiters and monopolists. Our resources are still great enough—if deforestation and erosion are checked in time, and if our mineral resources are properly conserved—to afford abundance, the good life, to all the inhabitants of These States.

And a fourth principle of the American Way is *opportunity*.

THE Progressive Party promises to safeguard the *right to life* by avoiding war—always the saddest failure of morality and now the potential destroyer of human society and the globe itself.

Whether or not we can avoid World War III, I don't know; but I do know this—that if we don't try to avoid it, nothing else is worth try-

LOUIS ADAMIC *Slovenian American author and lecturer, a foremost authority on national groups, he is a prolific writer. Among his works are My Native Land, Dinner at the White House, Two-Way Passage, Nation of Nations, My America. He also edits and publishes a current affairs bulletin, Trends and Tides, issued from his home in Milford, New Jersey.*

ing to do nowadays. It is futile to wonder about the kind of curtains you'll hang up in your living-room . . . futile to write or read books, to go to lectures or to school . . . silly to worry about being called a Red or a Communist, or whatever, or about being hauled up before the fantastic Un-American Activities Committee . . . futile to work at your job, whatever it may be . . . silly to worry about keeping on the good side of whoever can take that job away from you.

War or peace? I don't know; but if we want any sort of future for this country, for the rest of the world, for ourselves and the Russians, for you and me personally, then we'd better work for peace . . . stand up for peace . . . stand up with our new political vehicle, the Progressive Party.

The Progressive Party further proposes to safeguard the right to life by abolishing poverty. Cynics, presstitutes, and generally people without hope and vision say this can't be done. They say Henry Wallace is a starry-eyed visionary. We say it can be done if we will jealously maintain freedom, bear in mind the limitless capabilities of Americans, and keep the grip of monopoly from arrogating the resources that should serve all, and if we will insist upon the application of the ever more marvelous discoveries and techniques of science for the common good.

The Progressive Party proposes to safeguard *liberty* — not with more lip service, but by adhering fully to the Constitution, including the Bill of Rights and all subsequent amendments, in all their vitality and integrity, and by reviving and enhancing the programs and formulations of Roosevelt's New Deal. The Progressive Party proposes to guard liberty

(Continued on page 26)

A HALF HOUR OF MUSIC

with
**TWO DISTINGUISHED AMERICAN ARTISTS
OF SLAVIC DESCENT**

in a unique

Album of Recordings
Now on Sale

ZLATKO BALOKOVIC
Violinist

IVAN PETROFF
Baritone

By BALOKOVIC

HYMN TO THE SUN	Rimsky-Korsakoff
CROATIAN RHAPSODY	Lhotka
FOR ONE MOMENT OF JOY	Croatian Folk Song

By PETROFF

LEGEND	Bulgarian Folk Song
PEASANT'S LAMENT	Bulgarian Folk Song
ARIA PRINCE IGOR	Borodin

By BOTH

SONGS MY MOTHER TAUGHT ME	Dvorak
ELEGIE	Massenet

Prize selections for your library long to be cherished and enjoyed

FOUR RECORDS TO EACH ALBUM

$4 the Album

postage prepaid

USE CONVENIENT ORDER BLANK ➧

The American Way
(Continued from page 5)

against that danger which most disturbed the Founding Fathers—the power of the military. And note how all these things are inter-related. Liberty is imperiled by poverty, by monopoly, by war. Every measure which the new party proposes is a measure to safeguard liberty.

By *abundance*, the new party means that our rich land—and our skills, brought here by immigrants from the Old World in the last 300 years—shall produce all that is needed to make the good life available to every law-abiding and industrious man and woman here, and their children, regardless of color, race or religion; and that these fruits of enterprise and labor shall not be so ill-divided that a few are glutted with a surfeit of luxuries while many who toil and sweat must for reasons beyond their control still go "ill-fed, ill-clothed and ill-housed."

The pioneers who first possessed the Atlantic seaboard and later pressed westward through the forests and the prairies, could win abundance by strength and industry, by the wide swing of the axe, the true aim of the flintlock, and the firm hand on the plow. There was *opportunity galore*. Almost any man could get land for the asking or for a few dollars an acre, and become

(Continued on page 29)

AMERICAN SLAV CONGRESS
205 East 42nd Street
New York 17, N. Y.

$4 for album of 4 records

I enclose .... for ☐ album(s)

Name ....

Address ....

City & Zone ....

State ....

(Make checks and money orders payable to
AMERICAN SLAV CONGRESS

The American Way

(Continued from page 26)

an independent farmer. Any man could set up a little store in a new community and become a prosperous merchant as the town grew. Almost any man could start a paper, establish a factory or mill, or open a mine, and become an industrialist.

This is no longer true. Millions of square miles have been rendered useless for human use and habitation by irresponsible deforestation and by erosion. The number of family farms dwindles yearly; every day hundreds of independent merchants and small mining, milling and manufacturing companies are forced out of business by the power of monopoly, centered in Wall Street.

The relentless limitation of opportunity, the shrinking of abundance for millions, the violences done to liberty in defiance of the Constitution and in contempt of the tradition that began in 1776, the further threat against freedom in the ominous form of military rule, the denial of life itself to unnumbered victims of poverty, and the grave threat to all our lives in the probability of a war waged with atom bombs and bacteria —these developments, conditions and prospects now imperil the American Way of Life.

The Progressive Party proposes to restore and safeguard and extend that Way—the emphasis is on the word "extend." Nothing in nature stands still, and no more can human economic and social and political institutions. Change is the key principle of the American Way—growth, adaptation, progress. Had it not been for that principle, the USA would not exist—we would not now be debating the decisions made in an election; we would still be colonial subjects, or we wouldn't be here at all.

If we remembered more vividly what daring it took in 1776 to reject monarchy and form a republic, we would have less hesitation in rejecting the National Association of Manufacturers' notions of "free enterprise," and adopting measures more in keeping with today's facts of life. We would not hesitate to defy the greatest power on earth—that of monopoly corporations and cartels, whose agents have lately seized control of the U.S. Government.

Under Henry Wallace's leadership, the Progressive Party offers itself as a medium through which those who love their country and are also in favor of their own rightful individual interests can express themselves politically . . . in 1949 . . . 1950 . . . in 1952, assuming that the "next war," now being drummed up, won't destroy us all before then.

We know now that we have established a firm foundation for the new party under the leadership of Henry Wallace and Glen Taylor. Personally, I was not in this campaign only in reference to this year's election or because I think, as I do think, that Henry Wallace is a great American who should be in the White House in this crucial period. In the main, I was in this campaign because, like Wallace and Taylor, like many other Americans, I became convinced that neither of the old parties is fit to deal with the profound crisis which is coming to a climax in these middle years of the 20th century. I am in this movement because I want to help build a new people's party that will be capable of coping with the crisis now converging upon us and the rest of the world.

LIKE many Americans, I am foreign-born; and every once in a while I hear or read some remark to the effect that I have no right to be doing what I am doing—helping the growth of a new party which hopes to save the peace. Such remarks amuse me. It so happens that I have read rather extensively in American history, not as taught in most schools, but as it really happened; and I am impressed by this fact—that in all crucial or climactic periods in the career of this country, the so-called foreigners played important roles.

The Irish and German elements, for instance, were the big "foreign" groups around 1776, and it was they who became the backbone of General Washington's revolutionary army. The Irish and German elements also furnished the mass support to Thomas Jefferson when he started a new party 150 years ago. Jefferson did not triumph immediately (as Wallace didn't); his supporters stood it with him until he did (as I hope we will

(Continued on page 30)

Greetings From

MARY ANTONIC
BOZO BARANIC
MILO BARANIC
JOHN BEZELJ
PAUL BIAZEVICH
KAY BEGOVICH
FLORENCE FERKICH
GEORGE GELSOVICH
STEVE HROSTI
FRANK KURSOC
LJUBICA LOVRICH
ANTON PESUSICH
ERICA PETRAS
NICK PETRICH
A. PUJATCKY
LUCY LJUBENKO

Lodge 3172, A.R.F.S., Sioux City, Iowa

PETER ZAKUTONSKY
LOUIS KLYM
MARY KLYM
HELEN WONSOWIC
PAUL ROMANOV
MARY ROMANOV
BRANCH No. 14, LEMKO ASS'N, GARY, IND.
BRANCH No. 3295, IWO, CARPATHO-RUSSIANS, GARY, IND.
MILLIE KLYM
MICHAEL KLYM
ANNA SAMOZKA
WALTER IVANZOWICZ

A.S.C. of Newark, N. J.

JOHN J. KASKEVICH, M.D.
530 Summer Ave., Newark

JOHN BENKO
JOHN DOLINAJEC
MICHAEL DROBAN
STEVEN DZUROSKA
STEPHEN HRUSKA
TILLY JANOVITZ
MICHAEL KOLARIK
STEFAN LACKO
JOSEPH MATEJKA
MICHAEL MATEJKA
JOSEPH MEDVECKY
IMRO RIBAR
SHEPERO SHOE STORE
MATEJ STROMKO
STEFA TAL
JOSEPH TURZA
FRANK ZAVARTKAJ
JOSEPH ZILINEK

Delegates join in singing the National Anthem.

The American Way

(Continued from page 29)

with Wallace). The same was true again in the period of Andrew Jackson, when American democracy took another long step forward. When Lincoln came along and started a new party, his most steadfast backing came from the numerous new-immigrant groups—Germans, Finns, Poles, Scandinavians and others.

This was quite natural. As newcomers who came here seeking liberty, abundance and opportunity, they had a more acute sense of what America professed, and they took American principles more seriously than many of the old-line Americans who had begun to be matter-of-fact, if not smug, about the country. As newcomers, they were somewhat outside the mainstream of American life. By going behind the cause of Washington, Jefferson, Jackson and Lincoln, they became part of the mainstream. They promoted themselves from second-class citizens to first-class. It was Americanization at its very best. It made history, it enriched the traditions, it integrated the new Americans into the country as a whole.

And it is quite natural, and very fortunate, that many of us in the new-immigrant groups have joined with many old-line Negro Americans, with many white Americans of the earlier immigration waves, with Henry Wallace, in this movement to form a new party and make it competent to deal with the complex problems looming before us. Many of us Slavic Americans already in 1946 and early in 1947, sensed that Henry Wallace was right, and we became part of the growing impulse to form a new party.

Regardless of what some of our opponents have said, this fact is strictly and wonderfully in the American tradition. It is part of the Americanization process. It is according to the American Way. We are promoting ourselves from second-class to first-class citizenship. This is resented by some of the Americans of the older strains, the self-styled standard Americans; but don't let that worry you too much. They, too, are being Americanized or re-Americanized as you assume your full rights and duties of citizenship. Americanism has its standards, to be sure; very high standards; but it is not anything rigid or dead; it is alive, vital, open to change and enrichment.

Slavic Americans are part of the whole immense American dynamic which is as yet little understood, and is full of promises and dangers. By coming here, we of the new immigration greatly complicated the American civilization as it was, say, 90 or 100 years ago. Most Slavic immigrants became workers in the great industries, and now their energy is integral with the American scene as a whole. Most immigrants in the last 100 years or so worked hard, many of them too hard at too little pay, and helped to create a complex industrial machine which, lest it overwhelm us, now needs intelligent handling and control. It is our duty to take an active interest in finding an approach to the immense industrial, economic and social problems facing us; for, let me repeat, our coming here and our labors in the last several decades have helped to create these problems.

Most of us who came over were ordinary people. But in the new immigration waves were also some extraordinary human beings. There was, for instance, a man of genius, Nikola Tesla. His numerous inventions now are one of the most important factors in the immense American industrial scheme which throbs with the high promises that pulsated through Tesla's brain, but which are also full of dangers. Personally, as one who happens to be proud of being of the same background as was Tesla, I feel it is my special duty to help do what is necessary to insure that Tesla's work, as well as the work of ordinary men and women, will go into the fulfillment of promises in our American Way of Life, rather than contribute to the catastrophe now threatening.

IN 1942, Henry Wallace made his famous speech on "The Century of the Common Man." Nikola Tesla, who was a very uncommon man, publicly endorsed that speech in glowing terms. And I think that I speak not only for myself, but also for Tesla, when I assert that the American Way of Life is not the way of incredibly greedy monopoly profits and prohibitive prices for the necessities of life. Look at this picture: Millions of men in their best years who fought and suffered, many of whom will carry greater or lesser disabilities to their graves—veterans to whom we said "Nothing is too good for you"—are unable to secure homes of minimum decency and convenience. Their families cannot be adequately fed with meat at 70¢ to $1.20 a pound. Whatever wage increases they may secure

(Continued on page 32)

comments from our readers

Dear Editor:

Our small club of eight members, from a small mining community in Pennsylvania, until recently was known as the Rural Ridge Busy Knitters Club. We are now a chapter of the Congress of American Women.

We have only fifteen dollars in our treasury and out of this we are sending you $10, because of our desire to contribute to the work you are doing.

May it help in some way towards *The Slavic American's* fight for freedom and democracy.

Anna Tominac, Pres.
Anne Kondrick, Sec'y.
Julia Pukavina, Treas.
Rural Ridge, Pa.

Dear Editor:

I send you post haste my renewal subscription for *The Slavic American*.

In all sincerity—keep up the good work for you are doing an excellent job in the struggle against fascism.

I never miss an issue.

Rev. Eliot White
New York, N. Y.

Dear Editor:

How about more profiles on Slavic American writers and scientists like Nikola Tesla? The field for this type of material is virtually endless.

Anton Markulic
Los Angeles, Calif.

(See page 13—Ed.)

The American Way
(Continued from page 30)

through their unions, increased living costs still stay one jump ahead of them.

We of the Progressive Party say this is not the American Way of Life. And "we" includes great numbers of ex-GIs and young workers, old-stock Americans and immigrants: Americans of all breeds and backgrounds.

If all Americans are employed at better than mere-existence wages or are engaged in business or professional activities at a reasonable compensation; if all Americans are well clothed and fed; if all Americans are secure instead of uncertain and worried, as the majority are today, there will be no war. The Hearsts, Peglers, Forrestals and Bullitts won't get to first base in trying to propagandize us into fear and hate of other countries which are emerging out of backwardness and, because of their different historic experiences, are attempting a different system for providing benefits and opportunities for their citizens.

Why go to war to keep others from having their way of life? We in the Wallace movement, in the Progressive Party, insist on peace in order to keep the American Way of Life. If our approach prevails in time, there will be no war and Russia will be no danger to America, to the American Way of Life. The chief danger to this country and to our institutions under the Constitution lies in our present high-level politicians and wire-pullers who have raised the cry of Communism and of the Russian menace as a smokescreen to neutralize any possible militancy on the part of labor, to scare us in the new-immigrant groups, to frighten the Negroes, and to confuse the people generally so they won't be able to figure out who or what is responsible for high living costs. Henry Wallace clearly means what he says; so he and his active supporters were smeared, lest too many voters vote for him and in their own interest.

The old-line politicians and wire-pullers and their propagandists are not afraid of Communism, but of American democracy and of the American people; of the people getting wise to themselves and demanding a return to the American Way of Life—the Way defined in the Declaration of Independence and the Constitution of the United States.

That's what *they* are afraid of . . . that's what *we* Progressives stand for . . . and that's what will prevail if you and I, all of us and all of our neighbors wherever we come from, do everything in our power to build the new party that has come into being around the personality and political philosophy of Henry Wallace. We, all of us, will have to do all we can in this post-election period to make of the Progressive Party a party capable of saving the country and helping to bring about a world in which the American Way of Life will include not warlike antagonism, but constructive interest in the ways of life in other countries.

32

11/13/1943 SAVA KOSANOVISH, ALLEGED COMMUNIST

FEDERAL BUREAU OF INVESTIGATION

Form No. 1
THIS CASE ORIGINATED AT CINCINNATI, OHIO

NY FILE NO. 100-27583 MBJ

REPORT MADE AT	DATE WHEN MADE	PERIOD FOR WHICH MADE	REPORT MADE BY
NEW YORK CITY	11/13/43	10/6, 7, 25-28/43	MARTIN J. LUKOSKIE

TITLE: ▓▓▓▓ with aliases b7C

CHARACTER OF CASE: SECURITY MATTER — C.

SYNOPSIS OF FACTS:

Bureau letter dated January 21, 1943, reflects that SAVA KOSANOVICH is alleged Communist and supposedly helps finance every Serbian newspaper in the U. S. except "SRBOBRAN", published in Pittsburgh; and active among the Serbians in U. S. He was Yugoslav Minister of State and after coming to the U. S. was threatened with violence in 4/43 as being anti-Chetnik and pro-German. ▓▓▓▓▓▓▓▓▓▓ employed by U. S. DEPT. OF STATE. ▓▓▓▓▓ was former professor in Yugoslavia and is presently writing articles for a Cleveland Slovene newspaper and also reported to be member of Communist dominated organization in NYC. Address of ▓▓▓▓▓▓▓ NYC, is ▓▓▓▓▓▓▓ which reportedly has received funds for support ▓▓ from the Communist organization. Indices negative on ▓▓▓▓▓▓▓▓▓▓▓▓▓▓▓ and ▓▓▓▓▓▓▓ except as set forth below.

— R U C —

REFERENCE: Bureau File #100-118061
Report of Special Agent WILLIAM H. JAHN, JR., dated July 17, 1943 at Cincinnati, Ohio.

DETAILS: At New York, N. Y.

This investigation is predicated upon a request in

COPIES OF THIS REPORT	DO NOT WRITE IN THESE SPACES
5 - Bureau	100-118061-47 RECORDED & INDEXED
4 - Cincinnati (2-USA, Dayton) (#100-4983)	30 NOV 6 1943
2 - New York	

NY 100-27583

reference report that indices of the New York office be checked against the names of the persons discovered to be corresponding with the subject in Cincinnati.

SAVA KOSANOVICH first came to the attention of the Bureau in January, 1943, after the death of NIKOLA TESLA, one of the world's outstanding scientists in the electrical field. During his lifetime, TESLA conducted many experiments in connection with the wireless transmission of electrical power and just prior to his death, was interested in what is commonly called the "death-ray".

The notes and records of TESLA's experiments and formulae, together with designs of machinery necessary for their operation, were reported to be among TESLA's personal effects, after his death.

It was reported that KOSANOVICH claimed to be a nephew of TESLA, and he attempted to secure possession of TESLA's personal effects, and hired a private locksmith to gain access to TESLA's possessions. The Bureau was interested because of the supposedly vital importance of TESLA's inventions and the desire to keep them out of enemy hands, as one informant maintains that KOSANOVICH was pro-Axis in his sympathies. The matter was later handled as an alien enemy, custodial detention matter and no further investigation conducted by this office.

The Bureau advised by letter of January 21, 1943, that its files revealed confidential information concerning NIKOLA TESLA and his inventions and advised that one NICOLA TESLA, who might be identical with NIKOLA TESLA, made a speech in Springfield, Massachusetts on July 4, 1922 under the auspices of the Friends of Soviet Russia.

It was further advised that one SAVA KOSANOVICH, described as the Minister of Supply, arrived with other Yugoslavian Government Officials at Norfolk, Virginia on September 4, 1941. In another instance, the name of SAVA N. KOSANOVICH appeared on the stationery of the CENTRAL & EASTERN EUROPEAN PLANNING BOARD (Czechoslovakia, Greece, Poland, Yugoslavia). In this letterhead, KOSANOVICH was described as chairman of the board and Minister of State for Yugoslavia. It was stated that this board was interested in planning for post-war Europe. In still another Bureau file, it was disclosed that SAVA KOSANOVICH, a Serbian, was a member of one of the Yugoslavian minority parties and when an emergency government to overthrow an alliance with the Axis was formed, he was included as an official

- 2 -

1/30/1951   MEMORANDUM—WESTBROOK PEGLER

STANDARD FORM NO. 64

Office Memorandum · UNITED STATES GOVERNMENT

TO : MR. TOLSON   DATE: Jan. 30, 1951

FROM : L. B. NICHOLS

SUBJECT: WESTBROOK PEGLER

ALL INFORMATION CONTAINED
HEREIN IS UNCLASSIFIED
DATE 2-22-89 BY PIACCUM

Westbrook Pegler called yesterday and said he would be in town for the next two or three days and wanted to see me. I told him I would be glad to see him late yesterday or today at his convenience. He is coming in today at 2:30 p.m.

I asked him if there was anything special which would require my doing any checking. He stated there were two things he wanted to discuss.

1. The case of Nicola Tesla and Abraham N. Spanel, President of International Latex Corporation, that he Pegler gave some information to Rogers of the Senate Investigating Committee three or four years ago and Rogers brushed it off stating the witness Pegler wanted to present was unreliable.

Our files reflect that Nicola Tesla was one of the world's outstanding scientists and in fact designed the generators installed at Niagara Falls. He died in New York on January 7, 1943, and is supposed to have left details and plans for a so-called death ray. Spanel and Henry Wallace, according to Pegler, tried to get hold of it.

Our files also reflect that Colonel Erskine of Military Intelligence called us on January 9, 1943, advising that Tesla had died, that A. Spanel had communicated with the War Department regarding this death, that Tesla had a nephew named Sava Kosanovich who had taken possession of Tesla's papers and Spanel thought the papers might be used against our Government.

We made an immediate inquiry in New York and the first report was that Kosanovich and others entered Tesla's room with the aid of a locksmith, broke into a safe containing some of Tesla's valuable papers including formula.

Coincident with this, on January 8, L. M. C. Smith called Mr. Tamm regarding the death of Tesla and Smith stated he was talking to the Alien Property Custodian about seizing these items.

We interviewed Spanel who expressed concern over Tesla's effects and Spanel stated that Kosanovich had turned over the effects of Tesla to the Alien Property Custodian. Spanel further stated the day before Tesla died, he tried to get in touch with the War Department to make available certain notes by

COPIES DESTROYED   RECORDED - 18   MAR 2 1951

R94   EX - 8   INDEXED - 18

It turned out that Kosanovich at this time was secretary of state to the Yugoslav Government in exile in New York. He later became Ambassador and returned to Yugoslavia last year. We investigated him on various occasions as a possible espionage agent. However, there were no overt acts ever developed.

In 1945, we talked to a Private Bloyce Fitzgerald, who stated he had been associated with Tesla, and that the Army believed that Tesla's "death ray" is the only defense against atom bombs.

It was very clear we had no responsibility for Tesla's effects, that the Alien Property Custodian seized them and we learned later that Naval authorities made microfilms of all his papers.

Kosanovich communicated with the Bureau on March 29, 1950, and under date of April 3, 1950, in response to his request for the microfilms of the papers of Tesla, who was a relative of Kosanovich, we advised Kosanovich that this Bureau had never been in possession of Tesla's papers.

I see in the file there are conflicting reports on Kosanovich: some people say he is a Communist; others say he is not a Communist but is a Tito opportunist. On one occasion, on December 11, 1946, we observed Nathan Gregory Silvermaster and ▬▬▬▬▬ in a meeting with Kosanovich in New York City.

Senator McCarthy furnished the Bureau five communications received from a ▬▬▬▬▬▬▬▬▬ which pertained primarily to Abraham Spanel. This individual mentioned the FBI at length in these communications, pointing out that Mr. Foxworth had been called in on the Tesla case but was killed shortly thereafter. He further stated that he was associated with Fitzgerald and as such came in touch with Tesla. He stated the FBI investigated this matter but their hands were tied, that there was nothing the FBI could do as they had been stopped from a higher level, that Harvey Rath, the FBI Agent he dealt with, resigned and requested ▬▬▬▬▬▬ never to discuss the matter with him again, that he had a wife and family to consider and that the last hope was Congress. These communications were furnished to the Department on September 19, 1950.

The checks we have made on Spanel reflect allegations he is pro-Soviet and others that he is a patriotic American.

- 2 -

It is significant that Spanel filed suit against King Features in 1945 for $6,000,000, alleging libel on the part of Pegler.

We did have an Agent, Harvey E. Rath, who entered on duty February 16, 1942, resigned April 5, 1946. At the time he resigned, he stated he was going into the toy business with ▮▮▮▮▮ Avenue, and his residence was ▮▮▮▮▮ Street, East Orange, New Jersey. The file does not indicate that we have ever interviewed Rath on the basis of ▮▮▮▮▮ allegations.

I think we should see what specifics Pegler wants. I think we can tell him on the Tesla papers that when they were reported to us, the Department stated that the Alien Property Custodian was going to seize the papers and that we learned Spanel had called the War Department about the papers falling into the wrong hands. I think the less we can give Pegler the better as the libel suit might still be pending. Again, he may be looking for information to publicize Spanel and International Later.

2. Pegler stated that he wanted to find out something about ▮▮▮▮▮ who was ordered deported. He referred to the information he furnished to me last Fall about ▮▮▮▮▮ being in Houston. We made a check on that and found ▮▮▮▮▮ had some oil wells.

I will limit anything I furnish him on ▮▮▮▮▮ to public record material and will go only as far as needed to protect the Bureau's interest.

b7C

Why wasn't he interviewed?

MEMORANDUM—INTERNAL SECURITY

8/30/1946

Office Memorandum · UNITED STATES GOVERNMENT

TO : D. M. Ladd
FROM : E. G. Fitch
SUBJECT : INTERNAL SECURITY - R

DATE: August 30, 1946

b7C

Mr. Lyon of the State Department informed Mr. Roach that he obtained a note from Colonel Grombach, Special Intelligence, War Department, concerning the above mentioned individual. Mr. Lyon was of the opinion that the information supplied by Colonel Grombach may be of interest to the Bureau.

The information as obtained from Colonel Grombach by Mr. Lyon is quoted as follows:

[REDACTED] (pronounce: [REDACTED]) [REDACTED] in Washington and according to common saying his mistress, arrived apparently together with or shortly after [REDACTED]. It is supposed that she was sent over here in order to try to convince [REDACTED]. Apparently a [REDACTED] of great reputation and [REDACTED] and collaborator of Nicolas Tesla the well known scientist, residing in Cleveland, Oh., (probably American citizen)

RECOMMENDATION

It is suggested this memorandum be referred to the Internal Security Section for its information.

FD-72
(1-10-49)

FEDERAL BUREAU OF INVESTIGATION
SECURITY INFORMATION – CONFIDENTIAL

FORM NO. 1
THIS CASE ORIGINATED AT WASHINGTON FIELD

REPORT MADE AT	DATE WHEN MADE	PERIOD FOR WHICH MADE	REPORT MADE BY
WASHINGTON, D.C.	JUN 19 1952	5/9,10,13,16,26/52	[redacted] SECRET

TITLE	FOI/PA # 291860 APPEAL # CIVIL ACT. # E.O. # 12356	CHARACTER OF CASE
b7C		ESPIONAGE – R

SYNOPSIS OF FACTS: DATE 2-16-89 INITIALS GLM

Informants acquainted with the subject [redacted] describe him as pro-Tito. Subject in interview and signed statement says he believes he was a [redacted] member when at the [redacted] and also active in the [redacted]. Recalls being at CP Headquarters in [redacted] and says it is possible he attended [redacted] in [redacted] but does not specifically recall. Admitted he attended [redacted] and identified his pictures from a copy of the annual, but denied he knew it was a Communist school. States he was never a member of CP, and never involved in espionage. Denies BENTLEY allegations. [redacted] also denies BENTLEY's allegations.

Classified by [redacted]
Declassify on: OADR
#291860

ALL INFORMATION CONTAINED HEREIN IS UNCLASSIFIED EXCEPT WHERE SHOWN OTHERWISE

DETAILS: AT WASHINGTON, D.C.:

APPROVED AND FORWARDED: [signature] SPECIAL AGENT IN CHARGE

SECURITY INFORMATION – CONFIDENTIAL

100 - 356557 - 99 RECORDED - 19
INDEXED - 19
10 JUN 20 1952
SECRET

COPIES OF THIS REPORT
6 - Bureau (100-356557)
1 - San Francisco (100-29336)(Info)
1 - Los Angeles (65-5203)(Info)
1 - New York (65-14842)(Info)
3 - Washington Field (100-19816)

59 AUG 1 1952

PROPERTY OF FBI - This confidential report and its contents are loaned to you by the FBI and are not to be distributed outside of agency to which loaned.

WFO 100-19816

~~SECRET~~

████████████████████████████ and also one
████ who was directly responsible for ████████
████████ was a known Titoist Communist and ████ was
certain that ████ although he never admitted it, was also a Communist, however, ████ could not advise whether he was a Titoist Communist, because he had not seen ████ since the TITO-STALIN break.

████████ did not see or hear of ████ after his
████ until the ████ said he had heard from a mutual
acquaintance that the ████ was planning to terminate
employment of ████ as part of a concerted effort to eliminate
United States citizens from ████████.

████████ With regard to ████ the subject who recently
████████████████ of known reliability,
advised she is ████ who was born at ████ on
████ said that ████ ████ departed
████ on ████ where
they expected to ████ on ████ They
were destined for the residence of ████████
████ described ████ as ████ feet, ████ inches, tall,
and as having brown hair and brown eyes.

INTERVIEW OF THE SUBJECT

████████ was interviewed at the Washington Field
Office by SA ████████ and the reporting Agent, on May 9,
10, and 13, 1952, and by ████████ and the reporting Agent,
on May 26, 1952.

History Prior to Entering United States

████████ said he was born ████████ at
████████ where he spent his early youth. About
the age of ████ he began attending the ████████
████ and was at this school for ████ years. He said the
curriculum was comparable to that of a high school in the United States,
or a trade school, with an emphasis upon fundamental ████.
The subject said that while in attendance, he took ████ years instruc-
tion in the English language. Following graduation, he went to ████

~~SECRET~~

- 3 -

WFO 100-19816

plant, and that person took ███████████ and
███████████ Subject said he may have attempted to distribute some
labor literature ███████████ but that it was not Communist Party
literature. ███████ advised he was not ███████
which ensued, nor ███████████

Acquaintanceship with Officials in the Yugoslav Government

Subject said that he, in connection with his membership in
███████████ while in ███████████ made contact in
New York City with representatives of the Royalist government who came
as ministers for the Government in exile. ███████ admitted at this time
he was interested in Yugoslav matters, Yugoslav progress in engineering,
and their advances in equipment. He said he was also desirous of making
the acquaintance of NIKOLA TESLA, who was an outstanding Yugoslav scientist and one of the founders of Westinghouse. He said he first learned
of the London group (Yugoslav government in exile) in the newspapers and,
when visiting in New York City, he visited them in the office which was
on Park Avenue, as he recalled. By this means he first became acquainted
with SAVA KOSANOVIC. KOSANOVIC eventually became an important official
with the Tito government (being Yugoslav Ambassador to the United States),
and subject was friendly with him despite the fact he saw him infrequently.
Their friendship resulted from a mutual knowledge of persons ███████████
███████████ saw KOSANOVIC a couple of times
in ███████ concerning matters of Yugoslav relief which was sponsored
by LOUIS ADAMIC, and the last time he saw KOSANOVIC ███████
███████████ was in the ███████████ when he was
███████████
███████ originally met ███████ at the ███████████ held
in ███████████ and ███████████ were LOUIS ADAMIC
and VASO TRIVANOVIC, deceased, economist and writer, and ███████ who
was described by the subject as ███████████ and a
Yugoslav National who made a fortune as an ███████████
███████ said he did not see KOSANOVIC again until he was in ███████
when he saw him in ███████████ where both were staying
at that time. KOSANOVIC was Yugoslav Ambassador to the United States
from 1946 to 1950, and subject saw him upon occasion despite the fact he
has had little contact with the political representatives of that government since ███████████ He said KOSANOVIC was not a great

WFO 100-19816

administrator, but he has considerable respect for him in many ways. He believes that KOSANOVIC emphasized to the Yugoslav government that he (KOSANOVIC), would be especially effective as Ambassador because he was a nephew of TESLA (mentioned above) and a friend of Mayor LA GUARDIA, and other influential persons in this country. According to ▓▓▓ KOSANOVIC is believed to be in disfavor in Yugoslavia now because of an article he wrote in defense of the Yugoslav-Nazi Pact some years previous. He has been under attack by theoreticians of the Communist Party in Yugoslavia for this article. In ▓▓▓ opinion, KOSANOVIC is not a Communist, and he believes that KOSANOVIC is against Marxism.

With regard to ▓▓▓ who was eventually ▓▓▓ said he may have met him, and shaken hands with him in New York City, but he can recall no other occasion when he may have met him. He said ▓▓▓ was on a higher political level than KOSANOVIC, and had been ▓▓▓. He explained that under the Royalist government, ▓▓▓ was an important ▓▓▓ and he is uncertain how ▓▓▓ has resolved this philosophic conflict, in view of his high position in the Tito government.

Acquaintanceship with LOUIS ADAMIC

▓▓▓ said he first corresponded with ADAMIC after the publication of ADAMIC's book, "Native's Return," which was published a number of years ago. As a Yugoslav National in this country, ▓▓▓ was interested in ADAMIC's work and initiated correspondence with him. At a subsequent date, possibly in late 1941 or early 1942, ADAMIC was publishing a bulletin for distribution to persons in the United States who were of Yugoslav descent. ▓▓▓ and shortly thereafter ADAMIC got in touch with the subject. He estimated it to be in the fall or winter of 1942 when he first met ADAMIC. In the spring of 1943, a rally was to be held in the Slovene Hall on St. Clair Avenue, in Cleveland, Ohio, in an effort to obtain funds for Yugoslav relief, and ADAMIC at that time requested the subject to participate. He said he thereafter saw him four or five times before ▓▓▓ and of course it was ADAMIC ▓▓▓. After subject ▓▓▓ he saw ADAMIC in New York a couple of times, and also at Yugoslav Embassy receptions held in Washington, D. C. In the opinion of ▓▓▓ ADAMIC was too much an artist and "free spirit," and also too good a businessman to be a Communist.

- 16 -

9/8/1975 — THE UNITED AMERICAN YUGOSLAV CLUB OF NEW YORK

PAGE THREE NY [105-130915] SECRET

Report Form
FD-263 (5-2-55)

FEDERAL BUREAU OF INVESTIGATION

Reporting Office	Office of Origin	Date	Investigative Period
WASHINGTON FIELD	BUREAU	3/28/60	2/18 – 3/15/60

TITLE OF CASE

████████████ b7C

Applicant, Pan American Union, Washington, D. C.

Report made by: ████████ b7C

CHARACTER OF CASE

LOYALTY OF EMPLOYEES OF THE UNITED NATIONS AND OTHER PUBLIC INTERNATIONAL ORGANIZATIONS

REFERENCE

Bulet dated 2/15/60;
Bu airtels dated 2/25 and 3/10/60;
Seattle airtel dated 2/26/60;
Baltimore airtels dated 2/27 and 3/4/60;
Norfolk airtel dated 3/1/60;
San Francisco airtel dated 3/3/60;
New York airtels dated 2/26, 3/3,4,10/60;
Chicago airtel dated 3/5/60;
Springfield airtel dated 3/8/60;
New Haven airtel dated 3/9/60.

6 - Bureau (138-4457) (Enc)
1 - Washington Field (138-4085)

138-4457-93

MAY 24 1960

Property of FBI - This report is loaned to you by the FBI, and neither it nor its contents are to be distributed outside the agency to which loaned.

U. S. GOVERNMENT PRINTING OFFICE: 1955 O—344750

UNITED STATES DEPARTMENT OF JUSTICE
FEDERAL BUREAU OF INVESTIGATION

Copy to:

Report of:
Date: MAR 28 1960   Office: Washington, D.C.
                      SEE REVERSE
                      SIDE FOR
Field Office File No.: 138-4085 CLASSIFICATION   Bureau File No.: 138-4457
                      ACTION

Title:
Applicant, Pan American Union,
Washington, D.C.

Character: LOYALTY OF EMPLOYEES OF THE UNITED NATIONS AND OTHER PUBLIC
INTERNATIONAL ORGANIZATIONS

Synopsis:

CSC requested investigation based on membership in the ▓▓▓▓. Present employment ▓▓▓▓ verified. Former employment ▓▓▓▓ to ▓▓▓▓ verified. Employment ▓▓▓▓ from ▓▓▓▓ to ▓▓▓▓ verified through interviews. All employments favorable. Former co-workers at ▓▓▓▓ believe applicant loyal to U.S. While employed by ▓▓▓▓ doubted applicant's loyalty based on association with ▓▓▓▓. Another person regarded applicant as pro-communist while employed by ▓▓▓▓ employees ▓▓▓▓ references and neighbors comment favorably. ELIZABETH TERRILL BENTLEY alleged that ▓▓▓▓ was engaged in Soviet espionage which he has denied. PAUL CROUCH said ▓▓▓▓ attended CP meetings. ▓▓▓▓ was a member of the ▓▓▓▓. Applicant has been interviewed on various occasions and denied espionage activity or CP membership. He has admitted affiliation with or attending meetings of communist organizations. Credit record satisfactory. Police department records ▓▓▓▓ CSC and ONI nothing additional. HCUA information set out. No record ▓▓▓▓ investigative files. G-2 files have been utilized. Applicant unknown to informants.

- P -

This document contains neither recommendations nor conclusions of the FBI. It is the property of the FBI and is loaned to your agency; it and its contents are not to be distributed outside your agency.

WFO 138-4085
EDT:mjr

███████ explained that despite the fact that BENTLEY furnished inaccurate information concerning him, it is possible that either ███████ or ███████ (if they were agents, as she claimed) may have attempted to attribute some of the information they were furnishing to her as having come from ███████. He added that it was generally known by his acquaintances he was employed with ███████ and, also, that he was ███████. He recalled prior to ███████ he was a guest at dinner of ███████ and ███████. During the time prior to ███████ the applicant's family was not with him. In ███████ applicant went to ███████, on a week's leave, ███████ accompanied his family to ███████ and ███████. Thereafter he ███████.

███████ said the fact that he was employed at ███████ should indicate that ELIZABETH T. BENTLEY is incorrect when she accuses him of furnishing information from the files of ███████ because the Russians had highly-placed officials in ███████ so any information ███████ could furnish concerning that Agency would have been of little value compared to what the Russians who were more highly placed would have been able to furnish.

███████ admitted he had been ███████ in ███████. He said he was employed in ███████ at that time.

███████ attempted to distribute some labor literature ███████ said he may have but it was not Communist Party literature. ███████ advised he was not ███████ nor was he ███████.

███████ said that he, in connection with his membership in ███████ while in ███████.

WFO 133-4085
EDT:mjr

made contact in New York City with representatives of the Royalist government who came as ministers for the Government in exile. ███████ admitted at this time he was interested in Yugoslav matters, Yugoslav progress in engineering, and their advances in equipment. He said he was also desirous of making the acquaintance of NIKOLA TESLA, who was an outstanding Yugoslav scientist and one of the founders of Westinghouse. He said he first learned of the London group (Yugoslav government in exile) in the newspapers and, when visiting in New York City, he visited them in the office which was on Park Avenue, as he recalled. By this means he first became acquainted with SAVA KOSANOVIC. KOSANOVIC eventually became an important official with the Tito government (being Yugoslav Ambassador to the United States), and the applicant was ███ saw KOSANOVIC a couple of times in ███████████ concerning matters of Yugoslav relief which was sponsored by LOUIS ADAMIC, and the last time he saw KOSANOVIC ██████████ ████████████ was in the ██████████████ when he was in ██████████ originally met ██████████████ at the ██████████████ held in ████████████ was LOUIS ADAMIC and VASO TRIVANOVIC, deceased, economist and writer, and ████████████ who was described by the applicant as █████████████████████████ and a Yugoslav National who made a fortune as an ██████████ ██████████████ said he did not see KOSANOVIC again until he was in ████████ when he saw him in ████████████ ██████████ where both were staying at that time. KOSANOVIC was Yugoslav Ambassador to the United States from 1946 to 1950, and applicant saw him upon occasion despite the fact he has had little contact with the political representatives of that government since ████████████████████. He said KOSANOVIC was not a great administrator, but he has considerable respect for him in many ways. He believes that KOSANOVIC emphasized to the Yugoslav government that he (KOSANOVIC), would be especially effective as Ambassador because he was a nephew of TESLA (mentioned above) and a friend of Mayor LA GUARDIA, and other influential persons in this country. According to ████████ KOSANOVIC is believed to be in disfavor in Yugoslavia now because of an article he wrote in defense of the Yugoslav-Nazi Pact some

WFO 138-4085
EDT:mjr

years previously. He has been under attack by theoreticians of the Communist Party in Yugoslavia for this article. In ███████ opinion, KOSANOVIC is not a Communist, and he believes that KOSANOVIC is against Marxism.

With regard to ███████ who was eventually ███ in Yugoslavia, ███████ said he may have met him, and shaken hands with him in New York City, but he can recall no other occasion when he may have met him. He said ███████ was on a higher political level than KOSANOVIC, and ███████ He explained that under the Royalist government, ███████ was an important ███████ and he is uncertain how ███████ has resolved this philosophic conflict, in view of his high position in the Tito government.

███████ said he first corresponded with LOUIS ADAMIC after the publication of ADAMIC's book, "Native's Return," which was published a number of years ago. As a Yugoslav National in this country, ███████ was interested in ADAMIC's work and initiated correspondence with him. At a subsequent date, possibly in late 1941 or early 1942, ADAMIC got in touch with ███████ He estimated it to be in the fall or winter of 1942 when he first met ADAMIC. In the spring of 1943, a rally was to be held in the Slovene Hall on St. Clair Avenue, in Cleveland, Ohio, in an effort to obtain funds for Yugoslav relief, and ADAMIC at that time requested the applicant to participate. He said he thereafter saw him four or five times before ███████ and of course it was ADAMIC ███████ After ███████ he saw ADAMIC in New York a couple of times, and also at Yugoslav Embassy receptions held in Washington, D. C. In the opinion of ███████ ADAMIC was too much an artist and "free spirit," and also too good a businessman to be a Communist.

███████ said he went to ███████ where he spent approximately ███████ then ███████ was important as ███████ before

O/S
b7C
b7D

Freedom of Information Release

On

Subject: Nikola Tesla

File #: 100-2237
Pages Reviewed - 160
Pages Released - 160

Federal Bureau of Investigation

Weehawken, N.J., 9/24/40.

Department of Justice,
Atten. Mr. J. Edgar Hoover,
Washington, D. C.

Dear Mr. Hoover:

The appended article was printed in the New York Times issue of Sunday September 22, 1940 and if based on proven facts, should be of vital importance to our War Department as well as to that of other nations now controlled by insane dictators.

If, as the author states, the teleforce has been perfected by Nikola Tesla, it would be a measure of foresightedness to insure his constant guarding against his being molested, possibly kidnapped and tortured, by alien enemies for the purpose of seizing the secret of such an invaluable instrument of war and/or defense

The foregoing is offered just in case the article and its inferences have not been called to your attention.

Very truly yours

NY TIMES 9/22/40

"Death Ray" for Planes

Nikola Tesla, one of the truly great inventors who celebrated his eighty-fourth birthday on July 10, tells the writer that he stands ready to divulge to the United States Government the secret of his "teleforce," with which, he said, airplane motors would be melted at a distance of 250 miles, so that an invisible Chinese Wall of Defense would be built around the country against any attempted attack by an enemy air force, no matter how large.

This "teleforce," he said, is based on an entirely new principle of physics that "no one has ever dreamed about," different from the principle embodied in his inventions relating to the transmission of electrical power from a distance, for which he has received a number of basic patents. This new type of force, Mr. Tesla said, would operate through a beam one one-hundred-millionth of a square centimeter in diameter, and could be generated from a special plant that would cost no more than $2,000,000 and would take only about three months to construct.

A dozen such plants, located at strategic points along the coast, according to Mr. Tesla, would be enough to defend the country against all possible aerial attack. The beam would melt any engine, whether Diesel or gasoline-driven, and would also ignite the explosives aboard any bomber. No possible defense against it could be devised, he asserts, as the beam would be all-penetrating.

High Vacuum Eliminated

The beam, he states, involves four new inventions, two of which already have been tested. One of these is a method and apparatus for producing rays and other manifestations of energy in free air, eliminating the necessity for a high vacuum; a second is a method and process for producing "very great electrical force"; the third is a method for amplifying this force, and the fourth is a new method for producing "a tremendous electrical repelling force." This would be the projector, or gun, of the system. The voltage for propelling the beam to its objective, according to the inventor, will attain a potential of 50,000,000 volts.

With this enormous voltage, he said, microscopic electrical particles of matter will be catapulted on their mission of defensive destruction. He has been working on this invention, he added, for many years and has recently made a number of improvements in it.

Mr. Tesla makes one important stipulation. Should the government decide to take up his offer he would go to work at once, but they would have to trust him. He would suffer "no interference from experts."

In ordinary times such a condition would very likely interpose an insuperable obstacle. But times being what they are, and with the nation getting ready to spend billions for national defense, at the same time taking in consideration the reputation of Mr. Tesla as an inventor who always was many years ahead of his time, the question arises whether it may not be advisable to take Mr. Tesla at his word and commission him to go ahead with the construction of his teleforce plant.

Such a Device "Invaluable"

After all, $2,000,000 would be relatively a very small sum compared with what is at stake. If Mr. Tesla really fulfills his promise the result achieved would be truly staggering. Not only would it save billions now planned for air defense, by making the country absolutely impregnable against any air attack, but it would also save many more billions in property that would otherwise be surely destroyed no matter how strong the defenses are as witness current events in England.

Take, for example, the Panama Canal. No matter how strong the defenses, a suicide squadron of dive bombers, according to some experts, might succeed in getting through and cause such damage that would make the Canal unusable, in which case our Navy might find itself bottled up.

Considering the probabilities in the case even if the chances were 100,000 to 1 against Mr. Tesla the odds would still be largely in favor of taking a chance on spending $2,000,000. In the opinion of the writer, who has known Mr. Tesla for many years and can testify that he still retains full intellectual vigor, the authorities in charge of banking the national defense should at once look into the matter. The sum is insignificant compared with the magnitude of the stake.

RECORDED & INDEXED
EWT:ZM
100-2237-1

October 1, 1940

[redacted]
[redacted], New Jersey

b7C

Dear [redacted]

    I wish to acknowledge receipt of your letter dated September 24, 1940, together with its enclosure.

    Your courtesy and interest in bringing this information to my attention are indeed appreciated, and you may be assured your letter will receive appropriate consideration.

Sincerely yours,

John Edgar Hoover
Director

ALL INFORMATION CONTAINED
HEREIN IS UNCLASSIFIED
DATE 2-2-80 BY SP4 Jam/rtc

COMMUNICATIONS SECTION
MAILED
★ OCT 1 1940 ★
P M
FEDERAL BUREAU OF INVESTIGATION
U. S. DEPARTMENT OF JUSTICE

Mr. Tolson
Mr. Clegg
Mr. E. A. Tamm
Mr. Foxworth
Mr. Nathan
Mr. Ladd
Mr. Egan
Mr. Glavin
Mr. Nichols
Mr. Rosen
Mr. Tracy
Miss Gandy

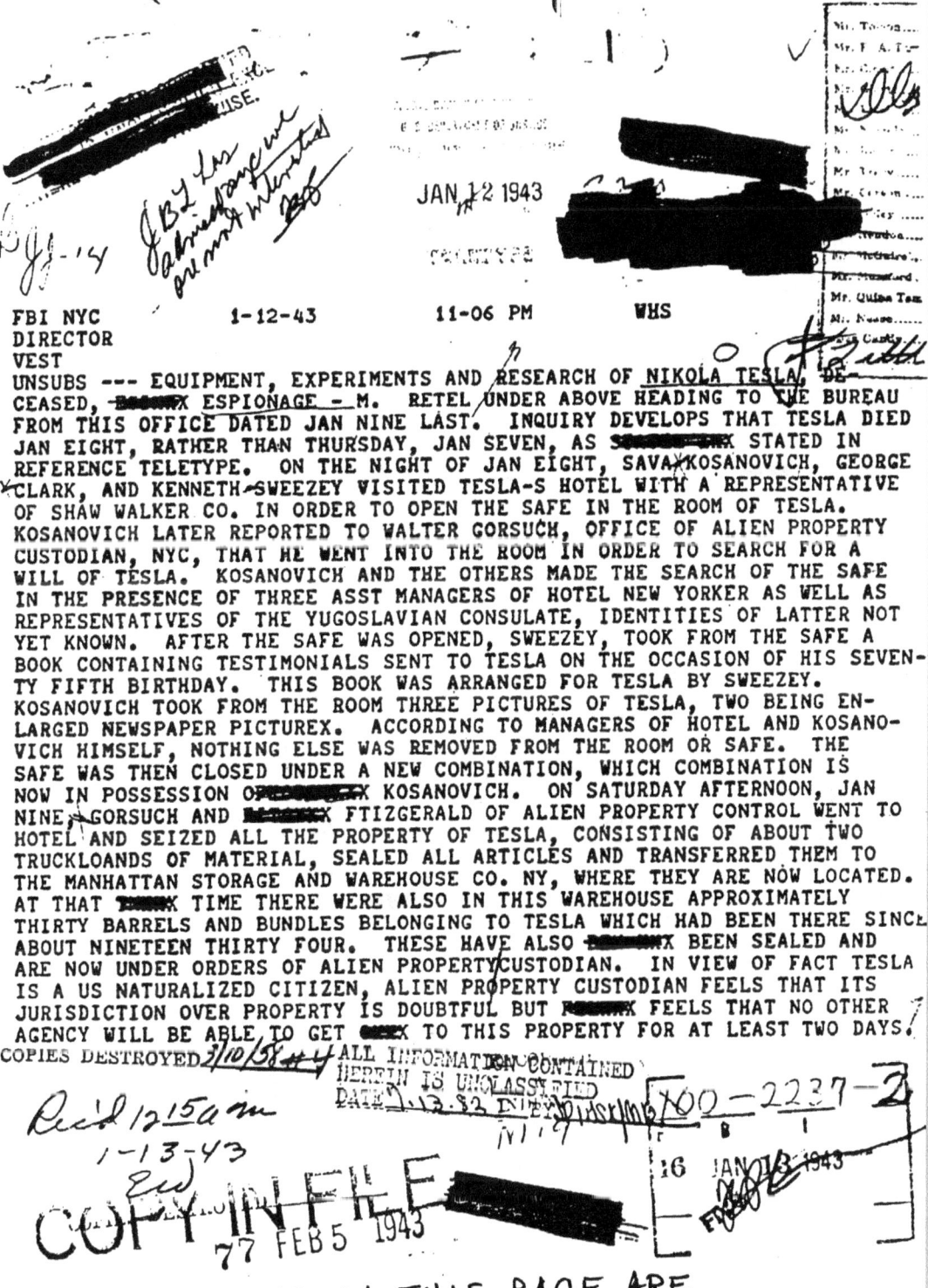

FBI NYC   1-12-43   11-06 PM   WHS
DIRECTOR
VEST

UNSUBS --- EQUIPMENT, EXPERIMENTS AND RESEARCH OF NIKOLA TESLA, DE-
CEASED, ~~XXXXX~~ ESPIONAGE - M. RETEL UNDER ABOVE HEADING TO THE BUREAU
FROM THIS OFFICE DATED JAN NINE LAST. INQUIRY DEVELOPS THAT TESLA DIED
JAN EIGHT, RATHER THAN THURSDAY, JAN SEVEN, AS ~~XXXXX~~ STATED IN
REFERENCE TELETYPE. ON THE NIGHT OF JAN EIGHT, SAVA KOSANOVICH, GEORGE
CLARK, AND KENNETH SWEEZEY VISITED TESLA-S HOTEL WITH A REPRESENTATIVE
OF SHAW WALKER CO. IN ORDER TO OPEN THE SAFE IN THE ROOM OF TESLA.
KOSANOVICH LATER REPORTED TO WALTER GORSUCH, OFFICE OF ALIEN PROPERTY
CUSTODIAN, NYC, THAT HE WENT INTO THE ROOM IN ORDER TO SEARCH FOR A
WILL OF TESLA. KOSANOVICH AND THE OTHERS MADE THE SEARCH OF THE SAFE
IN THE PRESENCE OF THREE ASST MANAGERS OF HOTEL NEW YORKER AS WELL AS
REPRESENTATIVES OF THE YUGOSLAVIAN CONSULATE, IDENTITIES OF LATTER NOT
YET KNOWN. AFTER THE SAFE WAS OPENED, SWEEZEY, TOOK FROM THE SAFE A
BOOK CONTAINING TESTIMONIALS SENT TO TESLA ON THE OCCASION OF HIS SEVEN-
TY FIFTH BIRTHDAY. THIS BOOK WAS ARRANGED FOR TESLA BY SWEEZEY.
KOSANOVICH TOOK FROM THE ROOM THREE PICTURES OF TESLA, TWO BEING EN-
LARGED NEWSPAPER PICTUREX. ACCORDING TO MANAGERS OF HOTEL AND KOSANO-
VICH HIMSELF, NOTHING ELSE WAS REMOVED FROM THE ROOM OR SAFE. THE
SAFE WAS THEN CLOSED UNDER A NEW COMBINATION, WHICH COMBINATION IS
NOW IN POSSESSION OF ~~XXXXX~~ KOSANOVICH. ON SATURDAY AFTERNOON, JAN
NINE, GORSUCH AND ~~XXXXX~~ FITZGERALD OF ALIEN PROPERTY CONTROL WENT TO
HOTEL AND SEIZED ALL THE PROPERTY OF TESLA, CONSISTING OF ABOUT TWO
TRUCKLOADS OF MATERIAL, SEALED ALL ARTICLES AND TRANSFERRED THEM TO
THE MANHATTAN STORAGE AND WAREHOUSE CO. NY, WHERE THEY ARE NOW LOCATED.
AT THAT ~~XXXXX~~ TIME THERE WERE ALSO IN THIS WAREHOUSE APPROXIMATELY
THIRTY BARRELS AND BUNDLES BELONGING TO TESLA WHICH HAD BEEN THERE SINCE
ABOUT NINETEEN THIRTY FOUR. THESE HAVE ALSO ~~XXXXX~~ BEEN SEALED AND
ARE NOW UNDER ORDERS OF ALIEN PROPERTY CUSTODIAN. IN VIEW OF FACT TESLA
IS A US NATURALIZED CITIZEN, ALIEN PROPERTY CUSTODIAN FEELS THAT ITS
JURISDICTION OVER PROPERTY IS DOUBTFUL BUT ~~XXXXX~~ FEELS THAT NO OTHER
AGENCY WILL BE ABLE TO GET ~~XXXX~~ TO THIS PROPERTY FOR AT LEAST TWO DAYS.

REDACTIONS ON THIS PAGE ARE NOT FOIA DELETIONS

PAGE TWO
AFTER THAT TIME IT IS POSSIBLE THAT A PUBLIC ADMINISTRATOR WILL BE
APPOINTED FOR THE PROPERTY WHO MAY TAKE THE PROPERTY INTO HIS CUS-
TODY. TESLA ALSO HAD SOME PROPERTY, ALLEGED BY INFORMANT
FITZGERALD IN THIS CASE, TO BE A WORKING MODEL OF AN INVENTION IN
A SAFE DEPOSIT BOX IN GOVERNOR CLINTON HOTEL IN NY. INQUIRY SHOWS
THAT THIS WAS PLACED HERE BY TESLA IN NINETEEN THIRTY TWO AS SECURITY
FOR FOUR HUNDRED DOLLARS OWED HOTEL. THIS BILL IS STILL OWED AND HOTEL
APPEARS UNWILLING TO RELEASE THIS PROPERTY TO ANYONE AT LEAST UNTIL
DEBT IS PAID, BUT THIS OFFICE WILL BE ADVISED IF ANYONE ATTEMPTS
TO PAY BILL AND OBTAIN PROPERTY. CONCERNING TESLA HOTEL MANAGERS RE-
PORT HE WAS VERY ECCENTRIC IF NOT MENTALLY DERANGED DURING
PAST TEN YEARS AND IT IS DOUBTFUL IF HE HAS CREATED ANYTHING OF VALUE
DURING THAT TIME, ALTHO PRIOR TO THAT HE PROBABLY WAS A VERY BRILLIANT
INVENTOR. THEREFORE, ANY NOTES OF VALUE WERE PROBABLY THOSE MADE
PRIOR TO THAT TIME. KOSANOVICH IS A NEPHEW OF TESLA WHO DESCRIBED
HIMSELF AS FORMERLY QUOTE YUGOSLAV MINISTER OF STATE UNQUOTE AND NOW
QUOTE PRESIDENT OF EASTERN AND CENTRAL PLANNING BOARD REP-
RESENTING YUGOSLOVIA, CZECHOSLOVAKIA, POLAND AND GREECE, UNQUOTE.
SWEEZEY IS A WRITER FOR POPULAR MECHANICS AND OTHER PUBLICATIONS WHO
IS DESIROUS OF PUBLISHING A BIOGRAPHY OF TESLA AND THERFORE WOULD
LIKE TO OBTAIN CONTROL OF HIS NOTES FOR THIS WORK. CLARK IS EMPLOYED
BY RCA AND WOULD ALSO PROVIDE STORAGE ROOM FOR TESLAS EFFECTS IN ORDER
TO USE THEM IN WRITING A BIOGRAPHY. TESLA AT ONE TIME REPORTED TO BE
WORKING ON EXPERIMENTS FOR YUGOSLAVIAN GOVERNMENT IN EXILE. IT IS
DESIRED THAT BUREAU ADVISE IMMEDIATELY WHETHER IT IS INTERESTED FURTHER
IN THIS PROPERTY FOR PURPOSES OF TAKING CONTROL OF IT. SUGGEST THAT,
IN VIEW OF FACT THAT THE NOTES AND OTHER MATERIAL WOULD BE HIGHLY TECH-
NICAL IN CHARACTER AND FOR THAT REASON COULD NOT BE REVIEWED
EXCEPT BY A TRAINED PERSON THE OFFICE OF SCIENTIFIC RESEARCH DEVEL-
OPMENT MIGHT BE INTERESTED.
FOXWORTH
END NYC S2 WHS
HOLD WA R 2 RSG

REDACTIONS ON THIS PAGE
ARE NOT FOIA DELETIONS

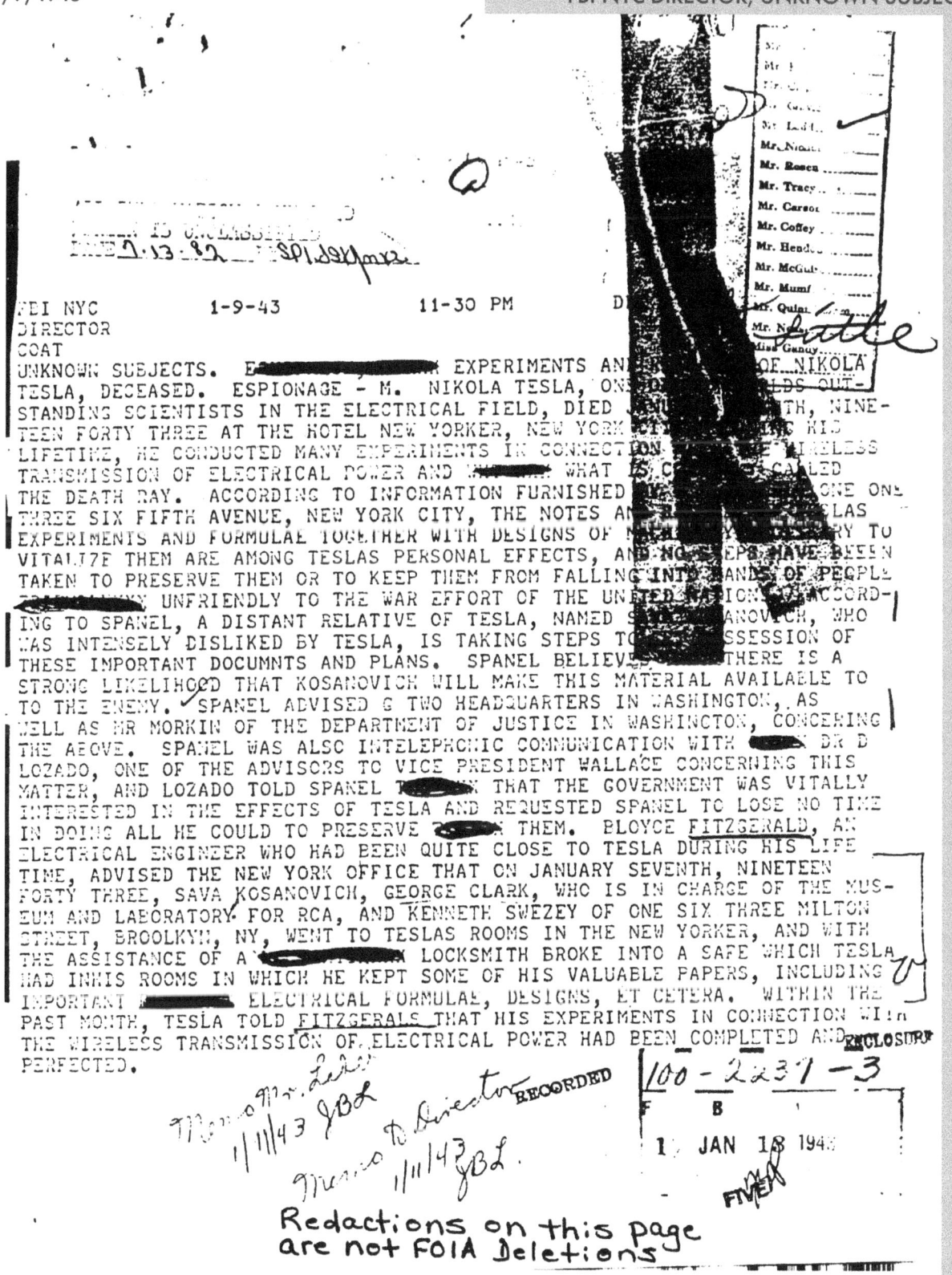

FBI NYC   1-9-43   11-30 PM
DIRECTOR
COAT
UNKNOWN SUBJECTS. ███████████ EXPERIMENTS AN████████ OF NIKOLA
TESLA, DECEASED. ESPIONAGE - M. NIKOLA TESLA, ON█████████ OUT-
STANDING SCIENTISTS IN THE ELECTRICAL FIELD, DIED ██████████, NINE-
TEEN FORTY THREE AT THE HOTEL NEW YORKER, NEW YORK █████████ HIS
LIFETIME, HE CONDUCTED MANY EXPERIMENTS IN CONNECTION ██████████
TRANSMISSION OF ELECTRICAL POWER AND ███████ WHAT IS C████ CALLED
THE DEATH RAY. ACCORDING TO INFORMATION FURNISHED █████████████ ONE ONE
THREE SIX FIFTH AVENUE, NEW YORK CITY, THE NOTES AN████████████ SLAS
EXPERIMENTS AND FORMULAE TOGETHER WITH DESIGNS OF ████████████ TO
VITALIZE THEM ARE AMONG TESLAS PERSONAL EFFECTS, AND NO STEPS HAVE BEEN
TAKEN TO PRESERVE THEM OR TO KEEP THEM FROM FALLING INTO HANDS OF PEOPLE
██████████ UNFRIENDLY TO THE WAR EFFORT OF THE UNITED NATIONS. ACCORD-
ING TO SPANEL, A DISTANT RELATIVE OF TESLA, NAMED S█████ ANOVICH, WHO
WAS INTENSELY DISLIKED BY TESLA, IS TAKING STEPS TO ███████SSESSION OF
THESE IMPORTANT DOCUMNTS AND PLANS. SPANEL BELIEVE██████ THERE IS A
STRONG LIKELIHOOD THAT KOSANOVICH WILL MAKE THIS MATERIAL AVAILABLE TO
TO THE ENEMY. SPANEL ADVISED G TWO HEADQUARTERS IN WASHINGTON, AS
WELL AS MR MORKIN OF THE DEPARTMENT OF JUSTICE IN WASHINGTON, CONCERNING
THE ABOVE. SPANEL WAS ALSO INTELEPHONIC COMMUNICATION WITH ███ DR D
LOZADO, ONE OF THE ADVISORS TO VICE PRESIDENT WALLACE CONCERNING THIS
MATTER, AND LOZADO TOLD SPANEL T█████ THAT THE GOVERNMENT WAS VITALLY
INTERESTED IN THE EFFECTS OF TESLA AND REQUESTED SPANEL TO LOSE NO TIME
IN DOING ALL HE COULD TO PRESERVE ██████ THEM. BLOYCE FITZGERALD, AN
ELECTRICAL ENGINEER WHO HAD BEEN QUITE CLOSE TO TESLA DURING HIS LIFE
TIME, ADVISED THE NEW YORK OFFICE THAT ON JANUARY SEVENTH, NINETEEN
FORTY THREE, SAVA KOSANOVICH, GEORGE CLARK, WHO IS IN CHARGE OF THE MUS-
EUM AND LABORATORY FOR RCA, AND KENNETH SWEZEY OF ONE SIX THREE MILTON
STREET, BROOKLYN, NY, WENT TO TESLAS ROOMS IN THE NEW YORKER, AND WITH
THE ASSISTANCE OF A ████████ LOCKSMITH BROKE INTO A SAFE WHICH TESLA
HAD IN HIS ROOMS IN WHICH HE KEPT SOME OF HIS VALUABLE PAPERS, INCLUDING
IMPORTANT ██████ ELECTRICAL FORMULAE, DESIGNS, ET CETERA. WITHIN THE
PAST MONTH, TESLA TOLD FITZGERALD THAT HIS EXPERIMENTS IN CONNECTION WITH
THE WIRELESS TRANSMISSION OF ELECTRICAL POWER HAD BEEN COMPLETED AND
PERFECTED.

Redactions on this page are not FOIA Deletions

PAGE TWO

FITZGERALD ALSO KNOWS THAT TESLA HAS CONCEIVED AND ░░░░░ A REVOLUTIONARY TYPE OF TORPEDO WHICH IS NOT PRESENTLY IN USE B░░░░░ THE NATIONS. IT IS FITZGERALDS BELIEF THAT THIS DESIGN HAS NOT B░░░░░ AVAILABLE TO ANY NATION UP TO THE PRESENT TIME. FROM STATEME░░░░░ TO FITZGEARLD BY TESLA, HE KNOWS THAT THE COMPLETE PLANS, ░░░░░ CATIONS AND EXPLANATION OF THE BASIC THEORIES OF THESE THIN░░░░░ OME PLACE IN THE PERSONAL EFFECTS OF TESLA. HE ALSO KNOWS THAT ░░░░░ A WORKING MODEL OF TESLAS WHICH COST MORE THAN TEN THOUSAND D░░░░░ O BUILD IN A SAFETY ░░░░░ DEPOSIT BOX BELONGING TO TESLA ░░░░░ GOVERNOR CLINTON H░░░░░ HOTEL, AND ░░░░░ FITZGEARLD B░░░░░ THIS MODEL HAS TO DO WITH THE SO CALLEDE DEATH RAY OR THE WIRE░░░░░ NSMISSION OF ELECTRICAL CURRENT. TESLA HAS ALSO TOLD FITZGEARLD ░░░░░ CONVERSATIONS THAT HE HAS SOME ░░X EIGHTY ░░░░░ TRUNKS INDIFFERE░░ ░░░CES CONTAINING TRANSCRIPTS AND PLANS HAVING TO DO WITH EXPERIMENTS ░░░░░ED BY HIM. BUREAU IS REQUESTED TO ADVISE IMMEDIATELY WHAT, IF A░░ ░░ION SHOULD BE TAKEN CONCERNING THIS MATTER BY THE NEW YORK FIEL░ ░░░░ION.

FOXWORTH

CORRECTION- THROUGHOUT THE ENTIRE TELETYPE THE NAME THAT SHOULD APPEAR
IS FITZGEARLD NOT FITZGERALD AS IT SOMETIMES IS
SPELLED

HOLD

Redactions on this page are not FOIA Deletions

1/11/1943 — FBI MEMORANDUM

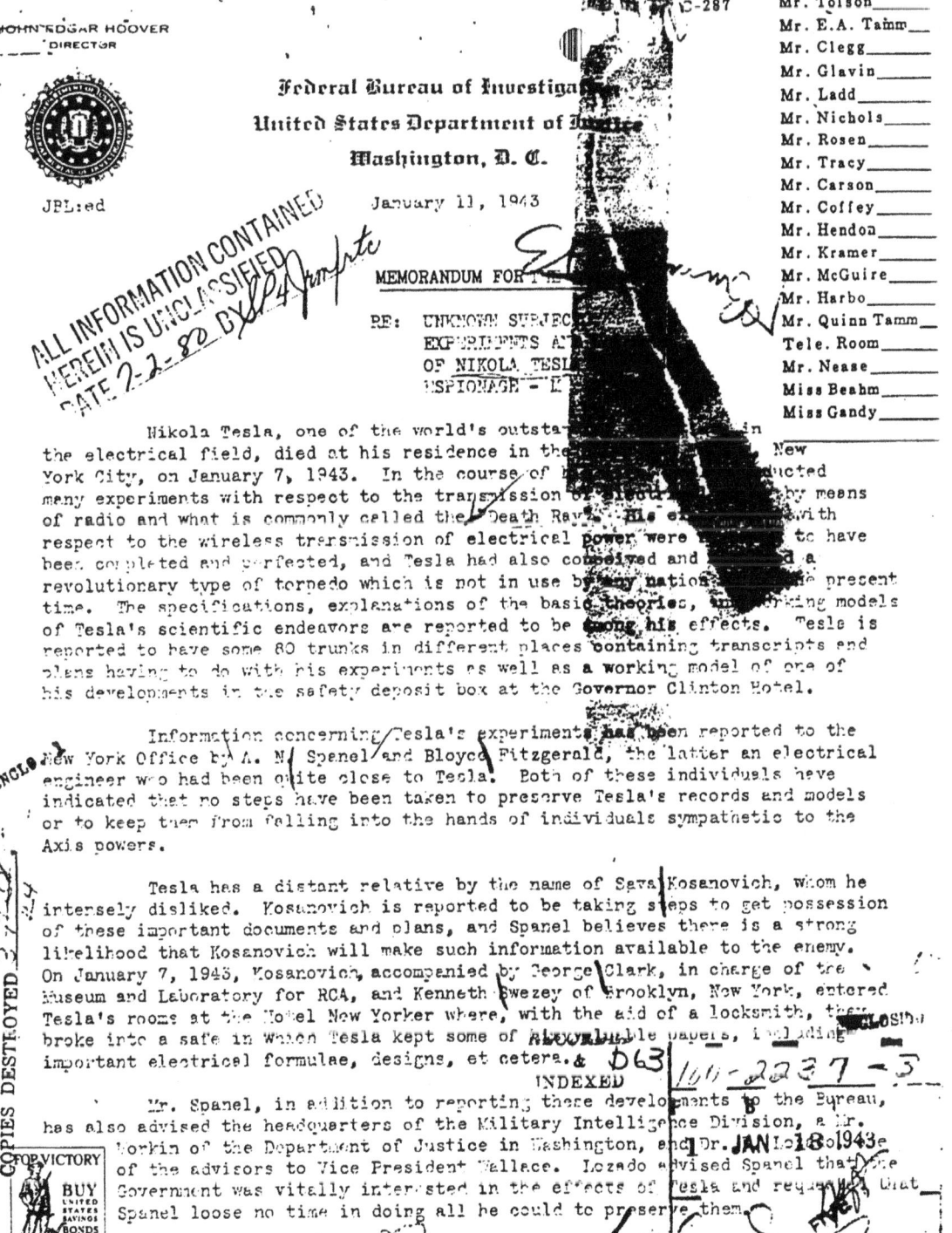

JOHN EDGAR HOOVER, DIRECTOR

Federal Bureau of Investigation
United States Department of Justice
Washington, D. C.

JPL:ed

January 11, 1943

MEMORANDUM FOR THE DIRECTOR

RE: UNKNOWN SUBJECTS;
EXPERIMENTS AND RESEARCH
OF NIKOLA TESLA
ESPIONAGE - L

Cc: Mr. Tolson, Mr. E.A. Tamm, Mr. Clegg, Mr. Glavin, Mr. Ladd, Mr. Nichols, Mr. Rosen, Mr. Tracy, Mr. Carson, Mr. Coffey, Mr. Hendon, Mr. Kramer, Mr. McGuire, Mr. Harbo, Mr. Quinn Tamm, Tele. Room, Mr. Nease, Miss Beahm, Miss Gandy

ALL INFORMATION CONTAINED HEREIN IS UNCLASSIFIED DATE 2-2-80

Nikola Tesla, one of the world's outstanding scientists in the electrical field, died at his residence in the Hotel New Yorker, New York City, on January 7, 1943. In the course of his life he conducted many experiments with respect to the transmission of electricity by means of radio and what is commonly called the "Death Ray." His experiments with respect to the wireless transmission of electrical power were reported to have been completed and perfected, and Tesla had also conceived and perfected a revolutionary type of torpedo which is not in use by any nation at the present time. The specifications, explanations of the basic theories, and working models of Tesla's scientific endeavors are reported to be among his effects. Tesla is reported to have some 80 trunks in different places containing transcripts and plans having to do with his experiments as well as a working model of one of his developments in the safety deposit box at the Governor Clinton Hotel.

Information concerning Tesla's experiments has been reported to the New York Office by A. N. Spanel and Bloyce Fitzgerald, the latter an electrical engineer who had been quite close to Tesla. Both of these individuals have indicated that no steps have been taken to preserve Tesla's records and models or to keep them from falling into the hands of individuals sympathetic to the Axis powers.

Tesla has a distant relative by the name of Sava Kosanovich, whom he intensely disliked. Kosanovich is reported to be taking steps to get possession of these important documents and plans, and Spanel believes there is a strong likelihood that Kosanovich will make such information available to the enemy. On January 7, 1943, Kosanovich, accompanied by George Clark, in charge of the Museum and Laboratory for RCA, and Kenneth Swezey of Brooklyn, New York, entered Tesla's rooms at the Hotel New Yorker where, with the aid of a locksmith, they broke into a safe in which Tesla kept some of his valuable papers, including important electrical formulae, designs, et cetera.

Mr. Spanel, in addition to reporting these developments to the Bureau, has also advised the headquarters of the Military Intelligence Division, a Mr. Yorkin of the Department of Justice in Washington, and Dr. Lozado, one of the advisors to Vice President Wallace. Lozado advised Spanel that the Government was vitally interested in the effects of Tesla and requested that Spanel loose no time in doing all he could to preserve them.

COPIES DESTROYED

FOR VICTORY BUY UNITED STATES SAVINGS BONDS AND STAMPS

INDEXED 100-2237-5

55 JAN 23 1943   1-13-43

Memorandum for the Director — 2 —

The New York Office was instructed to dis[creetly take] the matter up with the State's Attorney in New York City with the [view to] possibly taking Kosanovich into custody on a burglary charge and obt[aining] the various papers which Kosanovich is reported to have taken from Tesla's [safe]. It was pointed out that any activities pursued by the State's Attorn[ey shou]ld be handled in a most secret fashion in order to avoid any publicity [with r]espect to Tesla's inventions. The New York Office was also instructed [to contact] the Surrogate Court in order that stops could be placed against the [estate] of Tesla both in his hotel and any other points, in particular, the safe[deposit] boxes that he may have in order that no one may enter them without a Bureau representative being present and every precaution taken to preserve the secrecy of Tesla's inventions. The New York Office is to keep the Bureau advised of all developments.

Respectfully,

D. M. Ladd

L.M.C. Smith is handling this with alien Property Custodian so there appears to be no need for us to mess around in it.

EAT

Federal Bureau of Investigation
United States Department of Justice
Washington, D. C.

EAT:DS

January 12, 1943

MEMORANDUM FOR MR. LADD

Mr. Tolson	
Mr. E. A. Tamm	
Mr. Clegg	
Mr. Glavin	
Mr. Ladd	
Mr. Nichols	
Mr. Rosen	
Mr. Tracy	
Mr. Carson	
Mr. Coffey	
Mr. Hendon	
Mr. Kramer	
Mr. McGuire	
Mr. Harbo	
Mr. Quinn Tamm	
Tele. Room	
Mr. Nease	
Miss Beahm	
Miss Gandy	

On Friday, January 8th, Mr. L. M. C. Smith called me in connection with the death of Nikola Tesla. He advised me that he was concerned about the possibility of enemy agents confiscating some of the trunks of Tesla, who had died on January 7th. He understood that the War Department was interested in this matter and that apparently the Alien Property Custodian's office was taking some action. He desired to know whether the Bureau would take some steps to refrain relatives of Tesla from taking the contents of his trunks and whether the Bureau would seize possession of the trunks. Mr. Smith indicated that he was talking to the Alien Property Custodian along the same lines. I told him that in view of the fact he was going to handle the matter with the Alien Property Custodian's office, there did not appear to be any action which the Bureau could or should take.

Very truly yours,

Edw. A. Tamm

Milwaukee 6, Wis.
April 16, 1948

Mr. J. E. Hoover
Federal Bureau of Investigation
Washington D.C.

Dear Mr. Hoover,

I am a student at the Milwaukee School of Engineering, studying Electrical Engineering. I am also interested in the life and work of Nickola Tesla. I understand that at the time of his death, your department took his manuscripts and experiment data for national security. I am preparing a paper to be presented before the student branch of the American Institute of Electrical Engineers on Tesla.

If it is possible, I would appreciate material bearing on Tesla's theories and methods of Experiment.

This information would help me in a better presentation of this paper and consequently a far greater appreciation of his work in the field of science.

I know that a part of his experiments and theory have a secret classification, and I do not expect any of it.

I am interested in "Ground Current Transmission" as the basis of my thesis for graduation. If is possible to obtain this information, I would be very grateful.

Yours very truly,

b7C

LETTER FROM J. E. HOOVER — 4/22/1948

100-2237-3X   April 22, 1948

Dear

Your letter of April 16, 1948, has been received and I wish to express my appreciation to you for having written me as you did. The effects of Nickola Tesla were handled by the Office of Alien Property, and not by this Bureau. It is suggested you may desire to communicate with the Office of Alien Property, United States Department of Justice, 101 Indiana Avenue, Washington, D. C.

Sincerely yours,

John Edgar Hoover
Director

NOTE: This individual requests information relative to the work of Nickola Tesla relative to electrical experiments he was conducting, which Swain understands were taken by this Bureau and held for security reasons. Bureau file 65-47330 reflects that the effects of Tesla were handled by the Office of Alien Property.

VWP:jsc

April 3, 1950

b7C

Washington, D. C.

My dear

    Reference is made to your inquiry by telephone on March 29, 1950, concerning certain technical papers which belonged to the late Nikola Tesla.

    From an examination of our files, we have been able to determine that this Bureau has never been in possession, as had been indicated to you, of a copy of Dr. Tesla's papers.

Very sincerely yours,

J. Edgar Hoover

April 17, 1950

Director, FBI

SAC, New York

SAVA N. KOSANOVIC
INTERNAL SECURITY-YU
(Bufile 65-47953)

Rebulet dated April 3 last.

On April 7, 1950 agents of this office interviewed Mr. J.V. POTTS, Vice President of the Manhattan Warehouse and Storage Company, 52nd Street & 7th Avenue, New York City, and at that time MR. POTTS advised that the rules of his firm required that all persons gaining access to goods stored by Manhattan first had to fill out an appropriate form setting forth their names, date of visit, and reason for requesting access to the goods.

In a review of the file pertaining to the storage of the effects of NIKOLA TESLA, MR. POTTS revealed that only one such visit had been made by persons outside of the management of Manhattan Storage itself. This one occasion took place on January 26 and 27, 1943, at which time representatives of the Alien Property Custodian made a thorough review of the entire effects of the TESLA estate.

The TESLA effects are stored in rooms 5J and 5L of Manhattan Storage's warehouse at 52nd Street & 7th Avenue, New York City. MR. MICHAEL KING, who stated he had been Floor Supervisor for approximately 10 years on the floor in question, stated that he could recall only the one occasion in early 1943 when an examination was made of the TESLA effects. He stated that at that time numerous photographs were taken by the examiners. His description of the equipment used would tend to show that a microfilm reproduction was made of some of the papers of the deceased scientist. MR. KING added that several of the group making the examination wore U.S. Navy uniforms, and during the two days required to complete the examination the civilian assistants in the group were identified to him only as "FEDERAL AUTHORITIES". According to MR. KING, no other instance of microfilming of the records of the TESLA estate has taken place since that time.

It should be noted that the Bureau was informed of the examination mentioned above by New York letter (with attachments) dated October 17, 1945, entitled UNKNOWN SUBJECT; SAVA KOSANOVICH; Experiments & Research of NIKOLA TESLA (Deceased), Espionage-M.

cc: 65-12290

EFH:JJC
105-1391

Letter to Director, FBI
NY 105-1391

MR. POTTS stated that no inquiry had been received by Manhattan from SAVA N. KOSANOVICH, nor had Manhattan informed him, in any way, that an examination of the TESLA effects had been made by anyone. In fact, added MR. POTTS, the only correspondence relating to the TESLA estate has been in the form of bills for storage.

MR. POTTS stated that any personal inquires regarding the estate would of necessity be directed to him, and to date no such inquiries have been made.

Interviewing agents explained to MR. POTTS that the examination made, as mentioned above, was not instigated by the Bureau, nor had the Bureau taken part in that examination.

Unless advised to the contrary, this investigation is being placed in a closed status, and no further investigative action is contemplated by this office. CLOSED.

-2-

Minneapolis 14, Minnesota
August 18, 1952

Federal Bureau of Investigation
Department of Records
Washington, D. C.

Gentlemen:

In a manner of introduction, I wish to state that I am working toward a degree in Electrical Engineering at the Institute of Technology of the University of Minnesota.

For several years, I have been engaged in a study of extensive compass and detail concerning the researches and writings of the late, world renowned scientist, Dr. Nikola Tesla. At considerable expense, I have acquired an extensive collection of materials relating to Dr. Tesla and his works which include:

1) Personal letters written by Tesla to his close friend.

2) Numerous periodicals, some of which are to be found in only a few libraries throughout the United States.

3) A few rare books which have now become "collector's items".

4) A collection of issued patents.

Although the items listed are considerable in number, the specific information desired is lacking.

As I understand it, because of the nature of Dr. Tesla's role in scientific developments, all research papers, patent applications, etc., were secured by the Federal Bureau of Investigation at the time of Dr. Tesla's death in January of 1943.

The purpose of this seizure, as described in numerous articles, was to determine whether these papers contained suggestions leading toward advancements in the field of science.

Now it seems that sufficient time has elapsed for an investigation of this kind. If Dr. Tesla's Estate has been released by the department in charge, any records that can be made available for examination will be welcomed.

A letter from Harold I. Baynton, Assistant Attorney General, Director, Office of Alien Property, informed me that the Library of Congress listed certain works, writings and research studies prepared by the late Dr. Tesla. However, a letter addressed to the Library failed to bring results as the Library "has no files on the researches of Tesla".

A similar result was obtained from the Bureau of Naval Research and the Department of Commerce.

I am especially interested in the research work in which Tesla was engaged in his later years. There are various unpublished works, such as a 10-page typewritten statement presented in 1937 at a meeting of several well-known editors outlining his discoveries and giving a resume' of his work in the fields of gravity and cosmic ray research, etc. Also, Tesla prepared various papers, one of which was in effort to secure the Pierre Gutzman Prize from the Institute of France. My inquiry is in effort to determine whether any of these documents, as well as others, are at this time available.

I will greatly appreciate any information in regard to any records which you may have.

Very truly yours,

August 26, 1952

ALL INFORMATION CONTAINED HEREIN IS UNCLASSIFIED DATE 7-2-80 BY SP4 [illegible]

EX. - 28

[redacted]
Minneapolis [illegible] Minnesota

b7C INDEXED 68 RECORDED - 68 100-2237-4

Dear [redacted]

With reference to your letter of August 18, 1952, our files disclose that the effects of Nikola Tesla were taken into custody at the time of his death by the Office of Alien Property, and not by this Bureau. Consequently, you may wish to communicate further with that agency, which may be addressed as follows: (65-47953)

Assistant Attorney General
Rowland F. Kirks
Director, Office of Alien Property
United States Department of Justice
101 Indiana Avenue, N. W.
Washington 25, D. C.

RECEIVED AUG 26 6 07 PM '52

Sincerely yours,

John Edgar Hoover
Director

cc - 1 - Assistant Attorney General (with copy of incoming)
Rowland F. Kirks
Director, Office of Alien Property
United States Department of Justice
101 Indiana Avenue, N. W.
Washington 25, D. C.

MAILED 10
AUG 2 ? 1952
COMM-FBI

PJC:awy

100-2237

NOTE: No reference Bureau files on correspondent in Minnesota.. 8-22-52...per [redacted]

b7C

60 SEP 10 1952

Office Memorandum · UNITED STATES GOVERNMENT

TO : MR. A. H. BELMONT
DATE: May 5, 1953

FROM : Mr. L. L. Laughlin

SUBJECT: NIKOLA TESLA (Deceased)
INFORMATION CONCERNING

ALL INFORMATION CONTAINED
HEREIN IS UNCLASSIFIED
DATE 2-2-80 BY SP4/mfrte

A ▇▇▇▇▇▇▇ Ordnance Section of the Bureau of Standards (EM 2-4040, extension 623) called on the afternoon of May 4, 1953.

▇▇▇▇▇▇▇ stated that he had been reading a book entitled, "The Prodigal Genius - The Life of Nikola Tesla" by John J. O'Neill, whom ▇▇▇▇▇ described as a science writer for a New York newspaper (publisher - Ives Washburn). ▇▇▇▇▇ noted in this book that Bureau Agents went to Tesla's room following his death on January 7, 1943, opened his safe, examined his papers, and took over his personal files. ▇▇▇▇▇ said this appeared on page 277. Mr. ▇▇▇▇ stated that Tesla is the father of modern power engineering, being responsible for the invention of the A. C. generator, motor transmission, and other electrical engineering feats. He inquired (1) if the papers and works of Tesla were in the possession of the Bureau, and (2) if so, were they available for review in view of their scientific importance.

b7C

I told Mr. ▇▇▇▇ that the statement concerning the Bureau's taking Tesla's files did not seem very logical but that I would check on the matter.

The Bureau's files reflect that shortly after the death of Tesla in his hotel room in New York City on January 7, 1943, Sava Kosanovich, a distant relative, and other individuals entered his room and opened the safe, examining certain materials which he possessed. On January 8, 1943, Mr. L. M. C. Smith of the Department advised Mr. Tamm that he was concerned about the possibility of enemy agents confiscating some of the trunks of Tesla and apparently the Office of Alien Property Custodian was taking some action regarding these effects. Since the matter was being handled by the Office of Alien Property Custodian, the Bureau did not make any inquiries into this situation. (65-47953-6)

It is noted also that the Bureau received a letter dated April 16, 1948, from Mr. ▇▇▇▇▇▇▇ of ▇▇▇▇▇▇▇ Milwaukee, Wisconsin, explaining that he was studying electrical engineering at the Milwaukee School of Engineering and

100-2237-4X

LLL:mer
65-47953

1 - Mr. Nichols

was interested in the life and works of Tesla. ▇▇▇ stated that he understood at the time of Tesla's death the Bureau took his manuscripts and experiment data for national security. The Bureau on April 22, 1948, advised ▇▇▇ that the effects of Tesla were handled by the Office of Alien Property and not by the FBI. (65-47953-18)

I called Mr. ▇▇▇ this morning and told him that it was the office of Alien Property and not the FBI which took over the effects of Tesla following his death. Accordingly, I suggested that Mr. ▇▇▇ might wish to communicate with the office of Alien Property for further information concerning this matter.

The book "Prodigal Genius - The Life of Nikola Tesla" is not in the Bureau Library. A copy is being obtained from the Library of Congress. It will be examined to determine specifically the reference made to the Bureau's taking these papers. At that time a determination can be made as to what further action should be taken.

ADDENDUM: LLL:mer 5-14-53

Page 277 of the "Prodigal Genius - The Life of Nikola Tesla," describing Tesla's death, contains the following statement: "Operatives from the Federal Bureau of Investigation came and opened the safe in his room and took the papers it contained, to examine them for a reported important secret invention of possible use in the war."

Since this work was published in 1944, it is not felt that any particular purpose would be served by raising an objection with the publishers at this time. ▇▇▇ the individual who raised the question, has been set straight and, therefore, no further action is being taken.

- 2 -

Office Memorandum • UNITED STATES GOVERNMENT

TO : Director, FBI
FROM : SAC, New York
SUBJECT:
DATE: 8/19/54

Mr. GEORGE H. SCHERFF, JR., 149 Beacord Road, New Rochelle, New York, advised that he received two letters from LELAND I. ANDERSON, 127 Seymour Avenue Southeast, Minneapolis, Minnesota, photostatic copies of which are being furnished the Bureau and Minneapolis.

Mr. SCHERFF stated that he was an associate of Dr. NIKOLA TESLA in 1914 and that for many years his father had been Dr. TESLA'S private secretary. Mr. SCHERFF said that he never heard of LELAND I. ANDERSON nor did he ever hear of any of the names mentioned in ANDERSON'S letters.

Mr. SCHERFF stated that he has quite a bit of Dr. TESLA'S writings in his possession and he didn't know whether or not they would be of value to a foreign government.

Mr. SCHERFF is an Engineer with Consolidated Edison in New York. As the letters sounded "fishy" to him he thought they should be brought to the attention of the proper authorities in the U.S. Government.

Mr. SCHERFF stated that if there was anything wrong with the letters he would be willing to cooperate with the FBI.

No further action is being taken by the N.Y. Office, UACB.

Encs. (2)
1 - Minneapolis (2 Encs.)

EXP. PROC.

BEST COPY AVAILABLE

Leland I. Anderson
127 Seymour Avenue Southeast
Minneapolis 14, Minnesota

February 3, 1954

Mr. George H. Scherff, Jr.
149 Seacord Road
Westchester, NEW YORK

Dear Mr. Scherff:

re.: The Life and work of Dr. Nikola Tesla.

Recently, I have founded an organization in name and honor of Dr. Tesla in cooperation with several people who were intimately associated with Tesla during his lifetime, and with others who are interested in Dr. Tesla and his achievements from a scientific and historical standpoint. (See enclosed brochure.) I have had some difficulty locating a few of Tesla's associates, and, the name of George Scherff is among them. Therefore, it is my sincere hope that you, Mr. Scherff, are the person I seek as having been associated with Tesla.

I have personally studied the works of Tesla for a number of years, being particularly interested in elaborating upon his researches regarding high-tension radiant beams. Through some travel and other efforts, I have been fortunate to locate many original collections of Tesla's correspondence and manuscripts, and in a few cases obtained a number of interesting items.

I was in New York a short time ago on business, and while there I visited Mr. Kenneth M. Swezey. He intends to undertake some significant work on behalf of Tesla in the near future, and since he knew Tesla for so many years during his later life, it will be handled with great understanding.

I hope that you may have some interest in the work which I have initiated on behalf of Dr. Tesla. There are many matters that I wish to discuss with you, provided of course, that you are the Mr. Scherff related to the Tesla story. I would be most happy to hear from you at your earliest convenience, and will send you all publications of the organization if you wish to receive them.

Very truly yours,

Leland I. Anderson

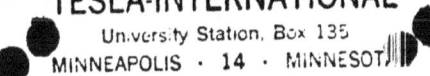
TESLA-INTERNATIONAL
University Station, Box 135
MINNEAPOLIS · 14 · MINNESOTA

To Those Who Are Interested in the Life and Work of
DR. NIKOLA TESLA

Following the death of Dr. Nikola Tesla on the 7th of January, 1943, Mr. John J. O'Neill, former Science Editor of the New York Herald Tribune, presented the biography

PRODIGAL GENIUS
The Life of Nikola Tesla

- a memorable tribute to one of the most outstanding figures in the entire field of electrical science. Many reading this biography learned of Nikola Tesla for the first time, despite his monumentous achievements with which he has won world-wide acclaim in scientific circles. Even those closely associated with the fields of science and engineering discovered a remarkable story not generally known of the brilliant genius Tesla whose sensitive personality and seclusion kept his fame in a shadow.

The TESLA-INTERNATIONAL organization is being established in the United States in name and honor of Dr. Nikola Tesla by those sharing a mutual interest in his life and works. The organization has as its objective the promulgation of the truth about Nikola Tesla; that a full recognition be made for his unparalleled research work on the effects of currents of high frequency and high potential, and for his achievements in the realms of polyphase power transmission and telecommunication. It would be the duty of the organization to do all in its power that the name of Tesla win in the eyes of the nation the fame deserving of a truly great American for his contributions to science, industry, and to this country.

A journal of the TESLA-INTERNATIONAL organization was issued beginning the month of November, 1953. In addition to items of recent and historical interest related to Tesla, the journal will include

1) A formal roster of all those who have an interest in the Tesla organization and wish to engage in its activities.

2) An opportunity of editorial exchange by members of the organization through the medium of the journal.

3) A comprehensive bibliographical listing of all available items concerning Tesla, which would include a cataloging of the various collections of Tesliana not generally known. Such a listing will be of particular importance to scholars in the research field.

4) A presentation of hitherto unpublished writings and analyses of Tesla's technical research studies as they become available.

The Journal of the TESLA-INTERNATIONAL organization will be forthcoming at intervals of 1½ - 2 months. Subscription rate is $1.00 for 10 issues. Membership in the TESLA-INTERNATIONAL organization is concurrent with subscription to the Journal.

REGISTERED MAIL

2/5/1954

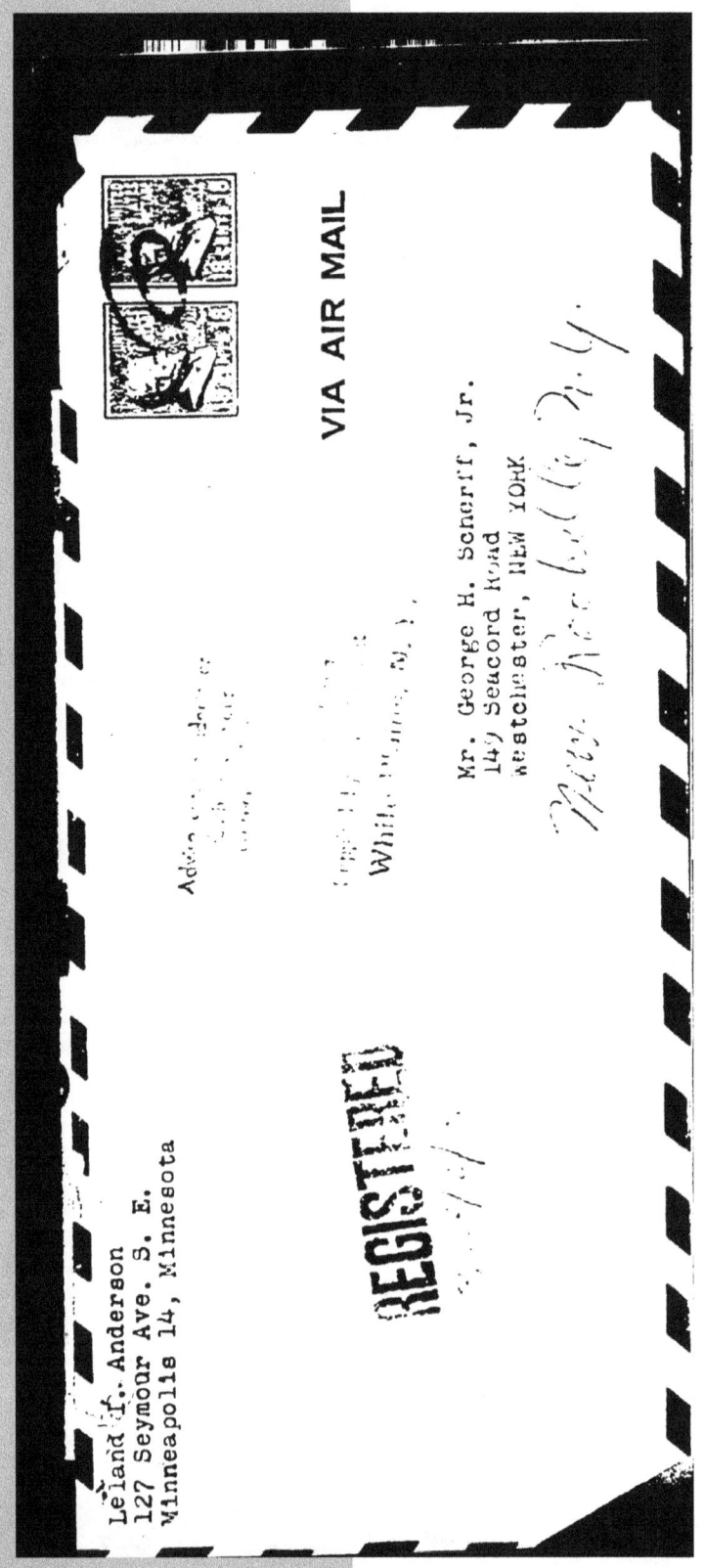

Leland I. Anderson
127 Seymour Avenue Southeast
Minneapolis 14, Minnesota

February 12, 1953

Dear Mr. Scherff,

It was so very rewarding to receive your reply concerning Dr. Nikola Tesla... I have initiated an undertaking on behalf of Tesla because I feel that in all right and justice something should be done to perpetuate the name of Tesla and see to it that his name becomes a part of the heritage of this nation. A great task perhaps, but as time goes on I believe the name of Tesla will become more significant in scientific developments. I hope that you may have an interest in the organization which I have proposed and established, and I will be honored to have you as a member. The organization is presently set up on the basis of those having a mutual interest in Tesla, with a free exchange of information between members. The first two issues of the Journal of the organization are being sent to you under separate cover, and should reach you in a day or two.

Some other members which may be of interest to you are; Muriel Arbus, Dorothy Skerritt, Kenneth Swezey and W. W. Wilhelm. The recent deaths of John O'Neill and Edwin Armstrong were very unexpected, and it is with a great sadness that I received the news and loss of these two members.

Do you know if Mr. Lowenstien had a daughter? The reason I ask is that a woman visited Mr. O'Neill before his death and told him that she inherited a great amount of Tesliana from her father — whom I presume to be Mr. Lowenstien. This woman was afraid of disclosing the information by reason of her mistaken notion and fear that she would rudely be raided by the army. You see Mr. O'Neill related to her that a few army officials visited his home with insistent requests for information. Of course all this sort of government interest was aroused by Tesla's "Death-Ray" rumors, played up by enterprising journalists. Well, the result of all this is that she refused to give Mr. O'Neill her married name — only that she married a Siamese prince no less, and moved to some mid-western city. If this woman has the amount of material that Mr. O'Neill intimated, it would certainly be important to locate her.

I believe that one of the valuable efforts of the Tesla organization would be to catalog every piece of information concerning Tesla. I have made a beginning effort along this line, and I hope that before too long all collections of Tesliana may be located, cataloged, and reproduced for fear of eventual loss. Through Mary A. Benjamin (of Walter R. Benjamin Autographs in New York) I have obtained a number of significant items of correspondence between Tesla and Robert U. Johnson. The entire collection of correspondence with Mr. Johnson numbers in excess of 70 pieces. I share this collection with Mrs.

Leland I. Anderson
127 Seymour Avenue Southeast
Minneapolis 14, Minnesota

-2-

James W. McChesney of Long Island. The period of this correspondence runs from 1894-1930. Mrs. McChesney has another group of correspondence between Tesla and George Sylvester Viereck which is very interesting in that it is from a period later in Tesla's life. (If you wish to receive any photostatic copies from these collections I will be happy to send them to you.)

I am interested to learn whether you have collected any mementoes, correspondence, writings, etc. of Tesla. For a long while I have been trying to locate a copy of the brochure which Tesla issued the first week of February, 1904. It came in a large square envelope bearing a large red wax seal with the initials "N.T." stamped thereon. Quite a number of them were distributed throughout New York and elsewhere by the Tesla enterprise in an effort to secure financial backing for the tower and power plant erected at Wardenclyffe, Long Island. You no doubt know of the brochure of which I speak. I thought it would be interesting to reproduce this brochure and distribute it among the members of the Tesla organization as a memento. Although I have written and inquired about this brochure extensively, I have not been able to locate a copy. Did you ever have one?

I have hopes that in 1956 (The Tesla Centenary) some significant observance may be organized here in the United States in honor of Tesla. The Tesla Museum in Yugoslavia has obtained the Tesla inheritance, which amounts to 9 tons of apparatus, writings, etc. It is the intention (so stated) of the Museum to publish the entire writings of Tesla, including those in the inheritance, on the Tesla Centenary. I don't know what sort of political propaganda might be injected in this publication, but it occured to me that it may be appropriate to arrange an advance publication in this country of Tesla's unpublished works. Unfortunately, there is not much to work on as yet. While the Tesla estate remained in this country, photostats of nearly every important paper in the estate were made under order of Wright Field Development Center in Ohio. If these photostats could be located there would be much material for a publication. However, in working with the Library of Congress in preparation of a file on Tesla, these photostats have escaped the most extensive search thus far.

Hoping that you may be interested in the efforts of the TESLA-INTERNATIONAL on behalf of Tesla and wish to associate yourself with it, I am,

Yours faithfully,

Leland I. Anderson

TESLA-INTERNATIONAL
University Station, Box 135
MINNEAPOLIS · 14 · MINNESOTA

IMPORTANT ANNOUNCEMENT

To: Members of the TESLA-INTERNATIONAL organization
and those interested in the works of
Dr. Nikola Tesla

RARE EDITION REPRINT --
"The Inventions, Researches and Writings of Nikola Tesla"
by
Thomas Commerford Martin

Through special arrangement, it is with great pleasure that the TESLA-INTERNATIONAL organization announces the reprinting of this classic of technical literature.

Long recognized as the most important and significant work on the early inventions of Tesla, a great demand for this book is anticipated. THIS REPRINTED EDITION IS STRICTLY LIMITED. This special offer will not be repeated when the supply is exhausted. Those desiring a copy of the book are therefore urged to reply promptly.

Cost of this book at the special printing rate is only $4.00 postpaid anywhere within the United States to members and friends of the TESLA-INTERNATIONAL organization.

UNDATED

SPECIAL DELIVERY—LETTER TO GEORGE SCHERFF

SAC, New York   March 10, 1954

Director, FBI

LELAND I. ANDERSON
MISCELLANEOUS; INTERNAL SECURITY - YU

    Reurlet 2-19-54 concerning the above-captioned individual. Relet forwarded to the Bureau two Photostats of two letters from Anderson which were received and made available to your office by George H. Scherff, Jr.

    There is returned herewith one set of the Photostats received by the Bureau as enclosures with your letter inasmuch as it appears this set was intended for retention in your office file.

Attachment

ETB:aas

ALL INFORMATION CONTAINED HEREIN IS UNCLASSIFIED
DATE 2-2-82 BY ___

MAILED 16
MAR 10 1954
COMM - FBI

Tolson
Ladd
Nichols
Belmont
Clegg
Glavin
Harbo
Rosen
Tracy
Gearty
Mohr
Winterrowd
Tele. Room
Holloman
Miss Gandy

KENNETH M. SWEZEY

163 Milton Street
Brooklyn 22, N.Y.
June 25, 1955

ALL INFORMATION CONTAINED
HEREIN IS UNCLASSIFIED
DATE 2-2-80 BY [signature]

Mr. J. Edgar Hoover
Federal Bureau of Investigation
Washington, D.C.

Dear Mr. Hoover:

Back in 1943, the local Alien Property Custodian searched through the belongings of the late electrical inventor, Nikola Tesla, stored in the Manhattan Storage Warehouse in New York City. Tesla had been a naturalized American for more than fifty years, so I believe that the search was made on the grounds that the property was to be sent to Yugoslavia, through Tesla's nephew and heir, Mr. Sava Kosanović (Mr. Kosanović had been Minister of State under the King's government, later became Ambassador to the United States from the present government, and is now a Minister serving in Belgrade).

According to the attorney who handled the Tesla estate, Mr. Philip Wittenberg, the Alien Property Custodian assured him that nothing had been held. I have a letter from the Office of Alien Property, dated March 15, 1955, which confirms this statement.

In gathering material to help in a nation-wide commemoration of Tesla's hundredth birthday next year---which will be participated in by leading scientific and engineering societies, museums, and universities---I have just discovered, however, that Tesla's solid gold Edison Medal somehow vanished during that search.

As a friend who had known Tesla well during his last twenty years, I was with Mr. Kosanović in Tesla's room in the Hotel New Yorker on the day he died. A safe expert was called in to unlock Tesla's safe. Among its contents were several honorary degrees, a volume of greetings which I had gathered for him on his seventy-fifth birthday, a bunch of keys, and the Edison Medal. We kept out the book of greetings (I mentioned this at the time to the assistant manager of the hotel and later to a Mr. Gorsuch of the Alien Property Custodian's office), but everything else, including the medal and the keys, was replaced and the safe was locked.

Except when it was inspected by the Alien Property Custodian, the safe was never reopened until it arrived in Belgrade (where Tesla's property was to be installed in a special Tesla Museum) and was there opened by Mr. Kosanović. According to his former secretary, both the bunch of keys and the medal were missing. The keys were later found in a tin box outside the safe; the medal was never found.

I learned of the disappearance of the medal only by accident. Mr. Kosanović had asked his former secretary to get permission from the American Institute of Electrical Engineers (who gave Tesla the Medal) to have it duplicated. This was given, but the cost, it turned out, would be about four hundred dollars. In the meantime, the Tesla Museum, in Yugoslavia, is quietly trying to raise the money to pay for it.

The irony of this situation is more disturbing than the money involved. By giving us a system which made electric power universally available, Tesla---probably more than any other one man---helped put America on top of the world. At the time he died, his gold Edison Medal was the only material evidence left of this country's appreciation. That this last token should have disappeared ---to have to be replaced by his materially poor countrymen overseas for whom he had done nothing---seems a tragic denouement.

John O'Neill, in his biography of Tesla, states that the FBI broke into Tesla's safe on the day he died, and an article in the current (June) Coronet repeats this. I know this isn't true. I did hear, however, that the FBI somehow lent a hand to the Alien Property Custodian during the latter's search in the warehouse.

If that is so, I thought that perhaps some of your men might remember the conditions under which the search was made and therefore might have a suggestion as to what could have happened to the medal. After this long time, I have no hope that the medal can actually be restored, and I am already trying to interest Americans in making a replacement. But future biographers might be spared a lot of wild guessing and wrong blaming if some hint could be obtained as to whether the original got lost, strayed, or stolen---and who might have been responsible.

With best regards and sincere appreciation for any help you can give,

Sincerely,

Kenneth M. Swezey

P.S.: I am enclosing an editorial from last month's POWER magazine which outlines Tesla's contribution to the electric power industry. K.M.S.

LOUIS N ROWLEY, EDITOR • MAY 1955 • ESTABLISHED 1882

Strange Genius

ASK ANY GROUP of power men to name those who laid the foundation for today's electrical generation and distribution. You'll wind up with an impressive list—Edison, Brush, Thomson, Westinghouse, many others. But there is almost sure to be a significant omission.

Yet this forgotten man conceived the polyphase ac motor—still basic—and devised a suitable system of generation and distribution for applying it. To grasp the magnitude of this contribution, we must turn back to the 1880's when the electrical era was being born, and the "battle of the systems" held sway.

Arc lights and motors were being operated on constant-current series systems. Edison's Pearl Street generating station had opened in 1882, supplying incandescent lamps and, later, dc motors on a constant-potential system. Under the leadership of Westinghouse and Stanley, the advantages of ac distribution were demonstrated. But there was no successful ac motor.

In May, 1888, a young Yugo-Slav engineer, but four years in the United States, read a paper before the American Institute of Electrical Engineers. In it he described a new ac system. Its heart was the induction motor with its basic and beautiful concept of the rotating magnetic field. The man was Nikola Tesla, the system he described was destined to sweep the field.

With characteristic vision, George Westinghouse realized the fundamental importance of the polyphase ac system and acquired the basic patents. Its first impact on the general public was at the Chicago World's Fair of 1893. There a 2-phase generator supplied motors and lamps, and, through rotary converters and motor-generators, a variety of dc equipment.

But it remained for the Niagara Falls power project to demonstrate in the most dramatic way possible that polyphase ac was the system of the future. Since 1886 when a charter to develop its power had been granted, the eyes of the world had been on Niagara. An international commission, headed by Lord Kelvin, had reviewed 17 proposals, found none acceptable. Later, just five years after Tesla's AIEE paper, it was officially decided to use the polyphase system.

In August, 1895, Niagara power was delivered to the first industrial customer and in 1896 ac transmission to Buffalo, 22 miles away, was begun. By that time, the steam turbine had been introduced in America and the modern age of electric power had truly opened.

For Nikola Tesla, these far-reaching inventions were but a beginning. Still to come was brilliant work in high frequencies, thinking basic to much of today's radio art. Yet by the time of his death in 1943, both he and his work had begun to slip into obscurity. Why?

A man of flashing insights and enormous brilliance, Tesla was largely indifferent to the development of his ideas. This he left to others while he followed the lure of new challenges. In later years, his projects became more grandiose, his ways more mysterious, his pronouncements more Olympian. And working alone, as he did, he formed none of the institutional ties that help to perpetuate a record of accomplishment.

Next year—July 10, 1956—will be the 100th anniversary of Nikola Tesla's birth. It would be fitting for our engineering societies to commemorate this occasion, to acknowledge our debt to this strange and lonely genius who changed our world for the better.

(REPRINTED BY PERMISSION)

АМЕРИКАНСКИ СРБОБРАН
THE AMERICAN SRBOBRAN
Second Class Mail Privileges Authorized at Pittsburgh, Pa.

THE LARGEST AND OLDEST SERBIAN DAILY NEWSPAPER IN AMERICA
Published Daily Except Sat's, Sundays and Holidays by SERB NATIONAL FEDERATION
3414 Fifth Avenue — Telephone MAyflower 1-6600 — Pittsburgh 13, Pa.

MOMCHILO SOKICH, Editor — JOVAN BRATICH, Ass't. Editor
MILAN M. KARLO, Editor English Section

RECOGNITION FOR TESLA

Largely thru a young American engineer's efforts, the world today is re-scanning the record and achievements of our inventive genius, Nikola Tesla. Of late, even the big-time magazines have devoted space to the amazing career and fascinating character of the pioneering electrical wizard.

The man behind this belated recognition for the one-time Serbian immigrant boy who made millions but died almost a pauper is Leland P. Anderson, head of the **Tesla Society**, which has headquarters at the University of Minnesota.

Thru travels, correspondence and detailed research, Mr. Anderson has dug up many friends of the late genius and induced them to join in his noble work. A good many of these are American-Serbians. They serve Mr. Anderson and he serves them, with information issued thru his TESLIAN publication. This is, at present, a mimeographed publication issued monthly which casts new light on the known life and record of the late Dr. Tesla.

The latest issue (March-June) informs of progress plans to honor Dr. Tesla even more. It also presents an account of a fascinating editorial, "Strange Genius", by the POWER magazine of the powerful McGraw-Hill publishing line. This editorial traces the introduction of Dr. Tesla's polyphase system, described by Mr. Anderson, as the **"most tremendous event in all engineering history."**

Editorialist Louis N. Bowler, according to the TESLIAN, answers the perplexing question why, in view of Tesla's important discoveries, he fell short of the comparative popularity won by Edison and Bell. Then in closing, he suggests: "It would be fitting for our engineering societies, in commemoration of the 100th anniversary of Nikola Tesla's birth (July 10, 1956), to acknowledge our debt to this strange and lonely genius who changed our world for the better."

This appears to be just what Mr. Anderson was waiting for. For now, in the same issue of his TESLIAN, he has prepared a form to petition Postmaster General Arthur E. Summerfield to issue a Tesla commemorative stamp next year.

We are printing this form in duplicate in this issue and we urge all our readers to endorse it with their signatures. Send the completed petition...

Office Memorandum • UNITED STATES GOVERNMENT

TO: L. V. BOARDMAN
FROM: A. H. BELMONT
DATE: June 29, 1955

ALL INFORMATION CONTAINED
HEREIN IS UNCLASSIFIED
DATE 7-2-80 BY [signature]

SUBJECT: NIKOLA TESLA
MISCELLANEOUS - INFORMATION CONCERNING (ESPIONAGE)

Nikola Tesla, a native of Yugoslavia, was a famous electrical inventor who died in New York City in 1943 where he had lived for many years. In attached letter to Bureau dated 6-25-55 Kenneth M. Swezey, Brooklyn, New York, advises he is gathering material to help in a nation-wide commemoration of Tesla's hundredth birth anniversary in 1956. Swezey relates he was present when Tesla's safe was opened by friends after his death and advises the contents were thereafter replaced and then impounded by the United States Alien Property Custodian. Later the safe was removed to Belgrade, Yugoslavia, to be installed in a Tesla Museum. Missing from Tesla's effects is a gold Edison medal he had been awarded. Swezey is seeking to locate the medal and has been advised by the Office of Alien Property (OAP) that OAP held none of Tesla's property. Swezey states he has heard the FBI assisted OAP in handling Tesla's effects while in storage, and accordingly, he asks whether Bureau could assist him in locating the Edison medal. Re FBI's assistance to OAP Swezey mentions that in the Tesla biography ("The Prodigal Genius" - 1944) by John O'Neill it was stated FBI broke into Tesla's safe the day he died (1-8-43 to protect contents from enemy hands). Swezey notes this same comment appears in article ("The Genius Who Walked Alone") by Alfred H. Sinks in the June, 1955, "Coronet." Swezey says he knows FBI did not do this. Bufiles not pertinent re Swezey. Bureau did not enter into Tesla safe matter upon Department's advice it was being handled by OAP. Bureau previously aware of comment in O'Neill's book. Per Bufiles Sinks was officer of American Civil Liberties Union in 1930-40; staff member of Communist line newspaper "The Anvil" 1933-37; member of League of American Writers ("CUA report 1944); close friend of [redacted] reported CP member and suspected underground member - In 1945 Sinks requested for his use as author data re Bureau's microfilm procedure. Was advised no such data available for publication.

Enclosure 6-20-55
100-2237
cc - 1 - 65-47953
Ticklers - Mr. Bird
Mr. Belmont
Mr. Boardman
ETB:jaa
(5)

RECORDED
EX-104
6 JUL 7 1955
JUL 11 1955

Memorandum For Mr. Boardman

RECOMMENDATION:

That the attached letter be sent to Swezey advising Bureau did not participate in the handling of Tesla's effects and that the matter was handled by OAP. Therefore, Bureau unable to be of assistance; that no action be taken relative to Sinks' comment in "Coronet" article.

Mr. Belmont
Mr. Boardman

June 30, 1955

INFORMATION CONTAINED
HEREIN IS UNCLASSIFIED
DATE 2-2-80 BY SP4 Jrw/Rt

Mr. Kenneth M. Swezey
163 Milton Street
Brooklyn 22, New York

(Original)

Dear Mr. Swezey:

    With reference to your letter of June 25, 1955, our files disclose the effects of *Nikola Tesla* were taken into custody after his death by the Office of Alien Property and not by this Bureau.

    Since we did not participate in the handling of Mr. Tesla's effects, we are unable to supply the information you requested.

                        Sincerely yours,

                        J. Edgar Hoover

                        John Edgar Hoover
                            Director

NOTE:

    A cover memorandum from Belmont to Boardman was prepared by ETB:jaa on 6-29-55 in connection with this outgoing mail.

    Bufiles contain no derogatory data re correspondent; reflect only that he was close friend and admirer of Tesla.

ETB:jda
(5)

Downey, California.

August 1, 1955.

Mr. J. Edgar Hoover,
Federal Bureau of Investigation,
Washington, D.C.

Dear Mr. Hoover:

In his book, "Prodigal Genius", The Life of Nikola Tesla, Mr. John J O'Neil says, on page 277, that the F.B.I. went to Tesla's hotel room, opened his steel safe and removed from it, the papers it contained.

Was there ever any publication of what these papers contained? If so, could you inform me where I might obtain a copy of such publication?

If there was no publication of the Safe's content, after more than 10 years, would it be improper to publish them?

If there was no publication of the safe's content, but there were no particular secrets found there in, could you inform me where I might learn what the safe contained?

Any information on this matter will be appreciated.

Thank you for your trouble.

Sincerely,

8/11/1955 — LETTER FROM J. E. HOOVER

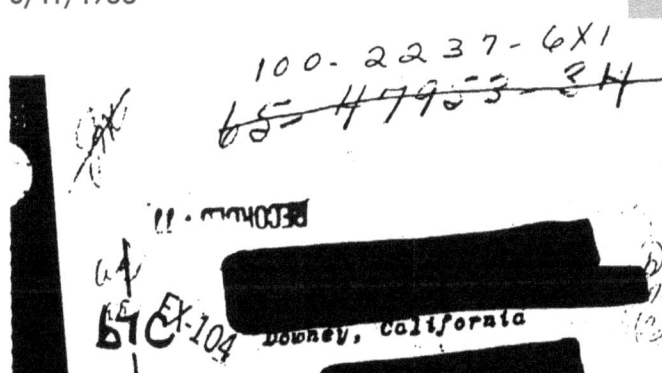

August 11, 1955

ALL INFORMATION CONTAINED
HEREIN IS UNCLASSIFIED
DATE 7-2-80 BY [signature]

Downey, California

Dear

Your letter dated August 1, 1955, has been received, and in response to your inquiry, I would like to advise that our files reflect that the effects of Nikola Tesla were taken into custody after his death by the Office of Alien Property and not by this Bureau.

Since we did not participate in the handling of Mr. Tesla's effects, we are unable to supply the information you requested.

Sincerely yours,

John Edgar Hoover
Director

NOTE: Bufiles reflect no record on correspondent. This type of reply utilized by Internal Security Division in answering similar inquiries on 6/30/55. (65-47953-33) Cover memo from Mr. Belmont to Mr. Boardman dated 6/29/55 set out background of this matter which concerned the death of Tesla, a famous electrical inventor. Bureau was not involved in this matter, and the opening of the safe mentioned was done by the Office of Alien Property.

JRH:sms
(3)

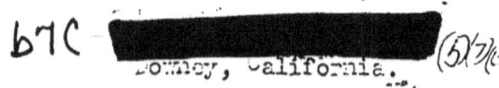

Downey, California.

September 10., 1955.

Mr. John Edgar Hoover,
Federal Bureau Of Investigation,
Washington 25, D.C.

Dear Mr. Hoover:

Referring to my letter to you August first, this year - your letter to me, August 11th., relative to the matter of the papers of Mr. Nikola Tesla.

On August 26, I wrote the office of Alien Property regarding this matter, indicating that I had received the information from you that it was their department which had taken the Tesla Property into custody - not yours..

I have a letter from Mr. Henry G. Hilken - that Department - File Number HGH:M SH:elk 017-3566, in which I am told that office "never had custody, nor has vested, any property of Nikola Tesla".

As I began this matter with you - because it was stated in Mr. O'Neill's book that it was your department who opened Tesla's safe - I am wondering if you have any further suggestions along lines I might follow to obtain some information in this regard?

Thank you for your time and trouble.

Sincerely

September 20, 1955

[REDACTED]
Downey, California

Dear [REDACTED]

I have received your letter dated September 10, 1955.

As you were advised by my letter of August 11, 1955, this Bureau was not connected in any respect with the acquisition or custody of the effects of Nikola Tesla, and it is therefore not possible to furnish you any additional information.

Sincerely yours,

John Edgar Hoover
Director

NOTE: By letter 8-11-55, we referred [REDACTED] to the Office of Alien Property, which Office was reported to have assumed custody of Tesla's effects subsequent to his death (65-47953-6)

JRH:vjs
(3)

RECOGNITION FOR TESTA

(Please fill out this form and mail to the address appearing below.)

THE TESLA SOCIETY
University Station, Box 135
Minneapolis 14, Minnesota

_____
(date)

_____
(city & state)

Hon. Arthur E. Summerfield
Postmaster General, Postoffice Dept.
Washington, D. C.

Dear Sir:

Nikola Tesla's contributions to science, industry, and to his adopted country have greatly inspired engineering progress. His electrical systems helped create an American economy of world pre-eminence.

We respectfully request issuance of a 1956 commemorative stamp to be issued on the centennial of Tesla's birth (1856-1943).

_____
(signed)

"AMERICAN SRBOBRAN"
June 29, 1955
Pittsburgh, Pennsylvania

The Genius Who Walked Alone

by Alfred H. Sinks

Nikola Tesla was a great inventor—and also a prophet without honor

COUNTER-ESPIONAGE WHEELS started turning early on the morning of January 8, 1943. Anxious FBI agents slipped into a room in the Hotel New Yorker where, late the night before, a chambermaid had discovered the body of Nikola Tesla, dead at 86, regarded by many as the greatest scientific genius of his time.

For years, Tesla had been making scientific predictions so fantastic as to be literally out of this world. Of late he had been working—or so he said—on revolutionary new weapons powerful enough to annihilate armies at a single blow.

There was only one Tesla, and the story might—incredible as it sounded—be true. The old man's safe might hold these secrets, and the Government could not risk the chance of enemy spies getting there first.

Half hoping to find something which would bring a sudden and decisive end to World War II, the G-men broke open the dead man's strong box. If anything of importance was discovered, it has never been revealed.

Yet, their quick action was justified, for you could never be sure about Tesla, one of the strangest men who ever lived. Most people took him with a grain of salt, yet no serious scientist dared shrug away his claims as nonsense. Not after Thomas Edison tried it and Tesla proved him wrong.

The world's leading physicists and electrical engineers had to eat crow back in the 1880s when Tesla solved a problem they had thought impossible. That one accomplishment—the invention of a practical alternating-current motor and generator—put Tesla's name among vorite was an "engine" powered by the world's top scientists.

From his inventions sprang the industrial age we live in. For without his alternating current, there would be no mass production of automobiles, aircraft, refrigerators; no great water-power dams and generating plants, no Diesel-electric trains; we could not have developed radio, television or atomic power.

The *direct* current that Edison worked with—a feeble force at best—could be sent no more than a couple of miles over wires because its power leaked away rapidly into the surrounding atmosphere. Lights near the power station might burn brightly and steadily, but those near the end of the line would be dim and fluttering.

Tesla sold his basic alternating-current patents in 1888, for a million dollars down. By 1895, the first great power station at Niagara Falls had been built, and by the end of 1896, two more Tesla generators had been installed. Within a few years, the pace of life over half the earth had changed from a crawl to a fast gallop—and it has been gathering speed ever since.

THE MAN WHO, by his brilliant idea of a "rotating magnetic field," changed the face of the earth and the living habits of the human race was a Croat, born in 1857 in Smiljan, a village in what is now Yugoslavia, but was then part of the old Austro-Hungarian Empire.

When he was about six, Nikola Tesla's father, the village priest, was transferred to a larger parish in the city of Gospic. There, the lad grew up and perfected his earliest "inventions." Of these, his fa-

16 June bugs, harnessed in sets of four to spokes which radiated from the drive shaft.

Nikola was a frail lad, often ill; and he nearly went blind from too much reading. He read everything he could get his hands on, not only science but also religion, philosophy, history, literature. By the time he finished high school, he was fluent in French, German and Italian, as well as his native Serbo-Croat.

He got his schooling—the best his doting family could afford—at Gospic, Carlstadt, Gratz, the University of Prague and, finally, at Budapest. At the University, he saw his first electric motor, a new type direct-current affair whose brushes and commutators sent out showers of crackling blue sparks.

"If we got rid of those brushes and commutators, with all that noise and loss of energy, we'd have a much better motor," Nikola told his professor. "Perhaps it might be done with an alternating current."

"Nonsense!" barked the professor. "An alternating current would never run anything. You're not the brilliant student I thought you were. Forget it!"

But Tesla could not forget. The teacher's ridicule only stamped the idea indelibly on his brain. It became an obsession, a passion - how to make an alternating current drive a motor. In every idle moment, wherever he went, he wrestled with this problem.

Tesla's mind had an unusual twist. Almost from infancy, he had been able to see things in his mind's eye so vividly—and in such minute detail—that often he had trouble telling the real from the imaginary.

Where the average engineer or inventor would reach instinctively for drawing board, paper and pencil, Tesla would simply switch on that uncanny magic lantern inside his brain. He would fix a mental image there. Then he would alter this detail or that, discard one plan, try another, without ever putting a line on paper.

Years later—from these mental images alone—he could give his workmen exact instructions on how to build each part of a new device, though it was unlike anything ever seen before.

Thus, needing no drafting room and few laboratory conveniences to work on an idea, Tesla could use every spare minute that he had to test and revise his theory of alternating current.

His first real job was manager of a newly organized telephone company in Budapest. But telephone circuits were dull stuff compared with the challenge of that one big idea. He moved to Paris where he became a kind of general trouble-shooter for the Continental Edison Company.

His brain was still chipping away at his big problem, but the trouble was, he couldn't share it with trained men who might have helped him work it out. For whenever he mentioned alternating current to an electrical engineer, the man would look at him as though he were crazy.

But then came the moment when he knew he had solved it. He was walking with a friend in the Bois de Boulogne. Suddenly, he stopped short and began jabbing with his cane at some invisible object in the air.

"See—it works!" he shouted. "It is the rotating magnetic field which causes the armature to turn. It pulls the magnets around with it, causing the shaft to revolve. As I oscillate this switch, causing the current to flow first in one direction, then the other . . ."

Never mind what his friend thought. Tesla had the answer.

At the office, his colleagues scoffed or looked blank. But the manager, listening to the outpourings of scientific jargon, suddenly thought of his boss back in the United States. If there *were* some truth in what the Croat said, surely the famous electrical wizard would be smart enough to see it.

So he gave Tesla a letter of introduction to Thomas Edison and urged him to try his luck in America. Thus, Tesla, now 27, arrived in New York. He was handsome, over six-feet-two, with a distinguished head and deep-set blue eyes. His Slavic face was broad across the cheekbones, his dark hair thick, his chin sharply pointed. Of worldly goods, he had the clothes on his back, four cents in cash, the letter to Edison, and the idea which was to change the world.

Edison thought less than nothing of the idea. It seemed so preposterous that he wouldn't even listen

JUNE, 1955

117

—and, of course, Tesla had no drawings with which any to convince him. But Edison gave him a job, for he had excellent training as an engineer and Edison needed trained men.

Busy with routine electrical work, Tesla waited nearly three years for a chance to turn his mental image into an actual motor he could show to others. In 1887, he was able to borrow enough money to start his own laboratory, and the following year the alternating-current motor and generator were practical realities—on a laboratory scale—though much practical engineering would still be needed to fit them to commercial use.

George Westinghouse, another inventor, was the first to see their value. He bought the patents and gave Tesla a job as engineer in his Pittsburgh factory.

But Tesla couldn't get along with the other Westinghouse engineers. From his standpoint, the alternating-current job was done. Even "schoolboys" could now iron out the few remaining kinks. Meantime, his brain had started to hatch even bigger dreams. He went back to his laboratory in New York.

"Be alone—" he once told a science writer. "That's the secret of invention. Be alone—that's where great ideas are born."

Alone he was. In the years that followed, Tesla had many admiring acquaintances, but seldom a friend. After his mother, no woman ever entered his personal life.

His manner toward others was cordial but reserved, distant. His words were as if uttered by some god, sitting on an Olympus high above the rest of humanity. Backed by his fame, those words made a tremendous impression.

He lectured at every scientific center in this country and in all the important capitals abroad. Things which, as yet, existed only inside that amazing brain of his were so real to him, he made them real to his listeners.

He described radar and radio broadcasting and even television. He advocated electro-therapy. He foresaw a day when man would control nature in every respect—even the weather—when machines of all kinds, and the power to run them, would be so cheap that poverty would vanish from the world.

Without wanting to be, Tesla was a superb actor. After listening to him and seeing his wonders, audiences were ready to believe nearly anything.

Tesla reasoned that you could sell electric power cheap if you could do away with the millions of poles and insulators, the millions of tons of copper wire used to transmit it from place to place. He thought he knew how to do it—and J. P. Morgan backed him with $300,000.

On Long Island, Tesla built a huge power plant with a 154-foot steel-ribbed tower topped by an enormous mushroom-shaped copper dome. From this dome he planned to bombard the earth's crust with millions of volts of electric energy. The power so added to the earth's permanent charge could be drained off at some other point—any point—on the earth's surface. Thus, it would be possible for electric power to be sent anywhere without conduits, poles or wires. Or so he thought, until he tried it.

CORONET

118

In November, 1898, Tesla announced that he could abolish war.

The inventor had designed a small, inexpensive, radio-controlled boat which, through its supposed ability to destroy the biggest battleships, would make great navies useless. Not many years later, he was talking of another super-weapon: a "death ray" which would annihilate whole armies.

Yet Tesla never suspected that the real super-weapon of the future would come from atomic fission. For Einstein's basic notion which led to smashing the atom, he had only ridicule. Alone in his middle age, he had fallen out of step with the world's great thinker.

Not all Tesla's later inventions were fantastic. Some, like his induction coils and oscillators, and pioneer work on "tuned" electrical circuits, were highly important.

Though he never succeeded in transmitting power without wires on a big scale, he did prove that a single wire is enough. And some of his brilliant prophecies inspired the more plodding scientists to work out the practical problems of induction heating, radio-telephone, radar and many other electronic marvels of today.

But as he grew older, he withdrew further and further within himself. His strange prophecies sounded like a voice from another planet. For companionship now, the old man had only his dreams, and they grew stranger with the years. Completely alone at last, a stooped, gaunt figure with thin, silvery hair, he used to slip from his hotel room, buy a bag of birdseed and trudge slowly over to a park where hundreds of pigeons awaited him. These were his friends. They needed him, though the world did not.

When he grew too ill to go out, each day he sent a Western Union messenger to the park. After feeding the birds, the boy was instructed to see if any of them seemed sick. If so, he was to bring them back to Tesla's room where the inventor would nurse them gently back to health.

Perhaps this sad little labor of love showed that the man who changed the world had, at last, discovered a great truth. Perhaps he knew now that the greatest power for good lies not in lonely thought but in a human heart pulsating—like his own "tuned circuits"—in tune with the hearts of his fellowmen. Or did he ever know? You could never be sure about Tesla.

Winnie Wit

IN THE EARLY 1920s, when Winston Churchill had offended both his own supporters and the political opposition, the late George Bernard Shaw wrote him: "I enclose two vouchers for the première of my new play, for yourself and a friend—if any."

Back to the playwright promptly came the theater checks with this note from "Winnie": "I regret I am unable to attend the première of your new play. Please send me two vouchers for the second performance—if any."

—BK*LING in (Cleveland News)

RECOGNITION FOR TESLA

At long last Serbians—American and Canadian—have acted to honor the memory and achievements of one of Serbia's greatest sons.

For the world-wide Centennial celebration of Dr. Nikola Tesla's birth next year, Serbs on this Continent plan to erect a bust statue of the electrical genius to stand before the entrance of the Monastery at Libertyville, Ill.

Steps looking towards that end were taken at the recent SNF convention following the reading of a letter by President Mile Radakovich from His Grace, Bishop Nicolai. As the universally-renowned churchman stated, erection of a suitable monument, by Serbians, would forever remind other Serbs of the honor and glory of Dr. Nikola Tesla . . . And that he was a SERBIAN, son of a SERBIAN ORTHODOX clergyman, born in the SERBIAN SELO of Smiljan in Lika.

Further, His Grace urged that the undertaking be a joint one and representative of ALL the Serbian organizations in the United States and Canada. He naturally looked to the SNF for leadership, and the greatest monetary contribution. But he also besought the help of the Serbian Nat'l Defense and the Jedinstvo beneficial society.

The Convention voted $1000 for the project and a hand collection was taken up among the delegates and guests, kinsmen Milos Konjevich of Joliet, Ill., giving $200. It is probable that the balance of the needed $3000 will be raised thru public good-will offerings and via cash gifts of the other two organizations mentioned.

And after a suitable bust has been erected for Dr. Tesla, Bishop Nicolai suggested a similar-like monument honor the memory of Dr. Mihailo Pupin, also a world-renowned scientist, author and educator.

This is a subject near and dear to all good Serbian hearts

"AMERICAN SRBOBRAN"
September 28, 1955
Pittsburgh, Pa.

SNF Opens Drive for Tesla Memorial at Libertyville

$2000 PUBLIC AID SOUGHT

PITTSBURGH, PA. — The Serb Nat'l Federation Executive Board has acted quickly to implement a Convention decision to honor the memory of the illustrious Dr. Nikola Tesla.

At its first meeting of October 8, the Board drafted a resolution calling on all SNF members and good Serbians to help finance a memorial project for the late scientist-inventor genius.

This would stand before the entrance of the Monastery in Libertyville, Ill.

Cost of the contemplated project, which would clarion to the world that Dr. Tesla was a Serbian, is estimated at $3000. The Convention voted $1000 to the cause and a hand collection among 122 delegates yielded several hundred dollars more.

Kinsman Milos Konjevich of Joliet, Ill., gave $200.

Public Aid Sought

Balance of the needed sum is now being sought thru good-will offerings of the general Serbian populace in the United States and Canada.

A fund, similar to the one being conducted to help defray mortgage expenses on Shadeland, has been established.

It is hoped to raise the necessary monies and complete the project in time for the world-wide Centennial celebration for the genius next year.

Spearheading the movement for recognition, especially among American elements, is the TESLA SOCIETY, founded by scientist-engineer Leland Anderson, a fanatical admirer of the late Dr. Nikola Tesla.

Mr. Anderson right now is conducting a search for a famous portrait of the Serbian electrical wizard done at the turn of the century in New York.

Seek Missing Portrait

In his current TESLAIAN publication, Mr. Anderson revealed the work, by Princess Vilma Lwoff-Parlaghy, is missing.

Reviewing developments, Mr. Anderson wrote:

"On March 1, 1916, the Princess gave a reception in her new studio in New York especially to exhibit her latest portrait of Nikola Tesla. An article in the NEW YORK TIMES for March 2, 1916, stated—

" 'It was one of the beliefs of Mr. Tesla that there was something unlucky about posing for a picture and he never sat to any before he entered the studio of the Princess. The room which she had chosen did not have a skylight in it and the much desired North exposure was missing.

" 'At the suggestion of Mr. Tesla, a cluster of powerful incandescents was put up in the corner of the apartment and the rays, filtered thru blue glass, were just the right quality. The portrait was shown under the same illumination.

At Ease for Sitting

" 'Mr. Tesla, having solved the problem of the artifical sun, fell to thinking about other parts of the universe, and there he sat oblivious to his surroundings.

" 'The painter was able to produce a likeness in which there is no evidence that the subject was conscious that anybody was watching him, much less studying his features from the other side of the easel.

" 'Among those who attended the reception were Mrs. C. B. Alexander, Henry P. Davison, the Countess de Rittenburg and Mrs. E. T. Isham.' "

After the Princess died, in 1923, her studio and all objects of art, was sold at auction.

The Tesla portrait, 53x48 inches, appeared on the cover of TIME magazine (July 20, 1931) and in the ELECTRICAL EXPERIMENTER (January 1919), Mr. Anderson says.

Its location is not now known.

AMERICAN SRBOBRAN
October 26, 1955
Pittsburgh, Pa.

TESLA F $1580

Half of $3000 Costs For Statue Pledged

Cadiz, O., Serb Gives $100 For Bust Image of Inventor To Be Placed at Monastery

Pittsburgh, Pa.—Half of the $3000 fund goal for a statue memorial of the late Dr. Nikola Tesla has been realized, the SNF announced today.

In fact, total contributions counted so far come to $1580.

The Fund is an outgrowth of a plea by Bishop Nicolai for Serbians to do honor for the memory of the noted electrical wizard during the world-wide Centennial celebration planned for the genius next year.

In the wake of the plea, voiced at the recent 7th Convention at Niagara Falls, Canada, the delegates approved a $1000 gift from the SNF and decided to raise, by public grant, the balance of $2000.

A hand collection among the 122 grass-roots leaders of the Society raised another $450. Then, at its first meeting October 5, the newly-elected Executive Board of the SNF appealed to the membership at large to fulfill the balance required.

First Contribution $100

A scant 24 hours after the appeal was published in the Society's "Srbobran" organ last Wednesday, Sime Zelich of Cadiz, O., gave $100.

The proposed memorial, a statue image, would be placed before the entrance of the St. Sava Serbian Monastery in Libertyville, Ill.

historians, writers, educators, scientists, etc., would not be misled, Bishop Nicolai believes.

Be that as it may, the SNF's goal is to amass the needed monies in time to erect and dedicate the memorial before the Tesla Centennial celebration ends.

Donors and the amounts of their donations are as follows:

SNF		$1000.00
Delegate M. Konjevich		200.00
"	Todor Drazich	50.00
"	Petar Borovich	25.00
SNF Counsel N. Stone		25.00
Delegate N. Stepanovich		20.00
"	Maxim Jakovac	20.00
"	Ilija Janjanin	20.00
"	Lou Balta	10.00
"	Jovan Vukcevich	10.00
"	Milan Kajganovich	10.00
"	Stevan Rogulja	10.00
"	Bogdan Dragisich	5.00
"	Milan Tomich	5.00
"	Todor Vuicich	5.00
"	Djuro Lukich	5.00
"	G. Stoisavljevich	5.00
"	R. Vukadinovich	5.00
"	Janko Mrmich	5.00
"	Petar Maravich	5.00
"	Mirko Baranin	5.00

a, the delegates approved a 000 gift from the SNF and cided to raise, b public int, the balance c .000.

hand collection among the grass-roots leaders of the So- raised another $450. Then, first meeting October 5, the ly-elected Executive Board of SNF appealed to the membership at large to fulfill the bale required.

First Contribution $100

A scant 24 hours after the ap- l was published in the Society's bobran" organ last Wednes-, Sime Zelich of Cadiz, O., e $100.

The proposed memorial, a tue image, would be placed be- e the entrance of the St. Sava bian Monastery in Libertyville.

"There it would proclaim to ns of thousands of Serbian sitors annually that Nikola esla was of Serbian immigrant ock and son of a Serbian rthodox clergyman," Bishop icolai declared.

For half a century and more, general American public has en misled anent the nationality the man who foretold the com- of atomic energy power.

Only recently, a prominent American magazine listed him, incorrectly, as of Croatian tock. The mistake was subse- uently publicly corrected with nologies by the publication. But lacking an image reference, th historical statistics, similar ors are likely in the future.

Old References Poor

The magazine publication, for tance, explained it obtained its erence material from an anti- ted guide book.

Since the misleading matter re was never challenged by rbians and other interested rties before, the magazine logi- ly assumed it was factual.

Erection of a bust statue. lso listing Dr. Tesla's date of irth, birthplace, parents, etc., ould counter the old guide nd make certain that future

Centennial celebration ends.

Donors d the amounts of their donat. e are as follows:

SNF		$ 1000.00
Delegate M. Konjevich		200.00
" Todor Drazich		50.00
" Petar Borovich		25.00
SNF Counsel N. Stone		25.00
Delegate N. Stepanovich		20.00
" Maxim Jakovac		20.00
" Ilija Janjanin		20.00
" Lou Balta		10.00
" Jovan Vukcevich		10.00
" Milan Kajganovich		10.00
" Stevan Rogulja		10.00
" Bogdan Dragisich		5.00
" Milan Tomich		5.00
" Todor Vuicich		5.00
" Djuro Lukich		5.00
" G. Stoisavljevich		5.00
" R. Vukadinovich		5.00
" Janko Mrmich		5.00
" Petar Maravich		5.00
" Mirko Baranin		5.00
" Stanko Jelich		5.00

* * *

Prof. Anthony Tomovich (Edmonton, Alberta, Can.)	10.00
Teta Andja Mamula (Pittsburgh)	5.00
Martha Mamula Bjelosh (Pittsburgh)	10.00
Sime Zelich (Cadiz, O.)	100.00
Milinko Alexich, war invalid (Omaha, Nebr.)	
Total	$ 1,

—the honoring, forever, of two of Serbia's best-known immigrant sons who contributed so greatly to the welfare and prosperity of their adopted America.

We hope to report developments as soon as they take place, remembering Bishop Nikolai's concluding remarks:

"Nikola Tesla, in the field of science, brought the Serbian name great glory—just as did the greatest Serbian knights on the field of battle."

23 June 56

Federal Bureau of Investigation
Washington 25, D.C.

Gentlemen:

During my senior year at Georgetown University I read J.J.O'Niel's Biography of Nikoli Tesla; the book, entitled "Prodigal Genius" described quite a few of Tesla's experiments, most of which I tried myself in the physics lab. I am interested in reviewing Tesla's experiments in wireless electric power transmission.

Unfortunately, Tesla died in 1945 just at the time he supposedly had developed a system of wireless power transmission. Since World War ll was then in progress his papers were seized and sealed by the F.B.I. I suppose that by now Tesla's papers have been released for publication, but a call to the Library of Congress produced no results. Therefore, I have two questions:

1) Does the F.B.I. now have Tesla's scientific papers?

2) If so, are they available for public inspection?
   If they were released, who has them?

I will certainly appreciate any help you can give me along these lines. Tesla published very little of his findings; this, coupled with the fact that wireless power is connected by most people with "Death Rays" and crack-pots has made it nearly impossible for me to find anything on the subject.

Yours very truly,

Arlington 3, Virginia

RECORDED - 86
INDEXED - 86
EX-122

ALL INFORMATION CONTAINED
HEREIN IS UNCLASSIFIED
DATE 2-3-80 BY [signature]

June 29, 1956

Arlington 3, Virginia

Dear

Nikola Tesla

Your letter dated June 23, 1956, has been received, and in response to your inquiry, I would like to advise that our files reflect that the effects of Nikola Tesla were taken into custody after his death by the Office of Alien Property and not by this Bureau.

Since we did not participate in the handling of Mr. Tesla's effects, we are unable to supply the information you requested.

Sincerely yours,

John Edgar Hoover
Director

COMM — FBI
JUN 29 1956
MAILED 24

NOTE: Bufiles reflect no record on correspondent and reveal the correct spelling of Tesla's name as "Nikola." Bufiles reflect this type of reply has been utilized by the Domestic Intelligence Division in answering similar inquiries. (65-47953; 100-2237) Cover memo from Mr. Belmont to Boardman 6-29-55, set out background of this matter which concerned the death of Tesla, a famous electrical inventor. Bureau was not involved in this matter, and the opening of the safe containing his effects was done by the Office of Alien Property.

Tolson
Boardman
Nichols
Belmont
Harbo
Mohr
Parsons
Rosen
Tamm
Sizoo
Winterrowd
Tele. Room
Holloman
Gandy

ELJ:jh:mmh
(3)

OFFICE MEMORANDUM—FLYING SAUCER

7/25/1957

Office Memorandum · UNITED STATES GOVERNMENT

TO : DIRECTOR, FBI
DATE: 7/25/57

FROM : SAC, NEW YORK (65-12290)

SUBJECT: NIKOLA TESLA (Deceased)
IS -YU

ALL INFORMATION CONTAINED HEREIN IS UNCLASSIFIED DATE 2-3-80 BY [signature]

[redacted] Street, New York 24, New York, a United States citizen of Yugoslav extraction, who on occasion, voluntarily furnishes the New York Office with information he considers to be in the interest of the Security of the United States Government, furnished Special Agent NICHOLAS J. MASTROVICH the following information on July 3, 1957:

[redacted] stated that a certain woman named Mrs. MARGARET STORM who lives with her husband, JOHN, at the Colonial Hotel, 51 West 81st Street, New York 24, New York, has been issuing newsletters which contain information pertaining to flying saucers and interplanetary matters.

[redacted] stated that in his opinion Mr. and Mrs. STORM are exploiting the reputation and genius of NIKOLA TESLA, deceased, inventor of Yugoslav extraction who achieved world wide fame as a result of his inventions in the United States.

TESLA was born in Smiljan, Yugoslavia in July, 1859 and came to the United States in 1894 and became a naturalized United States citizen. In 1886 TESLA designed the arc-lighting system and two years later he invented the Tesla motor and designed a plan for the transmission of alternating current. In subsequent years, TESLA's discoveries and inventions included such fields and appliances as wireless communication, electrical oscillation, radiant power and radio active matter. After 1900, communications and wireless power transmission occupied most of his research.

2 - Bureau (RM) (Encs.2)
1 - Los Angeles (Info) (Encl.1) (RM)
1 - New York (65-12290)

NJM:mcd
(4)

NY 65-12290

TESLA's only military invention was a method to which he once eluded but never fully described. This invention was a means whereby an inpenetrable "wall of force" can be erected around the United States' borders which would render helpless any military attack. TESLA disclosed the existence of his plan in 1934 and stated he intended to present it to the Geneva Conference but seldom referred to it afterward.

The "New York Times" dated 9/22/40, carried an article setting forth NICOLA TESLA's plan for a "Death Ray". This article included information to the effect that TESLA, on his 84th birthday, July 10, 1940, advised New York Times reporter WILLIAM A. LAWRENCE that he was ready to divulge to the United States Government the secret of his "teleforce", with which he said airplane motors would be melted at a distance of 250 miles so that an invisible Chinese wall of defense would be built around the country against any attempted attack by an enemy airforce no matter how large. According to TESLA, this "teleforce" was based on an entirely new principle of Physics that "no one has ever dreamed about" and was different from the principle embodied in his inventions relating to the transmission of electrical power from a distance, for which he received a number of basic patents.

TESLA stated that this new type of force would operate through a beam one hundredth millionth of a square centimeter in diameter and could be generated from a special plant that would cost no more than two million dollars and would take only about three months to construct. TESLA stated that a dzen such plants located at strategic points along the coast, according to TESLA, would be enough to defend the United States against all possible aerial attacks. TESLA stated that this beam would melt any engine and would also ignite explosives aboard any bomber. TESLA stated that no possible defense against it could be devised and he asserted that the beam would be all penetrating.

-2-

NY 65-12290

TESLA stated to Mr. LAWRENCE that he makes one important stipulation before he would divulge this secret to the United States Government and that was that should the United States Government decide to take up his offer, he would go to work at once but that the United States Government would have to trust him. TESLA stated that he would suffer "no interference from experts."

In this "New York Times" article Mr. LAWRENCE commented that with conditions as they were in 1940, and with the United States getting ready to spend millions of dollars for National Defense, Mr. TESLA's great reputation as an inventor, who always was many years ahead of his time, should be given careful consideration. Mr. LAWRENCE stated, in his opinion, the United States Government should take Mr. TESLA at his word and commission him to go ahead with the construction of his "teleforce" plant.

The New York file of Mr. TESLA bears no indication that any additional developments were carried on in connection with TESLA's invention and whether or not TESLA fully divulged his new plan to the United States Government.

TESLA died at the age of 85 on January 7, 1943.

Mr. ▮▮▮▮ provided a two page copy of the above mentioned newsletter which Mr. and Mrs. STORM have been distributing in connection with the alleged invention by TESLA, which, according to Mr. and Mrs. STORM, consists of a radio type machine known as the Tesla Set which was invented by Mr. TESLA in 1938 for interplanetary communication. Mr. and Mrs. STORM claim that TESLA's engineers did not complete the Tesla Set until after TESLA's death in 1943. Mr. and Mrs. STORM claim that this Set was placed in operation in 1950 and since that time TESLA engineers have been in close touch with space ships. etc.

b7D
b7C

- 3 -

NY 65-12290

    The Newsletter furnished by Mr. ▒▒▒ included   b7D
the following names: b7C

    MARGARET STORM
    JOHN STORM
    GEORGE VAN TASSEL, Yucca Valley, California
    DAN FRY
    GEORGE KING, London, England

    The files of the New York Office contained no pertinent information regarding any of the above mentioned individuals.

    Two photostatic copies of this newsletter are being sent to the Bureau for purposes of information while one copy is being submitted to the Los Angeles Office for information purposes.

- 4 -

Philadelphia, 34, Pa.

Mr. J. Edgar Hoover

Dear Sir:

I am hopeful that you can help me obtain certain information on records and data, which belonged to Dr. Nikola Tesla. He was an Electrical Engineer and prolific inventor.

He was born in Yugoslavia in 1856 and died in the United States, New York City, January 7th, 1943. He was a naturalized citizen of this country.

The only information I could find of his records was a report that the F.B.I. removed his papers for examination, and that the records were sealed by the custodian of alien property.

I have been doing some theoretical research of my own, which I believe may be along the same lines he followed in certain of his experiments. I also believe the development of his ideas would be in the interest of our country regardless of who developes them.

If it is at all possible for me to have access to at least some of his experimental work, I would certainly appreciate it. I am not able, by reason of the vast finances, which would be required, to conduct such experiments myself, so the data he made and collected would be invaluable.

Of course, it is possible that his records do not contain material pertinent to his electronics work, because from what I understand from reading about him, he kept most of his records in his head and wrote down very little of his data.

It is also possible that some of his ideas are impractical, but I feel sure that certain of his ideas will be of immense value to our country within the next several decades or even before, if they are developed at a rapid rate.

I would appreciate hearing from you on the subject, if you have any information pertaining to it, which you could make available to me.

Sincerely,

March 14, 1958

REC-13 100-2237-

▓▓▓▓▓▓▓▓▓▓▓▓▓▓▓▓▓▓
Philadelphia 34, Pennsylvania

ALL INFORMATION CONTAINED
HEREIN IS UNCLASSIFIED
DATE 2-3-80 BY ▓▓▓▓

Dear ▓▓▓▓▓▓▓:

Your letter postmarked March 7, 1958, has been received.

In response to your inquiry, I would like to advise that our files reflect that the effects of Dr. Nikola Tesla were taken into custody after his death by the Office of Alien Property in the Department of Justice and not by the FBI.

Since we did not participate in the handling of Dr. Tesla's effects, we are unable to supply the information you requested.

Sincerely yours,

John Edgar Hoover
Director

NOTE: Bufiles reflect no record on correspondent. Bufiles reflect above type of reply has been utilized in the past in answering similar inquiries. (100-2237-7) Cover Memorandum from Belmont to Boardman 6/29/55 set forth background of this matter which concerned the death of Tesla, a famous electrical inventor. Bureau was not involved in this matter, and the opening of the safe containing his effects was done by the Office of Alien Property.

DCL:abs

June 24, 1959

Federal Bureau of Investigation
Washington 25, D.C.

Dear Sirs,

I am doing a research study on the life of Dr. Nikola Tesla of New York City (1856-1943), and desire information which you may have. It was reported in the book "Prodigal Genius" that Dr. Tesla's papers were seized from his New York hotel room upon his death in 1943 by the F.B.I.. I am very interested in getting copies of his papers for my study and would like to know if this report is true and where I might obtain further information about them or if you are holding them.

Sincerely yours,

[redacted]

Milwaukee 15, Wis.

July 2, 1959

REG-91
EX 101

100-2237-10

[redacted]
Milwaukee 13, Wisconsin

Dear [redacted]

ALL INFORMATION CONTAINED
HEREIN IS UNCLASSIFIED
DATE 2-3-80 BY [signature]

Your letter dated June 24, 1959, has been received.

In response to your inquiry, I wish to advise that our files reflect that the effects of Dr. Nikola Tesla were impounded, after his death, by the Office of Alien Property of the Department of Justice and not by the FBI. Since we did not participate in the handling of Dr. Tesla's effects, we are unable to supply the information you desire.

Sincerely yours,

MAILED 5
JUL 2 1959
COMM-FBI

John Edgar Hoover
Director

NOTE: Bufile 100-2237 reflects that Dr. Tesla was a world-famous electrical inventor, and at the time of his death, all of his personal papers and effects were believed dangerous to the country's security if they fall into unauthorized hands. The book, "Prodigal Genius," by John J. O'Neil, alleges that the FBI took over a certain safe and opened it, appropriating his property. Bufiles clearly indicate that it was the Office of Alien Property of the Department who did so, and the above reply is forwarded in answer to related inquiries.

Tolson
Belmont
DeLoach
McGuire
Mohr
Parsons
Rosen
Tamm
Trotter
W.C. Sullivan
Tele. Room
Holloman
Gandy

DCL:mch
(3)

57 JUL 9 1959
MAIL ROOM ☐ TELETYPE UNIT ☐

OPTIONAL FORM NO. 10

UNITED STATES GOVERNMENT

Memorandum

TO : MR. TROTTER DATE: 12-6-60

FROM : A. K. Bowles

SUBJECT: **NIKOLA TESLA (DECEASED)
INFORMATION CONCERNING**

ALL INFORMATION CONTAINED
HEREIN IS UNCLASSIFIED
DATE 2-3-80 BY

[redacted] Boston, Massachusetts, telephoned December 6 and was referred to Ident by switchboard because he wanted to talk with someone in charge of records of deceased. [redacted] said he is making a research study for U. S. Air Force on subject of geophysics. His deadline is ten days from now. [redacted] said he just discovered a sentence in a book by John J. O'Neill entitled "The Prodigal Genius -- The Life of Nikola Tesla," which states the FBI took custody of papers from Tesla's safe after his death in New York City in 1943. Tesla was a world-famous Yugoslav scientist and inventor in the electrical field who died January 7, 1943, in New York City. [redacted] requested immediate access to Tesla's scientific works which may shed light on [redacted] research study. I told [redacted] we would have somebody from our Boston Office contact him immediately.

b7C

Bureau file 100-2237 shows no investigation of Tesla has been conducted by Bureau. Since erroneous statement concerning FBI's taking custody of papers from Tesla's safe after his death appeared in O'Neill's book published in 1944, Bureau has received numerous inquiries from scientists desiring to review Tesla's writings. Each inquiry has been answered by stating FBI did not participate in handling Tesla's effects, but information has come to our attention that Office of Alien Property of Department of Justice may have examined Tesla's effects. (File indicates that representatives of Office of Alien Property did actually review Tesla's possessions, including his writings, but file does not show what final disposition was made of Tesla's possessions.)

A teletype to Boston Division was prepared, but before it was sent [redacted] telephoned again to furnish me the exact page in O'Neill's book in which he refers to the FBI. At that time I told [redacted] the statement in the book was untrue -- that the FBI had not examined or taken custody of Tesla's papers. I suggested to [redacted] that he might contact Office of Alien Property. (Therefore, teletype to Boston was not necessary.)

ACTION:
For record.

Bu file 100-2237
1- Mr. Belmont

Ft. Wayne, Indiana
February 14, 1961

Federal Bureau of Investigation
Department of Information
Washington 25, D. C.

Dear Sir:

I am a college student who is doing a research paper on Nikola Tesla. As I was collecting the material for my paper, I discovered that at the time of Tesla's death, the department of the F.B.I. confiscated the data and papers that Tesla had collected from his research in the field of electricity. This confiscation of his material was stated in the PRODIGAL GENIUS by J.J. O'Neil, published in 1944 at New York city by Washburn Inc.

I have developed an interest in the discoveries and accomplishments of Tesla that is presently limited by the shortage of factual material. If in your files, you have any information concerning Nikola Tesla that you are permitted to release, I will sincerely appreciate your co-operation in helping me give the proper recognition to this great scientist and American. Below I have listed the facts that may be helpful to you;

1. Born in 1856 at Smiljan, Crotia, now Yugoslavia
2. Came to America in 1884 and was employed for a short time with the Edison Co. at Orange, N.J.
3. Died on January 7, 1943 at New York city

Thanking you for your time and co-operation that I have taken, I remain,

Sincerely Yours,

100-2237-12

February 23, 1961

[redacted]
Fort Wayne, Indiana

Dear [redacted]:

Your letter of February 14, 1961, has been received, and the interest which prompted you to write is appreciated.

In response to your inquiry, I wish to advise that our files reflect that the effects of Dr. Nikola Tesla were impounded, after his death, by the Office of Alien Property of the Department of Justice and not by the FBI. Since we did not participate in the handling of Dr. Tesla's effects, we are unable to supply the information you desire.

Sincerely yours,

John Edgar Hoover
Director

NOTE: No record could be located in Bufiles identifiable with correspondent. Bufile 100-2237 reflects that Dr. Tesla was a world-famous electrical inventor, and at the time of his death, all of his personal papers and effects were believed dangerous to the country's security if they fell into unauthorized hands. The book, "Prodigal Genius," by John J. O'Neil, alleges that the FBI took over a certain safe and opened it, appropriating his property. Bufiles clearly indicate that it was the Office of Alien Property of the Department who did so, and the above reply is forwarded in answer to related inquiries.

RWE:jab
(3)

November 21, 1962

Federal Bureau of Investigation
Washington 25, D.C.

Gentlemen:

I am making a study, motivated out of personal curiosity, into the life and works of Nikola Tesla. Mr. Tesla died on January 7, 1943 in the Hotel New Yorker. Since F.B.I. Operatives opened his safe and took his papers for examination, I wonder if these papers are available for perusal? If they are available, where would they be located, and are copies available to the public?

I am a citizen of the United States, and have been cleared for security--- the latest one being for work on Air Force Contracts for Eastman Kodak Company.

Thank you very much for any information or help you may be able to give me in this matter!!

Respectfully yours,

New York 23, N.Y.

ALL INFORMATION CONTAINED
HEREIN IS UNCLASSIFIED
DATE 7-3-80 BY

November 27, 1962

New York 33, New York

Dear

Your letter of November 21st has been received.

In response to your inquiry, I would like to point out that the effects of Dr. Nikola Tesla were impounded, after his death, by the Office of Alien Property of the Department of Justice and not by the FBI. Since this Bureau did not participate in the handling of Dr. Tesla's effects, I am unable to supply the information you desire.

Sincerely yours,

J. Edgar Hoover

John Edgar Hoover
Director

NOTE: Bufiles contain no record identifiable with correspondent. Bufile 100-2237 shows that Dr. Tesla was one of the world's outstanding scientists in the electrical field, and at the time of his death, all of his personal papers and effects were believed dangerous to the country's security if they fell into unauthorized hands. The book, "Prodigal Genius," by John J. O'Neil, alleges that the FBI took over a certain safe and opened it, appropriating Dr. Tesla's property. Bufiles clearly indicate that it was the Office of Alien Property of the Department which did so, and the above reply has been forwarded in answer to related inquiries. Dr. Tesla was born in Yugoslavia and died in New York City 1-7-43.

EFT:blc (3)

b7C

S_ AFB, Ill.
10 March 1964

Federal Bureau of Investigation,
Washington 25, D.C.

Dear Sir,

For some time, have been wondering about the matter of what was reported on the late Nikola Tesla, the inventor. He died during early January 1943, while in residence at the Hotel New Yorker, New York City. Understand it that his belongings (papers, etc.) were studied. Would appreciate knowing if anything can be learned about this.

Am hoping to be on leave, and in Washington, along the third week of April. This is mentioned, in case it is possible to review anything relating to the question.

Sincerely,

b7C

TRUE COPY

b7C

Scott AFB, Ill.
10 March 1964.

Federal Bureau of Investigation
Washington 25, D. C.

Dear Sirs,

For some time, have been wondering about the matter of what was reported on the late Nikola Tesla, the inventor. He died during early January 1943, while in residence at the Hotel New Yorker, New York City. Accounts have it that his belongings (papers, etc.) were studied. Would appreciate learning if anything can be learned about this.

Am hoping to be on leave, and in Washington, along the third week of April. This is mentioned, in case it is possible to view anything relating to the question.

Sincerely,

b7C

100-2237-14

March 18, 1964

b7C Scott Air Force Base, Illinois -

Dear

Your letter of March 10th has been received.

In response to your inquiry, I would like to point out that the effects of Dr. Nikola Tesla were impounded, after his death, by the Office of Alien Property of the Department of Justice and not the FBI. Since we did not participate in the handling of Dr. Tesla's effects, I am unable to supply the information you desire.

Sincerely yours,

J. Edgar Hoover

John Edgar Hoover
Director

NOTE: No record could be located in Bufiles identifiable with correspondent. Bufile 100-2237 reflects that Dr. Tesla was a world-famous electrical inventor, and at the time of his death, all of his personal papers and effects were believed dangerous to the country's security if they fell into unauthorized hands. The book, "Prodigal Genius," by John J. O'Neil, alleges that the FBI took over a certain safe and opened it, appropriating his property. Bufiles clearly indicate that it was the Office of Alien Property of the Department which did so, and the above reply is forwarded in answer to related inquiries.

SAW:mc
(3)

TRUE COPY

Sir,

According to "Prodical Genius, Nikola Festa" [Tesla] by J. J. O'Neil (a book) some papers were taken from the safe of Mr. Festa about 1945 yr. Is this true. If so are the papers declasified yet? If so may I obtain a copy?

Zip 62095
Wood River, Ill.

67C

REC- 15

June 22, 1964

ALL INFORMATION CONTAINED
HEREIN IS UNCLASSIFIED
DATE 7-3-80 BY [signature]

Wood River, Illinois 62095

Dear

Your card of June 16th has been received.

In response to your inquiry, I would like to point out that the effects of Dr. Nikola Tesla were impounded, after his death, by the Office of Alien Property of the Department of Justice and not by the FBI. Since we did not participate in the handling of Dr. Tesla's effects, I am unable to furnish the information you desire.

Sincerely yours,

J. Edgar Hoover

NOTE: No record could be located in Bufiles identifiable with correspondent. Bufile 100-2237 reflects that Dr. Tesla was a world-famous electrical inventor and at the time of his death, all of his personal papers and effects were believed dangerous to the country's security if they fell into unauthorized hands. The book, "Prodigal Genius," by John J. O'Neil, alleges that the FBI took over a certain safe and opened it, appropriating his property. Bufiles clearly indicate that it was the Office of Alien Property of the Department which did so and the above reply is forwarded in answer to related inquiries.

SAW:ufy (3)

OREGON STATE UNIVERSITY
SCHOOL OF SCIENCE

CORVALLIS, OREGON 97331

Reply to: DEPARTMENT OF GENERAL SCIENCE

March 28, 1967

FEDERAL BUREAU OF INVESTIGATION
Department of Information
9th Street & Pennsylvania Aven, N.W.
Washington 25, D. C.   20535

ALL INFORMATION CONTAINED
HEREIN IS UNCLASSIFIED
DATE 2-3-80 BY SP4 Jrm/rtc

Dear Sirs:

I am a student of the history of science at Oregon State University, and I am attempting to write a research paper on a very eccentric scientist who died in 1943. His name was Nikola Tesla, a naturalized American of Serbian extraction, and he died in his hotel room in New York City on January 8, 1943.

During the years leading up to World War II, Nikola Tesla supposedly invented a "Death Ray" which could destroy several hundred aircraft. Mr. Tesla was a very prolific and creative genius during his early years but gradually became something of a crackpot in his old age. As a student of the history of science, it is important to determine whether or not Tesla had any valid ideas in the plans for his death ray. Tesla invented the fluorescent light and also was one of the first scientists to discover X-Rays--hence there may be some possibility that his death ray might actually have been some crude type of laser.

In Tesla's biography, "Prodigal Genius", by John J. O'Neill, the author states on page 277:

> "Operatives from the F.B.I. came to Tesla's hotel room shortly after his death and opened the safe in his room. They took the papers that it contained in order to examine them for a reported secret invention of possible use in the war..."

I am trying to locate Tesla's secret and unpublished writings concerning his death ray. I have searched the literature quite thoroughly and have found nothing. Does the F.B.I. still have these papers or can you tell where I might be able to obtain these writings for examination? Any assistance or information that you may lend me will be very much appreciated.

Sincerely yours,

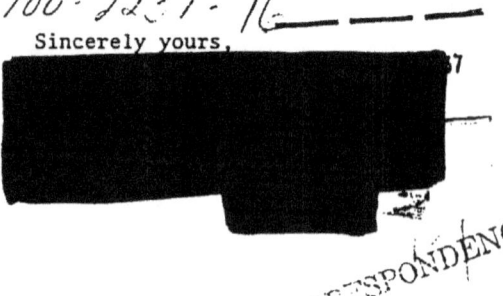

LRA:dg

April 3, 1967

REC 49 100-2237- 16

b7C [redacted]
Department of General Science
Oregon State University
Corvallis, Oregon 97331

ALL INFORMATION CONTAINED
HEREIN IS UNCLASSIFIED
DATE 2-3-80 BY [signature]

b7C Dear [redacted]

Your letter of March 28th has been received.

In response to your inquiry, the effects of Dr. Nikola Tesla were impounded, after his death, by the Office of Alien Property of the Department of Justice and not by the FBI. Since we did not participate in the handling of Dr. Tesla's effects, I am unable to furnish the information you desire.

Sincerely yours,

J. Edgar Hoover

John Edgar Hoover
Director

NOTE: No record could be located in Bufiles identifiable with correspondent. Bufile 100-2237 reflects that Dr. Tesla was a world-famous electrical inventor, and at the time of his death, all of his personal papers and effects were believed dangerous to the country's security if they fell into unauthorized hands. The book, "Prodigal Genius," by John J. O'Neil, alleges that the FBI took over a certain safe and opened it, appropriating his property. Bufiles clearly indicate that it was the Office of Alien Property of the Department which did so, and the above reply is forwarded in answer to related inquiries.

ED:emm (3)

Feb. 25, 1964

Dear Mr. Hoover,

In the year 1943 the F.B.I. confiscated all of the papers and maybe some of the machines of physicist, Nikola Tesla. These papers were his experiments and ideas at the time of his death. According to the books I've read, these papers were confiscated on the grounds of the enemy getting ahold of his ideas and apply them to war machines.

I have studied all of the material on this man and have found him to be more intelligent than the great "Brain" of his time, Thomas Edison. Why without Nikola Tesla there would be a Westinghouse Company as we know today. This is the man who harnessed Niagara Falls, and was the one and only man who could see the possibilities of Alternating Current when men like Edison said "it would never work."

What I am wondering is, maybe these papers could be reclassified from whatever "Top Secret" classification they now have and be made available for study by the people who understand and can gain knowledge from them.

I would be willing to pay for reproductions of his experiments if nothing else. He still has a great many ideas that have never been tried.

It disturbs me to think that everyone has forgotten about the ideas of this man when he was so advanced for his time.

I can say with assurance that no man alive can say that he knows all of Tesla's ideas. And studying other men's ideas is the way to advance in science faster.

I hope something can be done to get these papers released.

Thank you,

b7C

Fairmount, Indiana
46928

J. Edgar Hoover
Federal Bureau of Investigation
Washington D. C.

TRUE COPY

Feb. 25, 1969

Dear Mr. Hoover,

In the year 1943 the F.B.I. confiscated all of the papers and maybe some of the machines of physicist, Nikola Tesla. These papers were his experiments and ideas at the time of his death. According to the books I've read, these papers were confiscated on the grounds of the enemy getting ahold of his ideas and apply them to war machines.

I have studied all of the material on this man and have found him to be more intelligent than the great "Brain" of his time, Thomas Edison.

Why without Nikola Tesla there would be Westinghouse Company as we know today. This is the man who harnessed Niagara Falls, and was the one and only man who could see the possibilities of Alternating Current when men like Edison said "it would never work."

What I am wondering is, maybe these papers could be reclassified from whatever "Top Secret" classification they now have and be made available for study by the people who understand and can gain knowledge from them.

I would be willing to pay for reproductions of his experiments if nothing else. He still has a great many ideas that have never been tried.

It disturbs me to think that everyone has forgotten about the ideas of this man when he was so advanced for his time.

I can say with assurance that no man alive can say that he knows all of Tesla's ideas. And studying other men's ideas is the way to advance in science faster.

I hope something can be done to get these papers released.

Thank You,

/s/

Fairmount, Indiana 46928

March 4, 1969

100-2237-17

ALL INFORMATION CONTAINED
HEREIN IS UNCLASSIFIED
DATE 2-3-80 BY SP4 Jrm/ptc

b7C

Fairmount, Indiana 46928

Dear

Your letter of February 25th has been received.

In response to your inquiry, the effects of Dr. Nikola Tesla were impounded, after his death, by the Office of Alien Property of the Department of Justice and not by the FBI. Since we did not participate in the handling of Dr. Tesla's belongings, I am unable to furnish the information you desire. A copy of your communication has been referred to the Department of Justice.

Sincerely yours,

J. Edgar Hoover

MAILED 10
MAR 4 - 1969
COMM-FBI

NOTE: Bufiles contain no record of correspondent. Bufile 100-2237 reflects that Dr. Tesla was a world-famous electrical inventor, and at the time of his death, all of his personal papers and effects were believed dangerous to the country's security if they fell into unauthorized hands. The book, "Prodigal Genius," by John J. O'Neil, alleges that the FBI took over a certain safe and opened it, appropriating his property. Bufiles clearly indicate that it was the Office of Alien Property of the Department which did so, and the above reply is forwarded in answer to related inquiries. Copy of letter referred to Assistant Attorney General, Civil Division of the Department.
LEE:jls (3)

Tolson
DeLoach
Mohr
Bishop
Casper
Callahan
Conrad
Felt
Gale
Rosen
Sullivan
Tavel
Trotter
Tele. Room
Holmes
Gandy

54 MAR T 3 1969
MAIL ROOM ☐ TELETYPE UNIT ☐

LETTER TO FBI—TESLA'S PERSONAL EFFECTS

4/8/1970

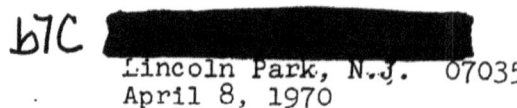

Lincoln Park, N.J. 07035
April 8, 1970

Federal Bureau of Investigation
Director of Central Records
Washington, D.C.

Dear Sir:

I am doing a research paper on Nickola [Nikola] Tesla and would appreciate it if you could please provide me with the following information.

That information being why did your Bureau impound his personal effects immediately after his death on January 7, 1943. Secondly, could you provide a list of those effects, and lastly, when were they released and to whom were they given.

Thanking you for the information

ALL INFORMATION CONTAINED
HEREIN IS UNCLASSIFIED
DATE 7-3-80 BY SP4 Jrn/stc

REC 44 100-2237-18

APR 15 1970

April 14, 1970

ALL INFORMATION CONTAINED
HEREIN IS UNCLASSIFIED
DATE 7-3-80 BY [signature]

Lincoln Park, New Jersey 07035

Dear

In reply to your inquiry of April 8th, the effects of Dr. Nikola Tesla were impounded, after his death, by the Office of Alien Property of the Department of Justice and not by the FBI. Since we did not participate in the handling of Dr. Tesla's belongings, I am unable to furnish the information you desire. A copy of your communication has been referred to the Department of Justice for any help it may be able to offer.

Sincerely yours,

J. Edgar Hoover

John Edgar Hoover
Director

NOTE: Bufiles contain no information identifiable with correspondent. Bufile 100-2237 reflects that Dr. Tesla was a world-famous electrical inventor, and at the time of his death, all of his personal papers and effects were believed dangerous to the country's security if they fell into unauthorized hands. The book, "Prodigal Genius," by John J. O'Neil, alleges that the FBI took over a certain safe and opened it, appropriating his property. Bufiles clearly indicate that it was the Office of Alien Property of the Department which did so, and the above reply is forwarded in answer to related inquiries. Copy of letter referred to Assistant Attorney General, Civil Division of the Department.

MHB:cfj (3)

MarVista 66, Calif.
July 8, 1970.

Mr. J. Edgar Hoover,
Director,
Federal Bureau of Investigation,
Washington D. C.

Dear Sir,

I am writing this to you as I believe that most of the government is infiltrated with foreign agents, and there is a very good chance this could be of extreme importance for the defense of our nation.

I met a man a number of years ago that was raised on Long Island in the neighborhood where Mr. Tesla, inventor of the Tesla Coil, had his lab. He told me of Mr. Tesla's notes blowing down the street when the junk men were dismantling his equipment. It would be a wonderful thing is some of these notes were salvaged and could be found.

Mr. Tesla was at least a century ahead of his time. He sent radio signals around the world seventeen years prior to Mr. Marconi, who received the credit, and pioneered many fields. He was so far advanced that he had to invent a special math to keep up with his work.

He, on several accasions talked before the scientists of the world and became very angry at their inability to understand him, and due to this was violently disliked and didnot receive acknowledgement for his discoveries. One of the notes read by this man told of the radio transmission of electricity being brought to a high degree of effiency.

Now here is the thing that should be investigated throughly. During my High School education, in the winter of either 19-25-26 or 1926-27, I made a currant events report on an article appearing in a small publication of that name that was received weekly at the Troy Highschool, Troy Montana. It stated in this article that Mr. Tesla had made an offer to the Congress of the United States that if they would install radio transmission towers at every 150 miles around the border of this country, that he would install equipment that would broadcast a vertical plane of energy beyond the atmosphere through which no material object could pass as it would shatter or lose it's monecular coohesion. It was refused.

There is a good chance that this data is in the files of congress. What a defence, and boy do we need it.

I have had some results along this line with structured vortices of magnetic fields, but do not have the technical equipment or knowledge to carry out further experiments. The theory is quite simple and deals with particle acceleration, and it works to the best of my knowledge.

Sincerely

July 15, 1970

REC-3 100-2237-19

ALL INFORMATION CONTAINED
HEREIN IS UNCLASSIFIED
DATE 7-3-80 BY ███

█████
Mar Vista, California 90066

Dear ███

Your letter was received on July 13th and the interest which prompted you to write to me is appreciated. With respect to your inquiry, the effects of Dr. Nikola Tesla were impounded, after his death, by the Office of Alien Property of the Department of Justice and the FBI did not participate in the handling of Dr. Tesla's belongings. In addition, this Bureau is strictly an investigative agency of the Federal Government and matters such as you mentioned do not come within the scope of this Bureau's authority.

Sincerely yours,

J. Edgar Hoover

John Edgar Hoover
Director

MAILED 9
JUL 15 1970
COMM-FBI

NOTE: Bufiles contain no record of correspondent. Bufile 100-2237 reflects that Dr. Tesla was a world-famous electrical inventor, and, at the time of his death, all of his personal papers and effects were believed dangerous to the country's security if they fell into unauthorized hands. Bufiles indicate that the Office of Alien Property of the Department appropriated his property and replies similar to the above have been used to answer related inquiries.

LEE:cnb (3)

LETTER TO FBI—HAVE THEM IN JAIL

12/6/1971

NABNASSET, MASS
01861

6 DECEMBER 1971

FEDERAL BUREAU OF INVESTIGATION
WASHINGTON, D.C.

Dear Sir:

I have recently begun a collection and reading file of all matters pertaining to Nikola Tesla. In so doing I was amazed to find that upon his death; January 7, 1943, in NYC, your bureau confined his papers. May I ask if you still "have them in jail". I am extremely interested in his work(s) and am trying to establish my own "Tesla" library. Your assistance would be greatly appreciated.

Very truly yours,

NABNASSET, MASS 01861

December 14, 1971

REC-28 100-2237-20

▮▮▮▮▮
▮▮▮▮▮
Nabnasset, Massachusetts 01861

Dear ▮▮▮▮▮

ALL INFORMATION CONTAINED
HEREIN IS UNCLASSIFIED
DATE 7-3-80 BY ▮▮▮▮▮

Your letter of December 6th has been received.

In response to your inquiry, the effects of Dr. Nikola Tesla were impounded, after his death, by the Office of Alien Property of the Department of Justice and not by the FBI. We did not participate in the handling of Dr. Tesla's belongings in any way. Copies of your communication and my reply have been referred to the Department of Justice.

Sincerely yours,

J. Edgar Hoover

John Edgar Hoover
Director

NOTE: Bufiles contain no record correspondent. Dr. Tesla was world-famous electrical inventor, and at death, his effects believed dangerous to country's security. "Prodigal Genius," by John J. O'Neil, alleges FBI took safe and appropriated his property. Above reply previously given to same inquiries. (100-2237) Material sent to the Assistant Attorney, Civil Division, of the Department.

MLN:jam (4)

Tolson
Felt
Rosen
Mohr
Bishop
Miller, E.S.
Callahan
Casper
Conrad
Dalbey
Cleveland
Ponder
Bates
Tavel
Walters
Soyars
Tele. Room
Holmes
Gandy

MAILED 2
FBI
58 DEC 21 1971
MAIL ROOM ☐ TELETYPE UNIT ☐

Federal Bureau Of Investigation
Ninth Street and Pennsylvania
Northeast Washington D. C. 20535

Dear Sirs,

Upon reading a biography on Nikola Tesla, I found the urge to read more on him and his works. At the end of the book it was stated that the F.B.I. went to his hotel room gathered up his papers and locked them in a vault. The thing I would like to know is the real reason they were locked up and if it would be possible to see some of these records and any other works of his.

I can think of only one possible reason as to cause of his records being locked up and that is because he was too far advanced for his time. This seems to be the only logical solution, but, with technology much more advanced now than in his time it would seem likely that scientists take over where he left off.

Please let me know If I can look at the records and if you can please answer my question of the real reason his records were locked up.

Thank You,

b7C

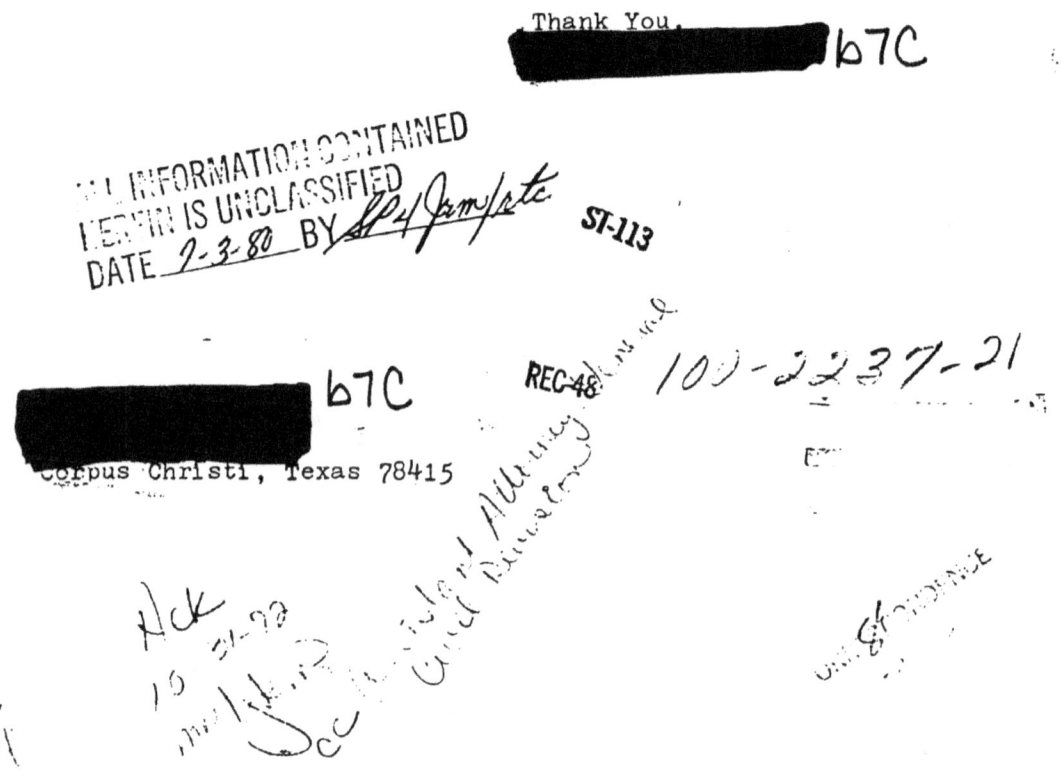

Corpus Christi, Texas 78415

October 31, 1972

Corpus Christi, Texas 78415

Dear

Your letter was received on October 26th.

In response to your inquiry, the effects of Dr. Nikola Tesla were impounded, after his death, by the Office of Alien Property of the Department of Justice and not by the FBI. Since we did not participate in the handling of Dr. Tesla's belongings, I am unable to furnish the information you desire. I am forwarding a copy of your communication and of this reply to the Department of Justice.

Sincerely yours,

L. Patrick Gray III

L. Patrick Gray, III
Acting Director

NOTE: Correspondent is not identifiable in Bufiles. Bufile 100-2237 reflects that Dr. Tesla was a world-famous electrical inventor, and at the time of his death, all of his personal papers and effects were believed dangerous to the country's security if they fell into unauthorized hands. The book, "Prodigal Genius," by John J. O'Neil, alleges that the FBI took over a certain safe and opened it, appropriating his property. Bufiles clearly indicate that it was the Office of Alien Property of the Department which did so, and the above reply is forwarded in answer to related inquiries. Copy of letter referred to Assistant Attorney General, Civil Division of the Department.

[REDACTED]
Liberty, North Carolina
April 3, 1973

Federal Bureau of Investigation
Washington
District of Columbia

Dear sirs:

Doing my research on Nikola Tesla, I found that the F.B.I. had confiscated his documents pertaining to his experiments. I would like to know if such information is available and, if so, how copies might be obtained.

I am an engineering student and hope possibly to resume where Tesla left off.

I have the honor to remain,

April 11, 1973

Liberty, North Carolina 27298

Dear [redacted]

Your letter was received on April 9th.

In response to your inquiry, the effects of Dr. Nikola Tesla were impounded, after his death, by the Office of Alien Property of the Department of Justice and not by the FBI. Since we did not participate in the handling of Dr. Tesla's belongings, I am unable to furnish the information you desire. A copy of your communication and of this reply have been referred to the Department of Justice.

Sincerely yours,

L. Patrick Gray, III
Acting Director

NOTE: Bufiles contain no record of correspondent. (Bufile 100-2237 reflects that Dr. Tesla was a world-famous electrical inventor, and at the time of his death, all of his personal papers and effects were believed dangerous to the country's security if they fell into unauthorized hands. The book, "Prodigal Genius," by John J. O'Neill, alleged that the FBI took over a certain safe and opened it, appropriating his property. Bufiles clearly indicate that it was the Office of Alien Property of the Department which did so, and the above reply is forwarded in answer to related inquiries. Copy of letter referred to the Assistant Attorney General, Civil Division of the Department.)

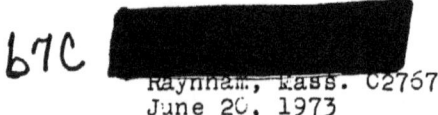

Raynham, Mass. C2767
June 20, 1973

Federal Bureau of Investigation
Department of Justice
Washington, D. C.

Gentlemen:

    I would like to know if any microfilm or other reproductions of Nikola Tesla's notes and papers exist at your office. Tesla was a famous scientist who died in New York City. The Federal Bureau of Investigation entered his safe shortly after this to remove his papers for examination for the war effort. After the war the papers were offered to any group that would start a museum to house them. No one accepted and the papers were finally sent to the Tesla Museum in Belgrade, Yugoslavia, sometime in the early 1950's, possibly just before 1954. Tesla was the inventor of all ac motors and the polyphase system, as well as all flourescent and neon lamps. He was a major pioneer in the early days of radio and discovered many of the early principles of radar. He declined nomination of a Nobel Prize. He was a naturalized citizen of America and said he valued his citizenship papers above all his awards and possessions. Despite this, all his papers were sent to another nation.

    I would like to examine some of his papers from 1899 and later without having to fly to Yugoslavia. I have only seen a condensed copy of his research from Colorado Springs, but am unable to obtain copies. The principles and equipment are rather out-of-date and well-known, but still useful in my research.

    I would greatly appreciate help in this matter.

Sincerely,

P.S. Tesla died in January of 1943 and shortly after ~~this~~ the papers were removed from his safe. The original copies of these papers were sent abroad prior to 1954, as I believe it was in that year the Yugoslavs founded the Tesla Museum (not to be confused with the Tesla Institute).

EX-109

REC-26 100-2237-23

June 27, 1973

ALL INFORMATION CONTAINED
HEREIN IS UNCLASSIFIED
DATE 2-3-80 BY [signature]

b7C

Raynham, Massachusetts 02767

Dear [redacted]

Your letter was received on June 25th.

In response to your inquiry, the effects of Dr. Nikola Tesla were impounded, after his death, by the Office of Alien Property of the Department of Justice and not by the FBI. Since we did not participate in the handling of Dr. Tesla's belongings, I am unable to furnish the information you desire. A copy of your communication and of this reply have been referred to the Department of Justice.

Sincerely yours,

William D. Ruckelshaus

William D. Ruckelshaus
Acting Director

NOTE: Bufiles indicate one letter to correspondent dated 4-15-66 in reply to his inquiry regarding the Air Force's Project Blue Book and UFO sightings. Bufile 100-2237 reflects that Dr. Tesla was a world-famous electrical inventor, and at the time of his death, all of his personal papers and effects were believed dangerous to the country's security if they fell into unauthorized hands. The book, "Prodigal Genius," by John J. O'Neill, alleged that the FBI took over a certain safe and opened it, appropriating his property. Bufiles clearly indicate that it was the Office of Alien Property of the Department that did so, and the above reply is forwarded in answer to related inquiries. Copy of letter referred to the Assistant Attorney General, Civil Division of the Department.)
mn:cmc (4)

54 JUL 6 1973
MAIL ROOM ☑ TELETYPE UNIT ☐

United States Senate

June 26, 1973

Respectfully referred to:

Congressional Liaison
Federal Bureau of Investigation
Department of Justice
Washington, D. C. 20530

Because of the desire of this office to be responsive to all inquiries and communications, your consideration of the attached is requested. Your findings and views, in duplicate form, along with return of the enclosure, will be appreciated by

Senator Bob Packwood
ATTN: U.S.S. Alan Holmer

Form #2

ENCLOSURE

Sparrevohn AFS
Alaska, 98746

20 June 1973

Dear Senator Packwood,

Though in Alaska temporarily working on a military contract, I still consider myself an Oregon resident, hence it is to you that I write.

During my days at Reed College, I became interested in a fascinating Czech physicist, Nicolai Tesla. Proffessor Tesla emmigrated to this country in the twenties, I believe, and did some of his most original work. Tesla had a peculiar bent of mind, in his younger days he was often called a mad scientist, and did not publish extensively when he came to the US. Most of the extant primary material is in untranslated Czech. Tesla was however, an extensive note taker. It is thought it strange that upon his death, none of his notes from his American period ever appeared. Upon discussing this with a friend, I was informed that all of Mr. Tesla's notes were confiscated by the FBI. I cannot conceive how these notes on physics and electricity can in any way endanger the national safety. It seems that Mr. Hoover in his zeal, had confiscated material whose only sin was a radical approach to science. There is indication that much of Professor Tesla's later work concerned a very novel approach to time theory. Needless to say, it has been radical approaches to physics that have been our greatest scientific advances in modern times, viz. Einstein, Heisenberg, et al.

I was wondering if your office might be able to determine if these papers are still extant, and if so, see to it that the public has access to them. It would be a shame to see all of Nicolai Teslas work to have been in vain.

Please excuse my typing; in all the thousands of words I typed trying to get a liberal education, I never did master the typewriter.

Sincerely yours,

1ENCLOSURE

July 5, 1973

ST-105
REC-15 100-2237-24

Honorable Bob ▮▮▮ Packwood
United States Senate
Washington, D. C. 20510

ALL INFORMATION CONTAINED
HEREIN IS UNCLASSIFIED
DATE 7-8-80 BY ▮▮▮

b7C

Dear Senator Packwood:

This is to acknowledge receipt of your communication dated June 26th enclosing a letter from your constituent, Mr. ▮▮▮▮▮▮▮ who is temporarily employed in Alaska. In response to Mr. ▮▮▮▮▮▮▮ inquiry, central files of the Federal Bureau of Investigation indicate that the effects of Dr. Nikola Tesla were impounded after his death by the Office of Alien Property of the Department of Justice and not by the FBI. Since we did not participate in the handling of Dr. Tesla's belongings, I am unable to furnish the information you desire.

I am returning your enclosure as you requested.

Sincerely yours,

William D. Ruckelshaus

William D. Ruckelshaus
Acting Director

Enclosure

1 - Portland - Enclosures (2)
1 - Congressional Services Office - Enclosures (2)
NOTE: Bufiles reveal prior cordial correspondence with Senator Packwood. Mr. ▮▮▮▮▮▮▮ is not identifiable in Bufiles Bufile 100-2237 reflects that Dr. Tesla was a world-famous electrical inventor, and at the time of his death, all of his personal papers and effects were believed dangerous to the countr[y] security if they fell into unauthorized hands. The book, "Prodig[al] Genius," by John J. O'Neill, alleged that the FBI took over a ce[rtain] safe and opened it, appropriating his property. Bufiles clearl[y] indicate that it was the Office of Alien Property of the Depar[tment] which did so, and the above reply is forwarded in answer to r[ecent] inquiries.

Mr. Felt
Mr. Baker
Mr. Callahan
Mr. Cleveland
Mr. Conrad
Mr. Gebhardt
Mr. Jenkins
Mr. Marshall
Mr. Miller, E.S.
Mr. Soyars
Mr. Thompson
Mr. Walters
Tele. Room
Mr. Baise
Mr. Barnes
Mr. Bowers
Mr. Herington
Mr. Conmy
Mr. Mintz
Mr. Eardley
Mrs. Hogan

b7C

Richardson, Texas 75080
12 July 1973

FEDERAL BUREAU OF INVESTIGATION
Washington, D.C.

ALL INFORMATION CONTAINED
HEREIN IS UNCLASSIFIED
DATE 2-3-80 BY [signature]

Dear Sirs,

It has come to my attention that upon the death of Mr. Nikola Tesla, the founder of modern A.C. power systems, and the original inventor of radio, and innumerable other devices, operatives of the F.B.I. opened his safe and removed his papers on 7 January 1943, within a few hours of his demise. Also, all records of his work have been siezed and held by our government since his death. I would like to know WHY, and also to be informed as to who was, and is responsible for keeping the lid on these records. I would also like to know where they are now.

I do hope you enjoy a good laugh over the aparent naievity of such a request as this, but it is a rather strange situation to exist in a country like this, that a man of such genius and achievement could be systematically cut out of history books, and that the facts about his works could be concealed to the degree they have been. I wish to obtain access to all those old records which have been concealed for thirty years. I would appreciate your kind consideration and attention to this matter, and any assistance you may care to give.

Sincerely,

LETTER FROM WILLIAM D. RUCKELSHAUS, ACTING DIRECTOR — 7/19/1973

July 19, 1973

REC-60 -2237-25

ALL INFORMATION CONTAINED
HEREIN IS UNCLASSIFIED
DATE 2-3-80 BY SP4 Jm/rtc

b7C

Richardson, Texas 75080   EX-105

Dear

Your letter was received on July 16th. In response to your inquiry, the effects of Dr. Nikola Tesla were impounded, after his death, by the Office of Alien Property of the Department of Justice and not by the FBI. Since we did not participate in the handling of Dr. Tesla's belongings, I am unable to furnish the information you desire. A copy of your communication and of this reply have been referred to the Department of Justice.

Sincerely yours,

C. M. Kelley

Clarence M. Kelley
Director

MAILED 4
JUL 19 1973
FBI

NOTE: Bufiles contain no record of correspondent. (Bufile 100-2237 reflects that Dr. Tesla was a world-famous electrical inventor, and at the time of his death, all of his personal papers and effects were believed dangerous to the country's security if they fell into unauthorized hands. The book, "Prodigal Genius," by John J. O'Neill alleged that the FBI took over a certain safe and opened it, appropriating his property. Bufiles clearly indicate that it was the Office of Alien Property of the Department which did so, and the above reply is forwarded in answer to related inquiries. Copy of letter referred to the Assistant Attorney General, Civil Division of the Department.)
jkb:cmc (4)

MAIL ROOM ☐   TELETYPE UNIT ☐

Richardson, Texas 75080

Clarence M. Kelley
Director
Federal Bureau of Investigation
Washington D.C. 20535

Dear Mr. Kelley,

Thank you for your letter of the 19th of July. I appreciate the information about the Office of Alien Property and its connection with the impounding of the effects of Dr. Nikola Tesla. In my letter of the 16th I did not mean to imply the FBI had impounded his effects, as I was aware of the O.A.P.s general part in the affair. The fact remains that to the best of my knowledge, it WAS agents of the FBI who did in fact break into his safe only hours after his death, and did remove the papers therein. Now, in so far as the Bureau was connected, I wish to understand that extent. I do appreciate your refering my communication to the appropriate persons in the Justice Department, but perhaps you could see that the above mentioned connection of the Bureau could be further looked into. I am curious as to who asked the Bureau to perform such an act, whether is was a person in the O.A.P. or what, and on what grounds they were carried out, and to whom they were responsible. Also, to what person were the perloined papers delivered? Names of the agents involved would be appreciated. As to what happened to any other effects of his, that is probably a question more ably answered by the O.A.P., yet if Bureau agents participated once, they may have done so on other occasions. If the persons who did open the safe were NOT FBI agents, then we are faced with the fact that persons aparently posed as Bureau operatives, an even more interesting situation. Perhaps this whets your own curiosity about

this affair, though on the surface it only has historic
interest. Are you aware that before the year 1900 he was
able to transmit thousands of watts of electric power to
any point on the globe WITHOUT WIRES. This and other feats
would make him a prime target for vested interest groups,
notably the J.P. Morgan combine with whom he had connections.
I am aware of the well earned tradition of the Bureau of NOT
serving any master but the common good, so again we have a
curious point if indeed strings were pulled. Quite frankly,
it looks as if someone went to a lot of trouble to see that
his ideas were not broadly available to ensure the stability
of their own electric technological apple cart financially,
at the expense of unguessable benefits to to humanity as a
whole. How would you like to be able to draw unlimited power
out of the air to run say a lightbulb with ONE wire? He did
it, and much more. My sincere thanks for your thought and
attentions to these matters.

Very best wishes,

b7C

REC 68 / 00 - 2237 - 26

August 2, 1973

ST-102

b7C

Richardson, Texas 75080

Dear

ALL INFORMATION CONTAINED
HEREIN IS UNCLASSIFIED
DATE 2-3-80 BY

Your letter, which was received on July 30th, has been reviewed and I would like to point out that FBI Agents were not involved in removal of papers from the safe of Dr. Nikola Tesla, nor did we at any time have custody of his property.

I realize there have been some written accounts that our Agents acquired Dr. Tesla's belongings; however, these accounts are simply not true. You can be assured we were absolutely not responsible and there was no impersonation involved.

Sincerely yours,

C. M. Kelley

Clarence M. Kelley
Director

NOTE: Correspondent had written in mid-July and asked about the effects of Dr. Tesla and he was advised that the Office of Alien Property had participated in removing his effects from his hotel room. A copy of his communication was referred to the Department of Justice. Bufiles indicate clearly that after Dr. Tesla's death some relatives opened the safe in his hotel room with the help of a locksmith and, thereafter, the Office of Alien Property confiscated all of his belongings. Bufile 100-2237 mentions that the FBI was advised of the existence of this property; however, inasmuch as the Office of Alien Property was handling Dr. Tesla's effects, the Bureau had absolutely no hand in the entire matter.

RWE:ncr (3)

MAIL ROOM ☐ TELETYPE UNIT ☐

June 9, 1975

Federal Bureau of Investigation
U.S. Department of Justice
Washington D.C. 20535

Sirs:

We recently contacted the San Francisco FBI office and a review of their files revealed information concerning the scientist Nikola Tesla or his papers which we understand to have been impounded.

If you could make a thorough investigation of all files and materials available to you, we would greatly appreciate the correspondence of any information that might be discovered.

Thank you,

July 7, 1975

100-2237-26X

San Jose, California 95117

Dear

This will acknowledge your letter of June 9th.

In response to your inquiry, the papers of Dr. Nikola Tesla were impounded, after his death, by the Office of Alien Property of the Department of Justice.

Sincerely yours,

C. M. Kelley

Clarence M. Kelley
Director

1 - The Deputy Attorney General - Enclosure
   Attention: Susan M. Hauser

NOTE: Bufile 100-2237 indicates that Dr. Tesla was a world famous electrical inventor, and at the time of his death his personal papers and effects were impounded by Office of Alien Property for national security reasons. Since Tesla's death in 1943 the Bureau has received numerous inquiries about the disposition of his technical papers. The above reply is forwarded in answer to these inquiries. Bufiles contain no information identifiable with requesters.

dbb:cgg (4)

MAILED 7
JUL 7 1975
FBI

Kensington, Md. 20795

13 November 1975

Mr. Clarence Kelley
Director
F.B.I.
Washington, D.C. 20535

ALL INFORMATION CONTAINED
HEREIN IS UNCLASSIFIED
DATE 2-3-80 BY ____

Dear Mr. Kelley:

In reply to the letter of 10 November from your office:

I restate that I was not asking about the existence or non-existence of any investigative information on Nikola Tesla, but on his technical papers seized on his death in 1943 and reported in the papers of that time.

The reason given in the reply from your office, the second paragraph, as to why I cannot get any information on Tesla's papers makes no sense in itself or in reply to my inquiry. The third paragraph stating the conditions under which a search will be made is a clear bureaucratic circumvention of the Freedom of Information Act and an excuse on the part of the individual handling my request for doing any work beyond the drafting of a letter. Will it be the decision of your office to let the situation stand like this?

As I stated in my first letter, I am following up the Tesla data for a magazine article. I am tempted to have your reply of the 10th printed and run nationally as an example of how bureaucratic manoeuvring is used to get around the FOIA. Does the bureau need more of this type of publicity?

It is disheartening to see an agency entrusted to uphold the law using its resources to mock the law.

Sincerely,

November 26, 1975

Kensington, Maryland

Dear

This will acknowledge receipt of your letter to the Bureau on November 14th.

In response to your inquiry, the papers of Dr. Nikola Tesla were impounded, after his death, by the Office of Alien Property of the Department of Justice.

Sincerely yours,

C. M. Kelley

Clarence M. Kelley
Director

1 - The Deputy Attorney General - Enclosure
    Attention: Susan M. Hauser

NOTE: Bufile 100-2237 indicates that Dr. Tesla was a World famous electrical inventor, and at the time of his death his personal papers and effects were impounded by Office of Alien Property for National Security reasons. Since Tesla's death in 1943 the Bureau has received numerous inquiries about the disposition of his technical papers. The above reply is forwarded in answer to these inquiries.

baf:gjd (5)

ROUTING AND TRANSMITTAL SLIP

TO (Name, office symbol or location)	ACTION	
1 Alan McCreight Rm. 5435 - JEH	INITIALS	CIRCULATE
	DATE	COORDINATION
2	INITIALS	FILE
	DATE	INFORMATION
3	INITIALS	NOTE AND RETURN
	DATE	PER CONVERSATION
4	INITIALS	SEE ME
	DATE	SIGNATURE

REMARKS

FOIA ▓▓▓▓▓▓▓▓▓▓▓▓▓▓▓▓▓▓▓ b7C

Do NOT use this form as a RECORD of approvals, concurrences, disapprovals, clearances, and similar actions

FROM (Name, office symbol or location)
Susan M. Hauser

DATE 10/21/75
PHONE 2145

OPTIONAL FORM 41
AUGUST 1967
GSA FPMR (41CFR) 100-11.206

Kensington, Md. 20795

17 October 1975

<u>Freedom of Information Act Request</u>

Deputy Attorney General
U.S. Department of Justice
Washington, D.C. 20535

Gentlemen:

I am writing an article for a magazine on early twentieth century inventors and want to obtain information on some papers of Nikola Tesla that were seized by the FBI on his death in 1943.

Tesla invented a number of electrical devices and because of the war and because Tesla was born a Yugoslavian national, it was probably considered a measure of preventitive safety to hold in safekeeping papers that might have any bearing on national security.

I would like to find out: 1) if the FBI still has the papers; 2) if they do have the papers, what must be done to see them; 3) if they do not have the papers, who does have them or what happened to them?

I would be very grateful for your help with this.

Sincerely

November 10, 1975

[redacted]
Kensington, Maryland 20795

Dear [redacted]

ALL INFORMATION CONTAINED
HEREIN IS UNCLASSIFIED
DATE 2-3-80 BY [signature]

This is to acknowledge receipt of your Freedom of Information-Privacy Acts (FOIPA) request forwarded to the FBI by the Department of Justice on October 22nd.

In response to your request for files pertaining to Nikola Tesla, please be advised that in order to preserve the privacy of an individual who may be the subject of a similar inquiry, it has been necessary for the FBI to maintain the practice of not indicating whether we do or do not have such information in our files.

If you can provide notarized authorization from Mr. Tesla's next of kin directing us to release to you any information our files may contain concerning him, we shall thereafter search our files and advise you accordingly.

Since we have not conducted a search of our files, please do not infer that we do or do not have the information you requested.

Sincerely yours,

C. M. Kelley

Clarence M. Kelley
Director

1 - The Deputy Attorney General - Enclosure
    Attention: Susan M. Hauser

baf/vas (5)

Raynham, MA 02767
April 20, 1976

Mr. Clarence Kelly
Director
F.B.I.
Washington, DC

Dear Mr. Kelly:

Mr. Allen and Mr. Ruchlehaus, former acting Director of the FBI, contacted me in 1973 regarding the unavailability of American microfilm records of Nikola Tesla's unpublished diary (now in the Belgrade museum, arranged by month per folder).

At the time I discounted the possibility that these unpublished discoveries had military significance. But because of experiments now under way at Hill AFB, I now suspect such military applications exist and feel it imperative that you be notified, particularly in view of the fact that the Soviets have primary access to the entire collection.

Two photos of each page exist.

After Tesla's death, scientists from the Navy and OSS performed a cursory examination of the diary and notes, which if my memory serves me correctly, was one month long, hardly enough time to decipher Tesla's torturous handwriting. Though Tesla wrote in English, his penmanship was small, blurred, and as difficult to translate as a foreign language.

According to the museum director (1971), the Soviets had made copies of some portions, but not the Colorado Springs diary, which numbers 500 pages, 20 that directly pertain to ball lightning, and 20 or so relevant to the equipment construction. (We copied the most significant portions, but feel more exists).

I have been associated with Project Tesla for four years, have just completed an article for my magazine, EDN (an electrical engineering magazine), but only with the very recent receipt of an unpublished manuscript from John J. O'Neill's book (PRODIGAL GENIUS) did I place credence on Tesla's later claim to military applications. Incidentally, some of O'Neill's descriptions were inaccurate and exagerated, as we have exceeded Tesla's results and are familiar with the experiments. At any rate, there are three possible military applications.

-2-

First, Tesla claimed that the lightning balls (which destroyed his equipment) could be used to destroy aircraft. I have talked to AF personnel --such as ▮▮▮▮▮ engineer at Micro Networks, who saw one inside his plane in flight--and found AF personnel fear these "rf balls," as they call them.

b7C

Second, it is a suspicion of mine that ball lightning, if injected with lithium, could produce a cheap fusion bomb.

Third--and this may be no more than a suspicion--the propulsion mode of ball lightning involves electro-gravitic interaction, by which means air vehicles of revolutionary configuration may be constructed. There are no presently-known laws of physics that can account for the propulsion (400 mph or so when following an airliner). Other hitherto unsuspected applications may exist.

None of these applications were the goal of Project Tesla, which centered on producing ball lightning as Tesla did and studying it as a plasma confinement technique for fusion reactors. Incidentally, Tesla's claim to setting up standing waves on the earth's surface (wireless power) was erroneous and involved techniques similar to Project Sanguine, that is, using the earth's atmosphere as a waveguide▮▮▮▮▮ is aware of our research).

b7C

Cordially

b7C

P.S. By a copy of this letter, along with the enclosures, I am notifying the C.I.A.

Enclosures: 2

DESIGN NEWS

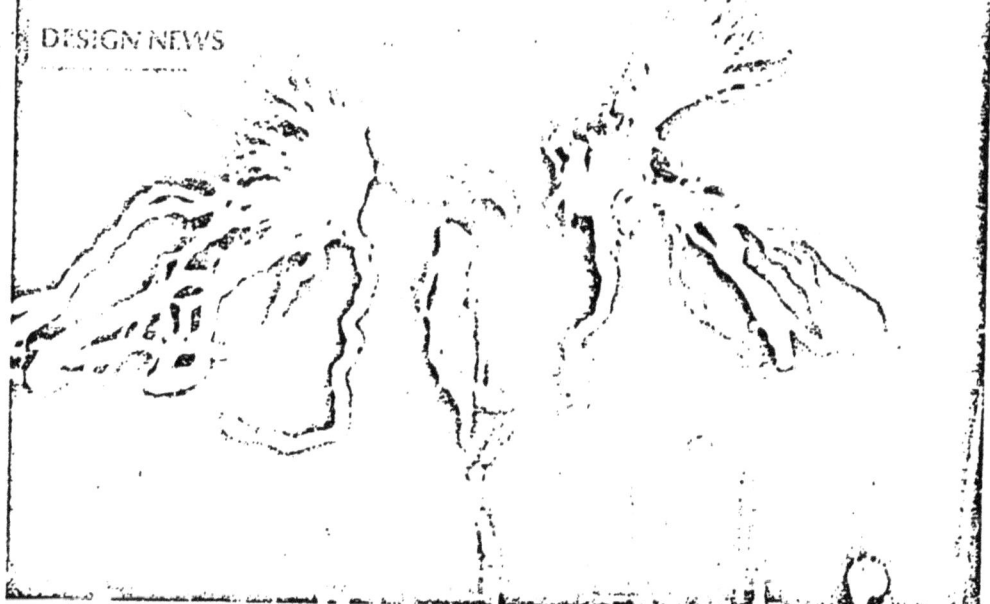

Fusion energy: will experiments in ball lightning provide the key?

Paul Snigier, Associate Editor

In the vast and empty hangar where the first atomic bomb was assembled, a man-made lightning storm is now being unleashed. The voltages of these lightning bolts—20 million volts—are the highest discharge voltages ever produced by man.

Project Tesla, headed by Robert K. Golka and Dr. Robert W. Bass, is an attempt to artificially duplicate one of nature's rarest and most terrifying phenomena—ball lightning. The experiments are based upon the unpublished notes of Nikola Tesla, who, in 1899 at his Colorado Springs laboratory, used a secret *magnifying transmitter* to produce 1.5-in. lightning balls that floated for 30 sec.

The energy surplus

Many physicists, including the eminent Dr. James Tuck, founder of the U.S. fusion program, believe that the lightning ball holds the key to a fantastic cheap and endless energy source—fusion power, or the energy source used by the stars and sun. The fuel is deuterium, or heavy water, that can be inexpensively extracted from ocean water to provide mankind

Highest voltage continuously oscillating damped-wave lightning generator (ever produced by mankind) creates a current of 1100A at 12.5 MV! Subsequent improvements raised this to a peak current of 2200A at 20 MV. Further improvements could conceivably produce bolts that exceed natural lightning (100 MV)!

with millions of years of ___ ___y. Unfortunately, prog___ in fusion research, which has centered on magnetic confinement and laser implosions, has been frustratingly slow and full of unpleasant surprises; and scientists warn that success could be as far off as four decades! But if these promising experiments under way at Wendover, UT, are successfu_, __ew ___nexpected confinement technique could unleash this energy source.

In search of nature's secrets...

Ball lightning, a glowing sphere of red, orange or yellow plasma, often materializes during lightning storms and floats about, often against a strong wind. The ball may bounce along the floor and, on occasion, the sphere will "slip" through glass without breaking it. (The author recently investigated one such case in a hospital, in which the lights were damaged.) At times it materializes inside or even outside aircraft in flight, seemingly impervious to deformation from the wind force.

Witnesses of ball lightning have included such notables as Niels Bohr and Victor Weisskopf, the Director of the MIT Physics Department. Another witness was Secretary of State Dean Acheson, who reported seeing it cross the breakfast table aboard the presidential plane.

The accidental formation of ball lightning has been observed about once per year for the past decade inside building 985 at Hill AF Missile Radiographic Facility, UT. The volleyball-size fireballs drop out of the space adjacent to the high voltage supply of the 25 Mev linear accelerator.

The ball of blue fire floats down to the floor, rolls around randomly and then rises again to the power-supply area where it dissipates without detectable damage. Despite troubleshooting, no explanation can be found for this occurrence.

On one occasion, lightning struck the building—a large concrete structure with a 60-ft. ceiling inside—and, simultaneously, an intense sphere of fire the size of a tennis ball formed above the conduit on the wall at ___rly shoulder level. It moved along the wall for a distance of some 30 ft., floated out and around the neck and shoulders of a person standing near the wall, moved back to the wall and continued along for several feet until it intercepted a duplex outlet on the conduit. At this the ball exploded, causing electrical damage throughout.

A new state of matter?

No presently known laws of physics can account for the stability and bouncing of fireballs unless it includes surface tension. This hitherto unobserved state of matter is a new concept, since plasmas have never previously exhibited such strong surface tension. Also, presently known laws cannot account for the propulsion.

Project Tesla has developed a rigorous mathematical model of the lightning ball's absolute, asymptotic, fluid-dynamical stability. Initial computer studies indicated a density range of 10^{13}-10^{14} cm^{-3}, with a temperature ___ 10^5-10^4 °K—or seven times hotte___ ___ ___e sun!

Chapter 34
TESLA TRIES TO PREVENT WORLD WAR II

When Tesla was talking as a scientist he was opposed to wars on moral, economic and all practical and theoretical grounds. But, like most scientists, when he stopped thinking as a scientist, and let his emotions rule his thoughts, he found exceptions in which he felt some wars and situations were justifiable. As a scientist he was unwilling to have the discoveries of scientists applied to the pruposes of war makers, but when the emotional phase of his nature took the ruling position he was then willing to apply his genius to devising measures that would prevent wars by supplying protective devices.

This attitude is exemplified in the following statement which he prepared in the twenties but did not publish:

"At present many of the ablest minds are trying to devise expedients for preventing a repetition of the awful conflict which is only theoretically ended and the duration and main issues of which I correctly predicted in an article printed in the Sun of December 20, 1914. The League is not a remedy but, on the contrary, in the opinion of a number of competent men, may bring about results just the opposite. It is particularly regrettable that a punitive policy was adopted in framing the terms of peace because a few years hence it will be possible for nations to fight without armies, ships or guns, by weapons far more terrible, to the destructive action and range of which there is virtually no limit. Any city at any distance whatsoever from the enemy can be destroyed by him and no power on earth can stop him from doing so. If we want to avert an impending calamity and a state of things which may transorm this globe into an inferno, we should push the development of flying machines and wireless transmission of energy without an instant's delay and with all the power and resources of the nation."

Tesla saw preventative possibilities in his new invention which embodied "death ray" characteristics and which was made several years after the foregoing statement was written. He saw it providing a curtain of protection which any country, no matter how small, could use as a protection against invasion. While he might offer it as a defensive weapon, however, there would be nothing to stop military men from using it as a weapon of offense.

While I did not know the nature of Tesla's plan I was convinced that it did embody many discoveries that would be of commercial value, and these were the angles he should seek to develop. I felt that if he could be induced to develop some minor phase of his work that would have immediate commercial use he could derive an income from it which would enable him to proceed with his more elaborate plans. To this end I sought to gain some insight into his thoughts, that would enable me to get a practical plan in operation. This was no secret to Tesla and he successfully parried every thrust I made.

The clearest conception I got, and that was largely from scattered remarks, and by making deductions from them, concerned a possible manner in which one phase of his curtain of protection might operate. This was a "war" angle and as such it did not interest me, but since it involved "lightning balls," or "fire balls," I was very curious. Fire balls had always fascinated me, and I had read everything I could lay my hands on about them.

A fire ball is a strange phenomenon associated with lightning. Some of the energy of the lightning stroke appears to become locked into a ball shaped structure which may be of any size from a couple of inches to a foot in diameter. It looks like a perfect sphere, brightly incandescent and floats like a bubble, being easily carried by air currents. They may last for a short time, from a fraction of a second to many seconds. In this interval, during which they stay fairly close to the ground, they may come close to many objects without damaging them or being damaged by them. Suddenly, for no known reason, the ball explodes doing as much damage as a bomb, if close to structures, and no damage if in the open.

The fire ball looked to me like a gigantically enlarged model of the tiny electron, one of the building blocks of matter, which acts as if it were just a spherical area of space in which an amount of energy was crystallized to give it structure. I felt that if it were possible to discover how a large amount of energy was stored in this fairy bubble structure of a fire ball a new insight might be gained into the structure of the electron and other fundamental particles of matter. Also this method of storing energy could be applied to a thousand useful purposes.

When I approached Tesla with pleas along this line to develop this possible phase of his discovery he would evade direct reply by indulging in a, not always, tolerant lecture on my gullability in believing theories about the complex structure of the atom. While he had in earlier years discussed some of his experiences with fire balls in his laboratory at Colorado Springs and explained his theory of their formation, he would not in the later years permit himself to be drawn into a discussion of them as a possible part of his system. This, of course, made me suspicious that the clue was "hot" but I could be completely wrong in my conclusions. Tesla was very quick in detecting my technique when I sought to narrow down a field by trying to get him to deny statements when he was adamant to direct questions.

Tesla became familiar with the destructive characteristics of fire balls in his experiments at Colorado Springs in 1899. He produced them quite by accident and saw them, more than once, explode and shatter his tall mast and also destroy apparatus within his laboratory. The destructive action accompanying the disintegration of a fire ball, he declared, takes place with inconceivabel violence.

He studied the process by which they were produced, not because he wanted to produce them but in order to eliminate the conditions in which they were created. It is not pleasant, he related, to have a fire ball explode in your vicinity for they will destroy anything they come in contact with.

It will be necessary to reconstruct his statements from very fragmentary notes and a long distance memory.

"Parasitic oscillations, or circuits, within the main circuit were a source of danger from this cause. Points of resistance in the main circuit could result in minor oscillating circuits between terminals or between two points of resistance and these minor circuits would have a very much higher period of oscillation than the main circuit and could be set into oscillation by the main current of lower frequency.

"Even when the principal oscillating circuit was adjusted for the greatest efficiency of operation by the dimination of all sources of losses the fire balls continued to occur but these were due to stray high frequency charges from random earth currents.

"From these experiences it became apparent that the fire balls resulted from the interaction of two frequencies, a stray higher frequency wave imposed on the lower frequency free oscillation of the main circuit.

"As the free oscillation of the circuit builds up from the zero point to the quarter wave length node it passes through various rates of change. In a current of shorter wavelength the rates of change will be steeper. When the two currents react on each other the resultant complex will contain a wave in which there is an extremely steep rate of change, and for the briefest instant currents may move at a tremendous rate, at the rate of millions of horsepower.

"This condition acts as a trigger which may cause the total energy of the powerful longer wave to be discharged in an infinitesmally small interval of time and at a proportionately tremendously great rate of energy movement which cannot confine itself to the metal circuit and is released into surrounding space with inconceivable violence."

It is but a step, from learning how a high frequency current can explosively discharge a lower frequency current, to using the principle to design a system in which these explosions can be produced by intent. The following process appears a possible one but no evidence is available that it is the one Tesla evolved: An oscillator, such as he used to send power wirelessly around the earth at Colorado Springs, is set in operation at a frequency to which a given warship is resonant. The complex structure of a ship would provide a great number of spots in which electrical oscillations will be set up of a much higher frequency than those coursing through the ship as a whole. These parasistec currents will react on the main current causing the production of fireballs which by their explosions will destroy the ship, even more effectively than the explosion of the magazine which would also take place. A second oscillator may be used to transmit the shorter wavelength current.

Somewhat later I learned the reason for Tesla's reticence to discuss details. This came shortly after Stanley Baldwin replaced Neville Chamberlin as Prime Minister of Great Britain.

Tesla revealed that he had carried on negotiations with Prime Minister Chamberlin for the sale of his ray system to Great Britain for $30,000,000 on the basis of his presentation that the device would provide complete protection for the British Isles against any enemy approaching by sea or air, and would provide an offensive weapon to which there was no defense. He was convinced, he declared, of the sincerity of Mr. Chamberlin and his intent to adopt the device & it would have prevented the outbreak of the then threatening war, and would have made possible the continuation - under the duress which this weapon would make possible - of the working agreement involving France, Germany and Britain to maintain the status quo in Europe. When Chamberlin failed, at the Munich conference, to retain this state of European equilibrium it was necessary to get rid of Chamberlin and install a new Prime Minister who could make the effort to shift one corner of the triangle from Germany to Russia. Baldwin found no virtue in Tesla's plan and preemptorially ended the negotiations.

Tesla was greatly disappointed by the collapse of his negotiations with the British Government. With it there collapsed his hopes of providing a demonstration of his most recent, and, what he considered, his most important discoveries. He did not, however, dwell on the subject; beyond the single conversation he did not mention the matter again. He did not get another chance to finance the demonstration of these discoveries.

During the period in which the negotiations were being carried on, Tesla declared, efforts had been made to steal the invention. His room had been entered and his papers examined but the thieves, or spies, left empty handed. There was no danger, he said, that his invention could be stolen for he had at no time committed any part of it to paper. He could trust his memory to preserve every fine detail of his investigations. This was true, he said, of all of his later major discoveries.

The nature of his system makes little difference now; he has gone and has taken it with him. Perhaps, if there is any communication from beyond the veil that separates this life from whatever exists hereafter, Tesla may look down upon earth's struggling mortals and find some way of dropping a hint concerning what he accomplished; but, if the situation is such that this cannot take place, then we must await until the human race produces another Tesla.

oOo

April 30, 1976

EX-115

REC-47 100-2237-29

Raynham, Massachusetts 02767

Dear

Thank you for your letter of April 20th, with enclosures. It was certainly most thoughtful of you to furnish us this information, and your interest and courtesy are indeed appreciated.

Sincerely yours,

C. M. Kelley

Clarence M. Kelley
Director

NOTE: Bufiles indicate limited correspondence with last outgoing 6-27-73, in reply to his request concerning papers of Dr. Nikola Tesla. Dr. Tesla was a world-famous electrical inventor, and at the time of his death in 1943, all of his personal papers and effects were believed dangerous to the country's security if they fell into unauthorized hands. The book, "Prodigal Genius," by John J. O'Neill, alleged that the FBI took over a certain safe and opened it, appropriating his property. Bufiles indicated the Office of Alien Property of the Department of Justice did so. Bufile 100-2237-23.

CAM:kmh (3)

United States Senate

JUN 16

To ensure proper handling please return all correspondence TO THE ATTENTION OF:

Pat

Respectfully referred to:

FBI

Please respond to the attached inquiry in duplicate and return the enclosure. Thank you for your cooperation.

Bill Proxmire, U.S.S.

ENCLOSURE

U.S. Senator Proxmire's Staff
New Senate Office Bldg
Room 5241, Washington DC 2510

Dear Sir.

I am a substitute in the Milwaukee Public School System. I do scientific experiments in high voltage electricity. I have studied all the available writings of the dead genius Nikola Tesla (1861 – January 7, 1943)

When Nicola Tesla died the Federal Bureau of Investigation came and opened the safe in his room and took the papers it contained, to examine them

...for a reported secret invention of possible use in WWII.

As a citizen & a scientist I would like to study these unpublished papers with hope of finding new ideas for producing an alternate source of energy. Something that Nikola Tesla knew about and because of his unfortunate financial status, was not able to develop into a working model.

Please help. —

With love in The Lc.

Milwaukee, Wisc. 53208

b7C

b7C

100-2237-30   June 23, 1976

Honorable William Proxmire
United States Senate
Washington, D. C. 20510

Dear Senator Proxmire:

b7C   This will respond to your communication of June 16th enclosing the letter of Mr. ▓▓▓▓▓▓▓▓▓▓▓ of Milwaukee, Wisconsin 53208.

The effects of Dr. Nikola Tesla were impounded, after his death, by the Office of Alien Property of the Department of Justice and not by the FBI. Since we did not participate in the handling of Dr. Tesla's belongings, I am unable to furnish the information you desire.

A copy of your communication and of this reply are being referred to the Department of Justice and the enclosure to your communication is being returned as requested.

Sincerely yours,

C. M. Kelley

Clarence M. Kelley
Director

Enclosure
1 - Assistant Attorney General - Enclosures (2)
    Civil Division
1 - Milwaukee - Enclosures (2)
1 - Office of Congressional Affairs - Enclosures (2)
NOTE: This response is consistent with past responses to inquiries of a similar nature. Bufile 100-2237 reflects that the Office of Alien Property took possession of Dr. Tesla's papers following his death.
DJC:mmd/mjb (7)

MAILED 10
JUN 23 1976
FBI

July 26, 1979

Dear Mr. Webster:

I am writing this letter in regard to some papers you have in your possession, by Nikola Tesla.

I have for some time now been studying the works of Mr. Tesla and I am involved in the research and further developement of his efforts. I have in my possession a copy of almost everything that was ever written by him.

However I have read that on the day following his death (he died the night of January 7th, 1943, so probably January 8th, 1943) the Federal Bureau of Investigation went to where Mr. Tesla had been staying - the Hotel New Yorker, New York City, New York and collected all notes and papers that he had with him there.

To further my studies and hopefully complete them it would be deeply appreciated if you would send me a copy of all the notes, papers, books, drawings etc. that were found there.

Thank you,

Royal Oak, Michigan 48073

August 6, 1979

OUTSIDE SOURCE

Royal Oak, Michigan 48073

Dear

Your recent letter requesting information concerning Dr. Nikola Tesla has been received.

The effects of Dr. Tesla were impounded, after his death, by the Office of Alien Property of the Department of Justice and not by the FBI. We have no preprinted material available for public distribution regarding Dr. Tesla. However, under the provisions of the Freedom of Information Act (Title 5, United States Code, Section 552), requests have been made in the past regarding your topic and there may be documents available to you under Title 28--Code of Federal Regulations.

If you are interested in seeking such documents under the Freedom of Information Act, you should make a separate inquiry, clearly marking the envelope and letter as a Freedom of Information Act request, and direct it to the Director, Federal Bureau of Investigation, 9th Street and Pennsylvania Avenue, N.W., Washington, D. C. 20535. In the letter you must request documents regarding the specific topic of interest to you.

Sincerely yours,

William L. Bailey
Assistant Director

1 — Mr. Underwood – Enclosure
Room 6958
(This correspondence response may engender a future FOIA inquiry.)

NOTE: Based upon available information, correspondent is not identifiable in Bufiles.

EHM:lch (4)

UNITED STATES GOVERNMENT — UNITED STATES DEPARTMENT OF JUSTICE
FEDERAL BUREAU OF INVESTIGATION

Memorandum

TO : Mr. Bresson

FROM : [redacted] b7C

DATE: 2/25/80

SUBJECT: FREEDOM OF INFORMATION ACT DISCLOSURE REGARDING DR. NIKOLA TESLA

ALL INFORMATION CONTAINED
HEREIN IS UNCLASSIFIED
DATE 2-3-80 BY [signature]

PURPOSE:

To reduce time spent on handling of requests for information on captioned subject and to promote uniformity of disclosure.

DETAILS:

A search of FBIHQ central records indices reflects that Dr. Nikola Tesla is carried as the subject of Bufile 100-2237. Virtually all information in this file is inquiry-type correspondence. For purposes of FOIA releases, copies of this material have not been made and requesters have been so advised. Copies of the remaining material in the file totalling 29 pages, however, has been processed for disclosure. Numerous requesters have sought information relating to Dr. Tesla under the FOIA. Therefore, it is recommended that the disclosure documents maintained in Bufile 190-16504-4 be considered the preprocessed release appropriate for responses by the Initial Processing Unit for any further requests for information on this subject.

RECOMMENDATION:

That the Initial Processing Unit, FOIPA Branch, Records Management Division, add captioned case to their list of preprocessed cases and handle any future requests for such information.

1 - Mr. Underwood
1 - Miss [redacted] b7C

100-2237
190-16504

MAR 27 1980

eah:vas (7)

Buy U.S. Savings Bonds Regularly on the Payroll Savings Plan

DEPARTMENT OF JUSTICE
FEDERAL BUREAU OF INVESTIGATION
INTERNAL ROUTING ACTION SLIP

(Rev. 10/10/79)

TO	BLDG.	ROOM	NAME/TITLE/ORGANIZATION		BLDG.	ROOM	NAME/TITLE/ORGANIZATION	
	JEH	7142	Mr. Colwell	235			DISCLOSURE SECTION	
	JEH	7110	Mr. Boynton	235	JEH	6995	Mr. Bresson/Normensen	314
	JEH	7110	Mr. Moore	235	JEH	6994	Mr. Lewis/Normensen	314
	JEH	5829	Mr. Bailey/Rogers	211	JEH	6927	CHIEF, UNIT A/Secretary	314
	JEH	5829	Mr. O'Brien/Lass	211			SA: _____ Team _____	
							RA: _____ Team _____	
	JEH	6296	Mr. Flanders/Woleslagle	3	JEH	6959	CHIEF, UNIT B	314
			OPERATIONS SECTION				SA: _____ Team _____	
	JEH	6992	Mr. Ervin/Poston	314			RA: _____ Team _____	
	JEH	6993	Mr. Tierney/Poston	314	JEH	6975	CHIEF, UNIT C/Secretary	314
							SA: _____ Team _____	
	JEH	6280	CHIEF, TAR/Secretary	314			RA: _____ Team _____	
			SA:		JEH	6986	CHIEF, UNIT D	314
			Attn:				SA: _____ Team _____	
	JEH	6987	CHIEF, FIELD COOR.				RA: _____ Team _____	
			SA:		JEH	6786	CHIEF, UNIT E	314
			Attn:				SA: _____ Team _____	
	JEH	6958	CHIEF, IPU/Secretary	314				
			SA:		JEH	6387	CHIEF, UNIT F/Secretary	314
			Attn:				SA: _____ Team _____	
	JEH	6363	File Duplication	314			RA: _____ Team _____	
	JEH	6268	Tickler/Index Group	314				
	JEH	6992	Leave Clerk	314				
	JEH	6348	Word Processing Center	314				
	JEH	6380	DCRU	314				
			Attn:					

ALL INFORMATION CONTAINED
HEREIN IS UNCLASSIFIED
DATE 2-14-82 BY SP6/RSM/mr9

b7C

I would prefer
IPU being alerted
that any request for Tesla file be
referred directly to _____ whereupon
she would see that request
return to work

☐ RECOMMENDATION/COMMENT   ☐ LOG   ☐ NECESSARY ACTION
☐ SEE REMARKS ON REVERSE   ☐ FILE   ☐ COORDINATE
☐ MAKE COPIES (NO.   )   ☐ SEE ME   ☐ PER INQUIRY
☐ RETURN (BY   )   ☐ CALL ME ☐ INFORMATION

FROM: Freedom of Information-Privacy Acts Branch
THOMAS H. BRESSON, SECTION CHIEF

FORM DOJ-359A
8-1-74

Tom —

It is my understanding that <u>every</u> case which is completed through disclosure is "preprocessed".

IPU's Reading Room maintains <u>only</u> those "preprocessed" cases which have been deemed to have sufficient public interest to warrant inclusion in the Reading Room.

The question, therefore, is: Does the TESLA material fit the criteria for inclusion in the FOIA Reading Room? I think not.

Thx
[signature]

OFFICE OF THE UNDER SECRETARY OF DEFENSE
WASHINGTON, D.C. 20301

RESEARCH AND ENGINEERING

FEDERAL GOVERNMENT

9 FEB 1981

MEMORANDUM FOR THE DIRECTOR, FEDERAL BUREAU OF INVESTIGATION

SUBJECT: Papers Recovered on the Death of Nicola Tesla (U)

(U) We understand that the FBI may have possession of a number of papers found after the death of Nicola Tesla in 1943. Nicola Tesla was a brilliant electrical engineer (i.e. the Tesla Coil) who was a pioneer in various aspects of electrical transmission phenomena.

(C) We believe that certain of Tesla's papers may contain basic principles which would be of considerable value to certain ongoing research within the DoD. It would be very helpful to have access to his papers.

(U) Since we have really no idea of the possible volume of these papers, we would be happy to provide a researcher who could assist you in reducing the magnitude of the search. If there are further questions, I am the point of contact within the DoD and can be reached at 695-6364 or 695-7417.

Allan J. MacLaren
LtColonel, USAF
Military Assistant
Strategic and Space Systems

Classifed by: DUSDRE/S&SS
Declassify on: February 1987

Lt. Col. Allan C. MacLaren, U.S.A.
Military Assistant
Strategic and Space Systems
Office of the Under Secretary
   of Defense
Washington, D. C. 20301

Dear Colonel MacLaren:

Your memorandum of February 9 requesting access to the scientific papers of Dr. Nikola Tesla which might be in our files has been referred to my office for reply.

A preliminary review of our files indicates that the FBI did not participate in the handling of Dr. Tesla's belongings following his death in New York City in January, 1943. His papers were examined by representatives of the Office of Alien Property, the Navy Department and the Office of Scientific Research and Development. In February, 1943, the papers apparently were released to Mr. Sava N. Kosanovic, Dr. Tesla's nephew and the administrator of his estate. Mr. Kosanovic's address at that time was 1 Central Park South, New York, New York.

A complete search of our indices is being made to determine if we have any information that might be useful to you. You will be notified of the results of this search at the earliest possible date.

Sincerely,

/s/

Roger S. Young
Assistant Director in Charge
Office of Congressional
   and Public Affairs

1 - ███████ (FOIPA) - Enc.
1 - Mr. Young - Enc.
1 - ███████ Enc.

NOTE: Reply discussed with ███████ FOIPA, RMD, who has handled similar requests for information in our files concerning Dr. Tesla. In numerous previous responses we have said that the Office of Alien Property, the Department of Justice impounded Dr. Tesla's papers after his death. However, the Office of Foreign Litigation, Civil Division, indicates that Dr. Tesla's papers are not in their possession.

March 23, 1981

Lt. Col. A. J. MacLaren
Military Assistant
Strategic and Space Systems
Office of the Under Secretary
 of Defense
Washington, D. C. 20301

FEDERAL GOVERNMENT

ALL INFORMATION CONTAINED
HEREIN IS UNCLASSIFIED
DATE _____ BY _____

Dear Colonel MacLaren:

A complete search of our retrievable files concerning Dr. Nikola Tesla shows that all notes and material in his immediate possession at the time of his death on January 7, 1943, were placed in the custody of the Alien Property Custodian under seal by the United States Government. These materials have never been in the care or custody of the FBI.

On January 26 and 27, 1943, Federal authorities made a thorough review of the effects of Dr. Tesla to determine if any ideas of significant value to the United States war effort could be found. His effects were examined at the Manhattan Warehouse and Storage Company at 52nd and 7th Avenue, New York, New York, where they apparently were taken after his death. Participating in this examination were representatives from the New York and Washington Offices of the Alien Property Custodian, the Office of Scientific Research and Development at the Massachusetts Institute of Technology, the Office of Naval Intelligence, and United States Naval Research. The FBI did not participate in this examination. (65-47953 section 1)

It was the considered opinion of a spokesman of those examiners "that there exist among Dr. Tesla's papers and possessions no scientific notes, descriptions of hitherto unrevealed methods or devices, or actual apparatus which could be of significant value to this country or which would constitute a hazard in unfriendly hands." There was thought to be no technical or military reason why further custody of the property should be retained. However, our files indicate that certain papers, which were regarded as typical of Nikola Tesla's writings and thoughts in the period of 1925 to 1942, were removed for the purpose of except to the office of the Alien Property Custodian. (65-47953 section 1)

MAILED 6
MAR 23 1981
FBI

1 -
1 -
1 -

MAIL ROOM

V-38 DE-113

(SEE NOTE PAGE THREE)

Mr. Col. L. R. Buchanan

A report dated October 17, 1945, from our New York Office said that at that time Dr. Tesla's effects retained at the Manhattan Storage Warehouse in some 75 packing boxes and trunks under seal by the New York Department of Taxation. The rental for this storage, approximately $15 per month, was being paid by Charlotte Muzar, 134 East 63rd Street, New York, New York, who was listed as an agent for Sava Kosanovich, Dr. Tesla's nephew and administrator of his estate. (65-47953-14)

On October 26, 1945, Private Bloyce Fitzgerald, U.S. Army, a young scientist who had been Tesla's protege, called in person at our New York Field Office. With him were Lt. David M. Pratt, Lt. Herbert O. Schutt and Lt. R. E. Houle from a research development unit at Wright Field, Dayton, Ohio. These men carried a letter signed by Brigadier General L. C. Craigee, Chief Engineering Division, Wright Field, requesting that the FBI allow the bearers of the letter access to the effects of Nikola Tesla. (65-47953-15)

It was explained to this military contingent that the FBI had no jurisdiction over Tesla's effects, and they were referred to the Office of the Alien Property Custodian. Bureau files do not indicate whether the men ever examined Tesla's belongings. (65-47953-15)

The Tesla effects remained in rooms 5C and 5L of the Manhattan Storage Company. In the 1950s, FBI Agents were told by company management that the only recorded visit had been made by "Federal authorities" in January, 1943. The floor supervisor recalled that the men had taken numerous photographs. His description of the equipment used would tend to show that a microfilm reproduction was made of the papers of the deceased. (65-47953-27)

Our files do not reflect any pertinent information on the Tesla materials since that date. Their current whereabouts or condition are not reflected in our files.

For further information regarding this matter, you may wish to contact the Office of the Alien Property Custodian and the other Federal agencies mentioned above.

I hope that we have been of assistance to you.

Sincerely,

Roger S. Young
Assistant Director in Charge
Office of Congressional
and Public Affairs

(CONTINUED - OVER)

- 2 -

Lt. Col. A. J. MacLaren

NOTE: On February 3, 1981, Col. MacLaren wrote to us inquiring about the scientific papers of Dr. Nikola Tesla. In a return letter of March 9, we informed him that a thorough review of our files would be made in search of the information he requested. This was done and he is being informed of the results. Tesla's papers have been the subject of numerous inquiries by various individuals and organizations since his death. FBI received over 20 FOIA requests on this matter during the period 1973-1980. Matter coordinated with FOIA Section, R&D.

- 3 -

OFFICE OF THE UNDER SECRETARY OF DEFENSE
WASHINGTON, D.C. 20301

RESEARCH AND
ENGINEERING

1 APR 1981

FEDERAL GOVERNMENT

Mr. Roger S. Young
Assistant Director in Charge
Office of Congressional and Public Affairs
Federal Bureau of Investigation
Washington, D.C. 20535

Dear Mr. Young,

Thank you very much for your letters of March 10 and March 20, 1981, in response to our request re Dr. Tesla. We very much appreciate the effort that must have gone into this. On behalf of the Deputy Under Secretary (Strategic and Space Systems), Dr. S. L. Zeiberg, I would like to thank you and the people who spent their time searching out the relevant data.

Sincerely,

Allan J. MacLaren
Colonel, USAF
Military Assistant
Strategic and Space Systems

21 July 1981

Director of the FBI
Washington, D.C.

Dear Sir:

While attending college, I came across an article about the electrical genius, Nicolai Tesla. Mr. Tesla was an electrical genius with such peers as EDISON and WESTINGHOUSE. Tesla designed the basic generator and was the first man to introduce alternating current to the people. The article, written in an underground SanFrancisco newspaper, stated that Tesla also worked with electromagnetic waves and supposedly built a plant that could harness the electromagnetic waves out of the earth's atmosphere sufficiently enough to use them as a source of electricity. The article stated that Tesla built such a plant and lit up a city street 150 miles away by sending the electromagnetism via radio waves. This method is presently being used in electronic warfare. After that, the article stated that the FBI confiscated his plans and buried them in your archives. Their reasoning was that such a free form of energy would knock out a big chunk of the oil, coal, and nuclear forms of energy and their contributions to the economy (money for research and employment). All I want to know is if there is any truth to this story and if so what was the FBI's reasons and when are the archives opened again so that Tesla's work could come to light again. Now bear in mind that this man was an electrical genius and even had a unit of electrical measure named after him. If he did figure out a way to utilize the earth's electromagnetic waves then I believe that we are ready to gradually phase out our dependence on oil, ease the volatile tension in the Middle East and put all that money presently going to the Arabs into space research, joint international research and deep-sea research to help solve our population problem. I am talking about huge sums of money being released that could speed up the experts present projected times of producing significant gains in these still relatively new fields.

You could at least take the time to check out what I am saying and judge for yourself whether or not the archives should be opened now to put the world back on a more secure heading.

Sincerely,

b7C

FPO SanFrancisco 96602

August 7, 1981

OUTSIDE SOURCE

FPO San Francisco 96602

Dear

Judge Webster has referred your letter of July 21st to me for a reply. A check of our files indicates Dr. Nikola Tesla's effects were impounded after his death by the Office of Alien Property of the Department of Justice and not by the FBI. While your interest is indeed appreciated, the FBI is unable to answer your questions as we did not participate in the handling or have anything to do with the storage of Dr. Tesla's belongings.

To be as helpful as possible, I am forwarding a copy of this communication to the Department of Justice.

Sincerely,

S

Roger S. Young
Assistant Director in Charge
Office of Congressional
and Public Affairs

1 - Acting Assistant Attorney General - Enclosure
    Civil Division

NOTE: ███████ is not identifiable in Bufiles. Dr. Tesla died on 1/7/43 and we have received much correspondence regarding his belongings which were impounded by the Office of Alien Property of the Department of Justice.

FD-36 (Rev. 8-26-82)

FBI

TRANSMIT VIA:
☐ Teletype
☐ Facsimile
☒ AIRTEL

PRECEDENCE:
☐ Immediate
☐ Priority
☐ Routine

CLASSIFICATION:
☐ TOP SECRET
☐ SECRET
☐ CONFIDENTIAL
☐ UNCLAS E F T O
☐ UNCLAS

Date 8/18/83

TO: DIRECTOR, FBI
ATTN: INTD, SUPERVISOR ~~[redacted]~~ (S)

FROM: SAC, CINCINNATI ~~[redacted]~~ (P)

NIKOLA TESLA
~~[redacted]~~ (S)
(OO: CI)

This communication is classified "Secret" in its entirety.

Re telephone call of SA ~~[redacted]~~ Cincinnati Division, to Supervisor ~~[redacted]~~ FBIHQ, on 8/11/83.

Enclosed for the Bureau and New York is one copy each of pertinent pages from the 1981 book titled "Tesla: Man Out of Time" by Margaret Cheney, with important passages underlined.

For information of Bureau and New York, a ~~[redacted]~~ research physicist with the Electro Optics Research Lab of the Avionics Division of the U.S. Air Force Aeronautical Systems Division at Wright-Patterson Air Force Base (WPAFB) and ~~[redacted]~~ physicist and intelligence specialist on Particle Beam Weapons Technology with the Foreign Technology Division (FTD) also at WPAFB, have both been in contact with SA ~~[redacted]~~ at the Dayton, Ohio RA regarding possible FBI

SECRET

Classified by: 8262
Declassify on: OADR

ENCLOSURE

2 - Bureau (Enc. 1)
2 - New York (Enc. 1)
2 - Cincinnati

DHF:mkg
(6)

Approved: _____ Transmitted _____ Per _____
(Number) (Time)

involvement in the seizing of Nikola Tesla's research papers and other documents and scientific instruments after his death on January 7, 1943.

They both explained that Tesla was a scientific genius and experimenter who was born in Yugoslavia of Serbian parents on 7/10/56, went to school later in Gratz, Austria, Prague, Czechoslovakia and Paris, France. He immigrated to the U.S. in the early 1880's, worked for Thomas Edison's laboratory for a couple of years, then started his own lab after being paid $1 million dollars for rights to his patents on his polyphase systems of alternating current dynamos, which lead to the harnessing of Niagra Falls for producing electricity and then the power system of the whole country. He was naturalized in 1889. He predicted wireless communication (radio). His later experiments in Colorado and elsewhere lead to his producing artificial lightning in the millions of volts. He also had patents on the concept of neon and flourescent lights, but he later made little money on his later inventions, although he continued to do experiments leading to devices of great potential worth, which he never patented. He became more reclusive in his later years, living in various hotels in New York City. In the 1930's he claimed he had developed the concept and method of building a "death ray", which could destroy planes at many miles distant, for defending America. Also, there are reports of resonance machines or devices whereby he could shake one or many large city buildings from some distance away.

Both ███ and ███ said that Tesla donated "some" of his papers (or copies thereof) to the Tesla Institute in Belgrade, Yugoslavia; set up in the 1930's in his honor by their government. Biographies on Tesla claim that either the custodian of Alien Property and/or the FBI seized his papers and other personal effects, including a safe or safes, and other property immediately after his death in 1943. This is elaborated on in the enclosed copies of certain pages of Margaret Cheney's book, "Tesla: Man Out of Time".

███ said that after World War II Tesla's papers were shipped to the Tesla Institute in Belgrade, Yugoslavia, by his nephew, Sava Kosanovic, who had become Tito's Ambassador to the U.S. There were reports that some microfilming of Tesla's papers by government agents while they were still in storage in New York under Kosanovic's custody.

-2-

CI ████(s) b1   SECRET

Also, the Soviet Union has allegedly had access to some of Tesla's papers, possibly in Belgrade and/or elsewhere, which influenced their early research into directed energy weapons, and Butler feels access to much of Tesla's papers on lightning, beam weapons and/or "death rays" would give him more insight into the Soviet beam weapons program. This is Butler's area of expertise and responsibility. He has been unable to locate any Tesla papers or copies of same in the classified or unclassified libraries at WPAFB. However, there are reports that some portions of them were shipped by the Custodian of Alien Property Office in Washington, D.C. to a technical research lab at WPAFB, possibly the "Equipment Lab", now closed for some years or reorganized into another organization.

b7C ████ and ████ are both desirous of learning the locations of such papers of Tesla as now exist in the U.S., for both intelligence and research purposes. Therefore, Butler would like to examine FBI files relating to Nikola Tesla and possibly any on Sava Kosanovic, his nephew who received the bulk of his papers after Tesla's death, and may possibly have been the subject of FBI investigation.

b7C ████ travels to the Washington, D.C. area on FTD business periodically and can review FBI files at FBIHQ relating to Tesla and Kosanovic.

REQUEST OF THE BUREAU

The Bureau is requested to conduct full indices checks on both Nikola Tesla and Sava Kosanovic.

b7C Should there be such files at FBIHQ, as well as at New York, it is requested that Bureau consider granting the above ████ of FTD, official access to same, in the interest of national security.

LEADS

NEW YORK

AT NEW YORK, NEW YORK

Will conduct same indices check as requested of Bureau and advise the Bureau and Cincinnati of results and confirm such files and references still exist there.

-3-   SECRET

 b1

CINCINNATI

AT DAYTON, OHIO

b7C   Will maintain contact with ▮▮▮▮▮ and

SECRET

"A VISIONARY GENIUS AS FERTILE AS ANY IN THE MODERN HISTORY OF SCIENCE...."*

Flamboyant, eccentric, almost supernaturally gifted, had he been born today he would still be ahead of his time. Called a madman by some, a genius by others, and an enigma by nearly everyone, Nikola Tesla was perhaps the greatest inventor the world has ever known.

He was a trailblazer who created astonishing, world-transforming devices, often without theoretical precedent. It was Tesla who harnessed the alternating electrical current we use today... Tesla who actually invented radio... Tesla who invented fluorescent lighting and the incredible bladeless turbine. He introduced us to the fundamentals of robotry and computer and missile science, which continue to create and transform the future.

This fascinating new biography, acclaimed by American Scientist as "excellent...a significant contribution to the recent history of science," is a riveting journey into the mind of the nineteenth-century wizard who was Edison's enemy, Mark Twain's friend, J. P. Morgan's client, and mentor to many of the twentieth-century's most famous scientists.

MARGARET CHENEY is a science writer and author of two other nonfiction books. She lives in California.

*The Sunday Times of London

MARGARET CHENEY

39077

0 71009 00495

ISBN 0-440-39077-X

The ill-fated Wardenclyffe tower built in 1901–03. It was intended for radio broadcasting and wireless transmission of power across the Atlantic. (Courtesy L. Anderson, after photo by Lillian McChesney)

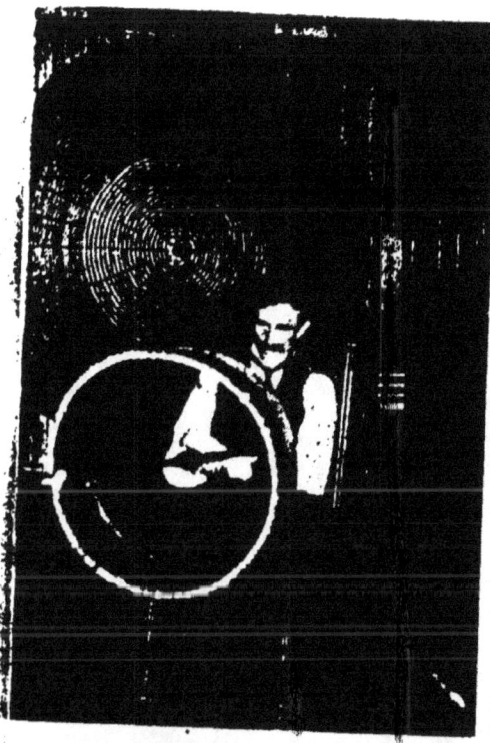

Tesla in his laboratory, 1898. The device shown is an unconnected coil illustrating the action of two resonating circuits of different frequencies—today one of the basic circuits used in computers. The pressure at the end of the coil facing the viewer (illuminated by streamers) is approximately one half million volts. (Courtesy L. Anderson)

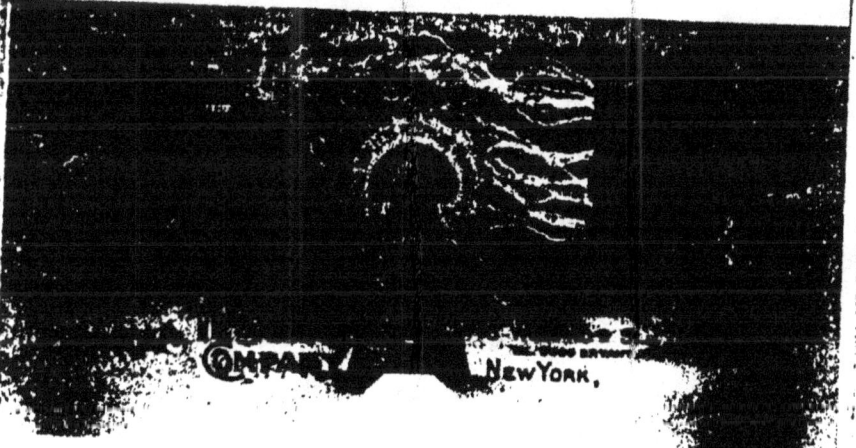

The letterhead of Tesla business stationery recalls some of his more important inventions. In the center is the Wardenclyffe tower as it was intended to look when finished. (Courtesy L. Anderson)

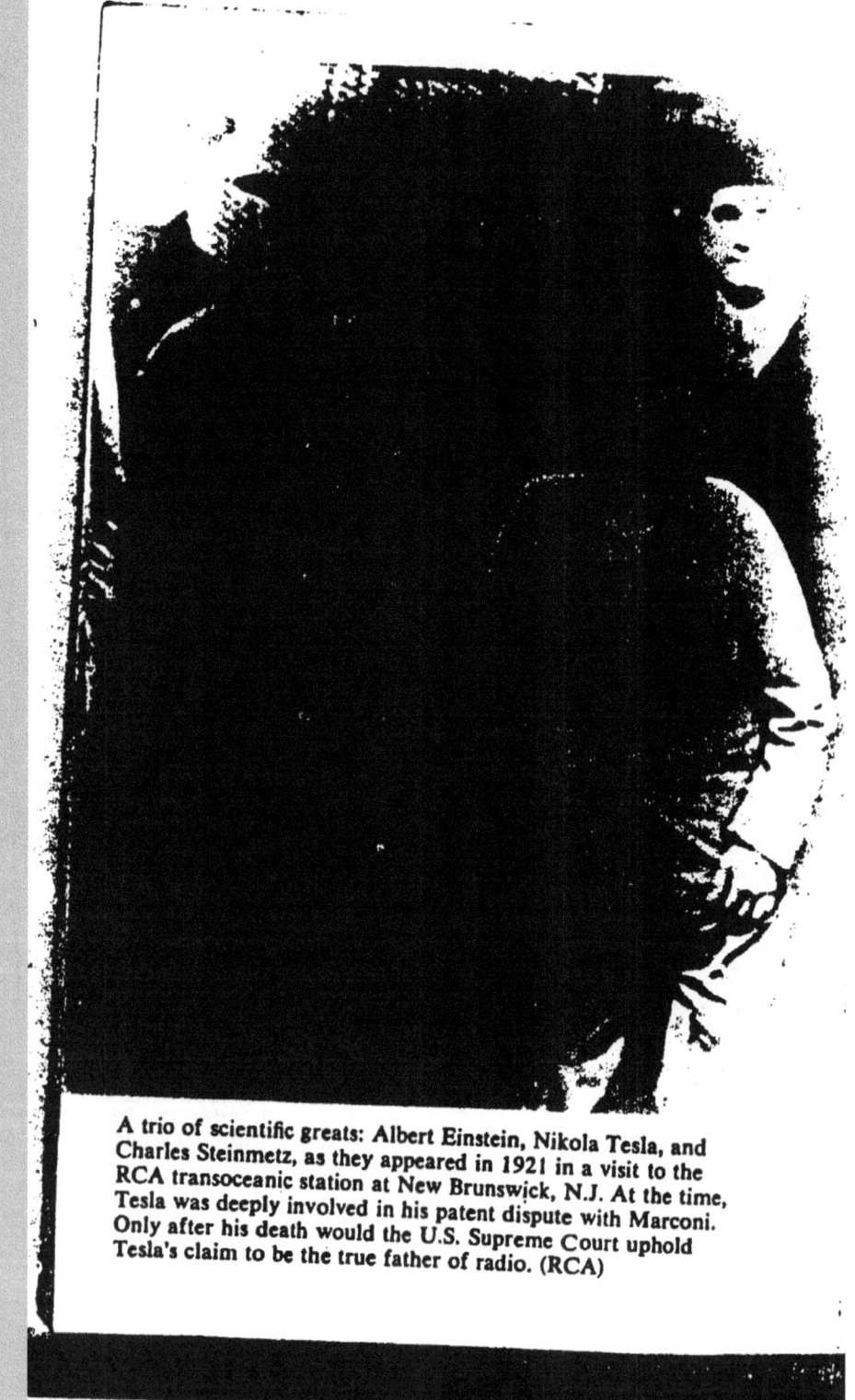

A trio of scientific greats: Albert Einstein, Nikola Tesla, and Charles Steinmetz, as they appeared in 1921 in a visit to the RCA transoceanic station at New Brunswick, N.J. At the time, Tesla was deeply involved in his patent dispute with Marconi. Only after his death would the U.S. Supreme Court uphold Tesla's claim to be the true father of radio. (RCA)

Tesla in his laboratory, 1898. The device shown is an unconnected coil illustrating the action of two resonating circuits of different frequencies—today one of the basic circuits used in computers. The pressure at the end of the coil facing the viewer (illuminated by streamers) is approximately one half million volts. (Courtesy L. Anderson)

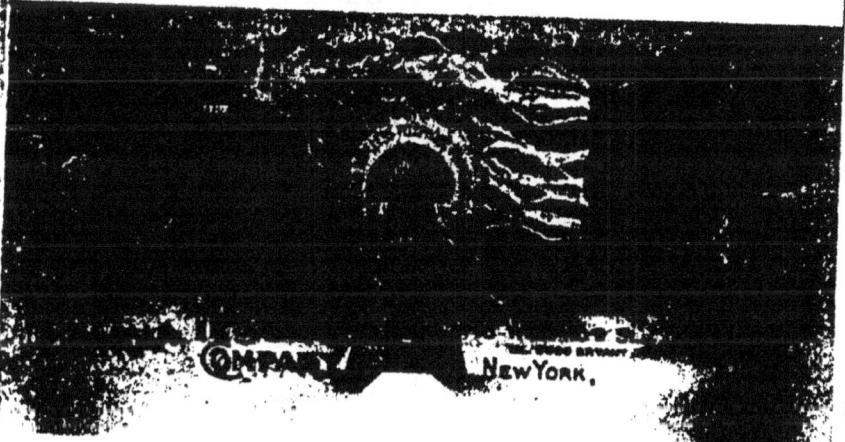

The letterhead of Tesla business stationery recalls some of his more important inventions. In the center is the Wardenclyffe tower as it was intended to look when finished. (Courtesy L. Anderson)

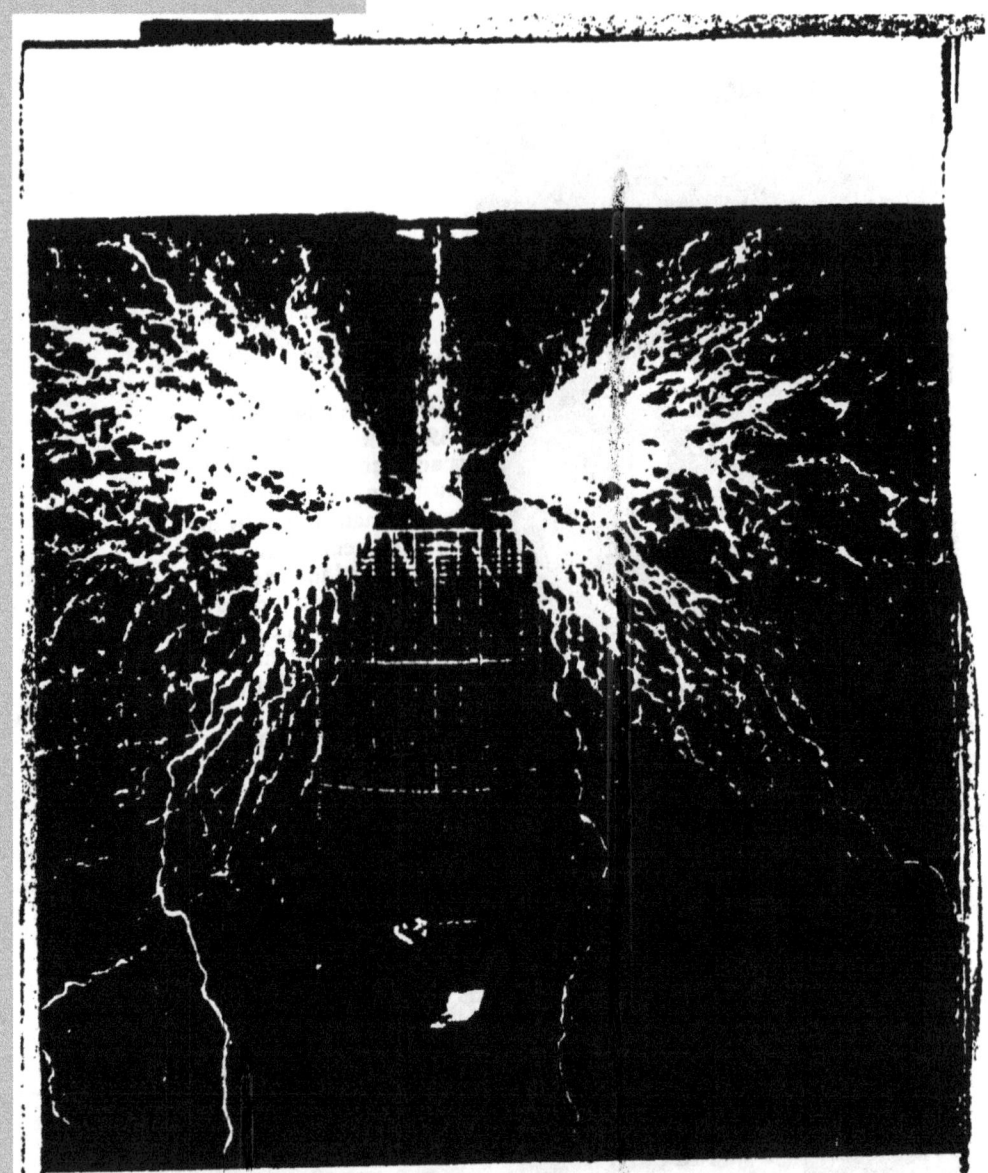

Discharge of several million volts cascading around Tesla in his Colorado Springs laboratory. The roar that accompanied such discharges could be heard ten miles away. (Burndy Library)

of low frequency, and would yield sinusoidal and continuous oscillations like those of an alternator.

"Taken in the narrowest significance of the term," however," Tesla wrote, "it is a resonant transformer which, besides possessing these qualities, is accurately proportioned to fit the globe and its electrical constants and properties, by virtue of which design it becomes highly efficient and effective in the wireless transmission of energy. Distance is then absolutely eliminated, there being *no diminution in the intensity of the transmitted impulses. It is even possible to make the actions increase with the distance from the plant* according to an exact mathematical law."[5]

Once this powerful equipment was built and the inventor began testing he was able to emulate the electrical fireworks of even the wildest mountain storms. When the transmitter was operating, lightning arresters in a twelve-mile radius from his station were bridged with continuous fiery arcs, stronger and more persistent than those produced by natural lightning.

For the first time he kept a careful daily diary in which he recorded every aspect of his research. And because visual effects were useful as well as thrilling, he devoted many hours to photographic experiments.

The equipment Tesla was perfecting would, he hoped, one day be adaptable for commercial use. But first, thousands of observations and delicate adjustments had to be made. He no longer trusted his legendary memory to store such a volume of information. His daily notes referred constantly to experiments that had failed to turn out as expected, and he would ask himself why. This process was at sharp variance with the one he claimed to have used throughout his earlier life. Now middle-aged, he may have felt his memory waning slightly. Certainly he felt driven by the pressures of his self-imposed deadline.

In his Colorado journal his lifelong fascination with visual phenomena is underscored. The flashing lights that he had always experienced on the screen of his mind were dramatically externalized, and his descriptions, among the mass of mathematical formulas, are detailed, loving, almost erotic in their lingering portrayal of the colors and grandeur of his Colorado electrical storms.[6]

Nights when experiments were being made with the magnifying transmitter the prairie sky exploded with sound and color. Even the earth seemed alive and the crash of thunder from the spark gap could be heard for miles. Butterflies were sucked into the vortex of the

28
Death and Transfiguration

The new government of King Peter, with broad popular support, confronted the Germans and refused to ratify the compromise agreement that had been made with Hitler by Prince Paul. Almost at once reprisals began.

On Palm Sunday, 1941, three hundred Luftwaffe bombers swept over the Yugoslav capital of Belgrade. Methodically they crisscrossed the city street by street, strafing everything that breathed. By noon 25,000 civilians were dead, and the wounded lay everywhere. Most public buildings were left in ruins, including the modern laboratory known as the Tesla Institute.

The combined armed forces of Germany, Italy, Hungary, and Bulgaria invaded the doomed country. Within only days the Yugoslav Army was crushed, and King Peter was sent to England for safety. His government-in-exile would operate from London for the remainder of World War II.

This, however, was only the beginning of the war for Yugoslavs. Accustomed to successive invasions for a thousand years, the people were resilient. The remnants of the Army and Communist factions withdrew into the mountains, from which they launched guerrilla attacks on the invaders. These armed fighters, men and women, were supplied with food grown by the old people and children remaining in undefended villages.

Against them the Nazis and Fascists carried out murderous reprisals. In the fishing villages and along the stony slopes of the Adriatic, half the people in every hamlet were systematically shot.

Soon, however, it became apparent to military strategists in the United States and England that, not only were Axis forces killing Yugoslavs, but rival guerrilla factions of monarchists and Communists had begun to vie for Allied support and were shooting each other as well as the invaders.

Col. Drazha Mihailović, a Serbian army officer, led a faction called Chetniks (the "Yugoslav Army in the Fatherland"), composed mainly of Serbian and Bosnian monarchists. With close ties to King

DEATH AND TRANSFIGURATION ⟷ 259

Peter, they became the first major resistance movement in Europe.¹ The initial British aid to Yugoslavia went to the Chetniks, but it was short-lived. The National Liberation Army or Partisans, led by Josip Broz Tito of the Communist Party, was swiftly rising to prominence.

Allied strategists knew little of Tito. It was said he had been left wounded on a battlefield in 1917 and captured by the Russians. There he was trained as a Communist leader and sent to France during the Spanish Civil War to aid the Loyalists or Republicans.

A Croat, Tito had little reason to love the monarchy, for he was imprisoned after returning to Yugoslavia. On release, he became active in organizing a metal workers' union and helped to build the Yugoslav labor movement. His emergence as head of the Partisans in World War II was that of a natural leader who inspired his fighters and maintained rigorous discipline. He was looking ahead to a time when the Slavs could rebuild a free and united country without oppression either by foreigners or kings.

Tito's goal was to set up committees of popular liberation after the Russian style, while Mihailović and the Chetniks favored local administrative authorities under the monarchy. Both factions kept on killing Germans and Italians but, unfortunately, they also continued murdering each other.²

Prof. Bogdan Raditsa*, then director of the information service of the Yugoslav Embassy in Washington, D.C., recalls, "The situation became rather complicated when Yugoslavia collapsed in 1941 and when, at the end of that year, a Royal Yugoslav Mission came to this country." It was composed of members of King Peter's government and the Ban (Governor) of Croatia, Dr. Ivan Šubašić. Sava Kosanović, Tesla's nephew, then a member of the Democratic Party, also arrived as a minister of the exiled government.

"As soon as Kosanović came to the States," says Professor Raditsa, "he tried to reorient Tesla from the exclusive Serbian policy, and he succeeded. Tesla, even before, never felt himself a Great Serbian chauvinist. He used to say, 'I am a Serb but my fatherland is Croatia.'"³

The conflict between Serbs and Croats in exile intensified as the war went on, paralyzing normal Slav diplomatic activities in London, Washington, and New York.

"Kosanović, though a Serb," recalls Raditsa, "was leading the struggle for a brotherhood between the Serbs and Croats against Fotić and many other Serb members of various Yugoslav missions.

*Raditsa belonged to a family in southern Croatia that had always favored a union of Croatians and Serbs.

DEATH AND TRANSFIGURATION ←→ 260

Thus he began using Tesla for the policy directed against the Great Serbians.

> "Tesla himself ... was not aware of the deep conflict between the Serbs and Croats, and as basically a scientist and in old age, he was very candid in politics."

Raditsa said he seemed happy that he finally had a man of his own blood near him in New York and noted that Tesla began to rely upon Kosanović's opinion on everything. During this period the inventor was receiving about $500 per month from the royal government as an honorarium.

Various political messages elicited from Tesla for home consumption, says Raditsa, were actually written by Kosanović.[4]

Toward the end of 1942 the Yugoslav Information Center was opened in New York in the Royal Mission headquarters on Fifth Avenue. Raditsa and Kosanović worked together at this office, issuing bulletins and other publications. But a crisis broke out when news reached them of the fighting between Mihailović and Tito.

> "Kosanović," he said, "joined Tito and began to popularize the National Liberation Movement for a new Yugoslavia. He had a terrible time to convince Tesla that monarchy was losing in Yugoslavia and that a new Yugoslavia was beginning to come out from the fratricidal civil war. As the largest majority of Serbs in Croatia were joining Tito, Kosanović convinced Tesla that he too should join the movement that was largely shared by the masses of the people, Serbs and Croats. So Tesla's message to the Serbs and Croats was written by Kosanović."[5]

On the walls of the Tesla Museum in Belgrade one may read a vastly enlarged photocopy of the words allegedly sent by Tesla to his embattled countrymen only months before his own death. American Vice-President Henry A. Wallace also had a hand in its drafting. Typewritten, it has many cross-outs and interlinings in Tesla's own handwriting yet the style is that of an ideologue, which the inventor was not:

> Out of this war ... a new world must be born, a world that would justify the sacrifices offered by humanity. This ... must be a world in which there shall be no exploitation of the weak by the strong, of the good by the evil, where there will be no humiliation of the poor by the violence of the rich; where the products of the intellect, science, and art will serve society for the betterment and beautification of life, and not the individuals for achieving wealth. This new world shall not be a

DEATH AND TRANSFIGURATION ⟷ 261

world of the downtrodden and humiliated, but of free men and free nations, equal in dignity and respect for man.

The inventor's name also appeared on another message—sent to the Soviet Academy of Sciences on October 12, 1941, urging joint struggle against the Axis powers by Russia, Great Britain, and America, in aid of the revolutionary struggle of the Yugoslav people. This message is not to be seen in the Museum, however, presumably because nostalgia Russian-style has ceased to be politic.

Kosanović became chairman of the Yugoslav Economic Mission advocating a New Yugoslav federation versus the centralistic prewar royalist Yugoslavia. This new organization also began working for a new Central East European Federation. Raditsa too became a member of the Tito movement.

King Peter was desperately seeking for Mihailović the support of President Franklin Delano Roosevelt and Prime Minister Winston Churchill, as well as that of his own Uncle Bertie, who was King George VI of England. The British, at first sympathetic to the Chetnik cause, began to change as they received reports of the aggressive actions of Tito's Partisans.

In 1942 King Peter visited Washington to intercede with FDR. Yugoslav pilots were being trained in Tennessee. FDR told him that America would send airplanes to the Chetniks as soon as they could be spared from the war in the Middle East. The monarch visited New York City, attending a large reception for the American Friends of Yugoslavia at the Colony Club. The Colony, the first female socialites' club in America, had been founded at the inspiration of energetic Anne Morgan. She attended the function, as did the King's mother, Queen Marie, and Mrs. Roosevelt. It was the sort of affair Tesla himself would have delighted in had he not been weak and ill. So King Peter went to him.

In his diaries (*A King's Heritage*), under date July 8, 1942, the young Peter II writes: "I visited Dr. Nicola Tesla, the world-famous Yugoslav-American scientist, in his apartment in the Hotel New Yorker. After I had greeted him the aged scientist said: 'It is my greatest honor. I am glad you are in your youth, and I am content that you will be a great ruler. I believe I will live until you come back to a free Yugoslavia. From your father you have received his last words: "Guard Yugoslavia." I am proud to be a Serbian and a Yugoslav. Our people cannot perish. Preserve the unity of all Yugoslavs—the Serbs, the Croats, and Slovenes.'"

DEATH AND TRANSFIGURATION ⟷ 262

The King added that he was deeply touched and that both he and Dr. Tesla had wept. He then visited Columbia University, to be warmly welcomed by President Nicholas Murray Butler and to find another link with his own country in the Pupin Physics Laboratory.

Returning to Washington, he was assured by FDR that food, clothing, arms, and ammunition would be dropped over Yugoslavia. But he was shocked when, in 1943, the British Mission in Yugoslavia made official contact with Tito. Peter asked to be parachuted into his country, but Churchill demurred. Tito openly accused Mihailović of being a traitor.[6]

At the Teheran Conference in November there occurred, largely at Churchill's instance, what the King described as a "fatal change" of Allied policy. It was decided that "the basic force fighting the Germans in Yugoslavia recognized by the Allies was the National Liberation Army, under the command of Tito, and the Partisan force received full recognition as an Allied Army. Mihailović was thus denied and abandoned."[7]

Winston Churchill overnight became a hero of modern Yugoslavia. And when the young monarch frantically wrote to FDR for support, the ailing President replied urging him to accept Churchill's advice "as if it was my own." Within months Roosevelt died.

Tesla's nephew Kosanović, along with certain other diplomatic representatives of King Peter, had been dismissed by the monarch at the height of the 1942 crisis. He often told Bogdan Raditsa in those days that he felt Tesla had been terribly shocked by his nephew's exclusion from the royal government. In fact, Kosanović believed that the inventor's death was actually precipitated by his own "setback."

"He thought," Kosanović repeatedly told Raditsa, "that I was punished, and that eventually I would be arrested or something of the kind, but I succeeded to convince him that it was inevitable in politics."[8]

During this period Kosanović was frank in saying that he tried to keep Tesla from seeing members of the royal government. Ambassador Fotić had become "the enemy" since he still favored a Great Serbian policy as opposed to the changes ahead. Tesla's relationship with this old friend became "lukewarm."

"There is no doubt," says Professor Raditsa, "that the whole internecine tragedy of Yugoslavia from 1941 to 1943 must have had a rather depressing impact upon Tesla. Very often he would ask me, could I explain to him what was going on among us, and why we cannot agree...."

DEATH AND TRANSFIGURATION ⟷ 263

After the war, Mihailović would be executed by a "People's Court" for alleged collaboration with the enemy, and the Republic of Yugoslavia declared to exist, with Tito as President for life and the Communists firmly in charge.

A count of Yugoslavian casualties at the end of World War II disclosed that 2 million persons had died; tragically, many thousands had been killed by fellow Yugoslavs.

"After the war," recalls Professor Raditsa, "Kosanović became a minister in the Tito-Subašić Government, and I was his assistant in the Ministry of Information from 1944 to 1945, when I left the country, for I couldn't become a Communist. Later on in 1946, Sava Kosanović became Tito's ambassador in Washington but I never saw him again after I left Belgrade in October of 1945. Kosanović had accepted totally the Communist system in Yugoslavia and remained loyal until his death."

There had not been a time in ten centuries when the Yugoslavs had not been ruled and ransacked by invaders—by Venetians, Romans, Turks, Bulgars, Austrians, Hungarians, Germans, Italians, when they were not living under threat of torture, prison, or violent death. Now a marvelous truth began to dawn upon them: that they were free, in a manner of speaking.

Tesla would not live to see this. Whether he could ever have accepted the new government, with its Soviet-type Constitution and a Soviet alliance, whether he could ever have accepted the permanent exile of his beloved monarch, are unanswerable questions.

Unfortunately, however, all this was to have a bearing on how he would be remembered in the West. The fading of his scientific reputation, the forgetfulness of Americans in the postwar period, resulted in large degree from the disappearance of most of his scientific papers behind that new Cold War phenomenon, the Iron Curtain.

In 1948 Yugoslavia ceased to be an Iron Curtain country, declaring its independence from the Soviet doctrine of "limited sovereignty." America and her allies then were generous in sending economic and military aid to the Slavs; but the damage had been done. America had not raced to Tito's wartime support with the alacrity that Churchill had shown. In the future it would not be made easy for American scholars to draw on Yugoslav sources to document the achievements of Nikola Tesla.

The inventor became very feeble in the winter of 1942. His fear of germs was so obsessive that even his closest friends were

DEATH AND TRANSFIGURATION ⟷ 264

required to stand at a distance, like the subjects of a neurotic Tudor. (Pigeon germs did not seem to worry him.) He had heart trouble and suffered occasionally from fainting spells. No longer able to feed his beloved birds, he often relied upon a young man named Charles Hausler, who owned racing pigeons, to take care of them for him.

Hausler had worked for Tesla in this capacity from around 1928 onward, his job being to go to the New York Public Library at noon each day with grain and then to walk around the four sides of the building looking for young or injured birds on window sills or behind large statues. He would take them to Tesla's hotel for rest and recuperation. Then, he has recalled, "I would release them at the library for him." He remembered that the cages in Tesla's rooms had been built by a fine carpenter— "as Mr. Tesla was in all his doings it had to be done right." The pigeons also enjoyed a curtained shower bath.

Hausler and Tesla spent many hours together, talking mostly of pigeons. Once Tesla confided to him that "Thomas Edison could not be trusted." The boy remembered his employer as "a very kind and considerate human person," and there was one incident that stood out in his mind long afterward. "He had a large box or container in his room near the pigeon cages and he told me to be very careful not to disturb the box," said Hausler, "as it contained something that could destroy an airplane in the sky and he had hopes of presenting it to the world." He believed it probably was stored in the cellar of the hotel later."

On a bitter day in early January 1943, Tesla called his other messenger boy, Kerrigan, and gave him a sealed envelope addressed to Mr. Samuel Clemens, 35 South Fifth Avenue, New York City. The boy set forth into the whipping wind and searched fruitlessly for the number. As it turned out, this had been the address of Tesla's first laboratory; but now South Fifth Avenue was West Broadway, and no one by the name of Samuel Clemens lived in the area.

Kerrigan made his way back to the Hotel New Yorker and reported to the sick man. In a weak voice, Tesla explained that Clemens was the famous Mark Twain and that everyone knew of him. He sent Kerrigan forth once more, and this time asked him also to take care of the pigeons. The perturbed messenger fed the birds and then consulted his supervisor, who told him that Mark Twain had been dead for twenty-five years. Once again Kerrigan trudged through the cold afternoon to Tesla's rooms, where he explained and tried to return the envelope.

DEATH AND TRANSFIGURATION ←→ 265

The inventor was indignant and refused to hear that the humorist was dead. "He was in my room last night," he said. "He sat in that chair and talked to me for an hour. He is having financial difficulties and needs my help. So—don't come back until you have delivered that envelope." Once again the messenger went to his supervisor and together they opened the envelope. It contained a blank sheet of paper wrapped around twenty five-dollar bills—enough to help an old friend through a little fainting spell.

On the fourth of January, the inventor, although very weak, went to his office to make an experiment that George Scherff was interested in. Scherff dropped in to help him prepare for it. The work was interrupted, however, when Tesla felt a recurrence of some sharp pains in his chest.

Refusing medical aid, he returned to his hotel. Next day a maid came in and cleaned. As she left, he asked her to put the *Do Not Disturb* sign on his door to keep visitors away, and not to bother cleaning. The sign remained there the following day and the one after that.

Early on the morning of January 8, Alice Monaghan, a maid, ignored the sign and entered the apartment to find the inventor dead in bed, his sunken, "emaciated face composed." Assistant Medical Examiner H. W. Wembly examined the body, placed the time of death as 10:30 P.M. on January 7, 1943, and gave his opinion that the cause of death had been coronary thrombosis. Tesla had died in his sleep, and the examiner noted that he had found "No suspicious circumstances." The inventor was eighty-six years of age.

Kenneth Swezey was notified at once; and at ten o'clock that morning he telephoned to Dr. Rado at New York University. King Peter's headquarters, then at 745 Fifth Avenue, was advised by the professor. Tesla's nephew, Kosanović, then wartime president of the Eastern and Central European Planning Board for the Balkan countries, also was notified.

Then the FBI was called. Swezey and Kosanović summoned a locksmith and Tesla's safe was opened and the contents examined.

The body was removed to the Frank E. Campbell Funeral Home at Madison Avenue and 81st Street and a sculptor was engaged by Hugo Gernsback to prepare a death mask of the inventor.

Just before Tesla's death, Eleanor Roosevelt had tried to intercede in his behalf with President Roosevelt—perhaps with the idea of conferring some honor upon him. In the Tesla Museum at Belgrade three brief notes on White House stationery may be read. On

January 1, at the request of author Louis Adamić, Mrs. Roosevelt had promised to ask the President to write to Tesla and said that she herself would call on him on her next trip to New York. The second note is headed, "Memo for Mrs. Roosevelt" and is signed FDR: "I was having this looked into but the papers yesterday carried the story that Dr. Tesla had died. Therefore I am returning the enclosures herewith." A third note of January 11 from Eleanor Roosevelt to Adamić forwards the President's message and adds her sorrow at learning of the inventor's death.

Adamić wrote a moving eulogy to Tesla that was read by New York Mayor Fiorello H. LaGuardia over station WNYC on January 10.[u] Meanwhile the extreme tensions between Serb and Croat factions in the United States were making the planning of funeral services difficult. The body lay in state but, according to an unpublished letter of O'Neill's, "only twelve people, some of whom were newspaper reporters," came to view it.

When state services were held at four o'clock on January 12, in the Cathedral of St. John the Divine, however, more than two thousand people crowded in. Serbs and Croats were seated on opposing sides of the cathedral, Bishop William T. Manning having exacted from both factions a promise of no political speeches. The service was begun in English by Bishop Manning and concluded in Serbian by the Very Rev. Dusan Sukletović.

Among Balkan diplomats present were Ambassador Fotić, the Governor of Croatia, a former Prime Minister of Yugoslavia, and the Minister of Food and Reconstruction. In the front row with Kosanović, chief mourner and head of the important new trade mission, sat Swezey. Dr. Rado had been too ill to attend as an honorary pallbearer.

Figures important in American science and industry who did attend as honorary pallbearers included Professor Edwin H. Armstrong, Dr. E. F. W. Alexanderson of General Electric, Dr. Harvey Rentschler of Westinghouse, engineer Gano Dunn, and W. H. Barton, curator of the Hayden Planetarium of the American Museum of Natural History. Newbold Morris, president of the New York City Council, headed this group.

When word of Tesla's death spread abroad to war-stricken Europe, telegrams of tribute and sorrow began pouring in from scientists and governmental leaders alike. In the United States three Nobel prizewinners in physics, Millikan, Compton, and James Franck, joined in a eulogy to the inventor as "one of the outstanding intellects of the world who paved the way for many of the important technological developments of modern times."

The President and Mrs. Roosevelt expressed their gratitude for Tesla's contributions "to science and industry and to this country." Vice-President Wallace, in the spirit of the new Yugoslavia, declared that, "In Nikola Tesla's death the common man loses one of his best friends."

Although Louis Adamić wrongly eulogized Tesla as one who had cared nothing for money, he could not have been more accurate when he said that Tesla was not really dead: "The real, important part of Tesla lives in his achievement, which is great, almost beyond calculation, and an integral part of our civilization, our daily lives, our current war effort.... His life is a triumph...."[12]

Among the honors that had come to Tesla in his life were many academic degrees from American and foreign universities; the John Scott Medal, the Edison Medal, and various awards from European governments. In September 1943 the Liberty ship *Nikola Tesla* was launched, an honor that would have pleased the scientist. But not until 1975 was he inducted into the National Inventors Hall of Fame.

Eight months after Tesla's death, the U.S. Supreme Court handed down the decision that he had been confident would come eventually—ruling that he was the inventor of radio.

His body was taken to Ferncliffe Cemetery at Ardsley-on-the-Hudson in the deep cold of the winter afternoon. In the car that followed the hearse rode Swezey and Kosanović. The inventor's remains were cremated and his ashes later returned to the land of his birth.*

In almost every nation in the world, the fighting and dying continued.

---

*Charlotte Muzar, formerly secretary to Sava N. Kosanović, carried Tesla's ashes to the Tesla Museum in Belgrade in 1957. Throughout the years Kosanović had spoken of leaving the ashes in America and had hoped an appropriate memorial to the inventor would be raised in the United States as their resting place.
—Archives, Tesla Memorial Society.

29
The Missing Papers

In addition to his acknowledged achievements, Tesla left a legacy of riddles. To pose only three of the most major: Was his unrealized concept for the wireless transmission of energy through the Earth scientifically valid? What actually was he doing in his experimentation with death/disintegrator beam weapons? And what became of his unpatented research papers and other sensitive documents in the days immediately following his death?

In the category of subquestions, what turn of affairs rekindled the intense interest of the U.S. intelligence establishment in Tesla's work (as something surely did) in the late 1940's?

Like Einstein he had been an outsider and, like Edison, a wide-ranging generalist. As he himself had said, he had the "boldness of ignorance." Where others stopped short, aware of what could not be done, he continued. The survival of such mutants and polymaths as Tesla tends to be discouraged by modern scientific guilds. Whether either he or Edison could have flourished in today's milieu is conjectural.

The example set by Tesla has always been particularly inspiring to the lone runner. At the same time, however, his legacy to establishment science is profound for his research, although sometimes esoteric, was almost always sweeping in its potential to transform society. His contribution was major rather than incremental. His turbine failed in part because it would have required fundamental changes by whole industries. Alternating current triumphed only after it had overcome the resistance of an entire industry.

But there was an unfortunate corollary to Tesla's lone battles with the scientific-industrial establishment. Since he was part of no group or institution, he had no colleagues with whom to discuss work in progress, no formal, accessible repository for his research notes and papers. He worked not just in private, but—his love of flamboyant announcements to the press notwithstanding—in secret. Thus any inventions which he did not patent or give freely to the world were more or less shrouded in mystery. And, because of the handling of the

268

papers he left behind after his death, the range of his achievement continues to remain a partial mystery.

If this has been frustrating to the scientists who have succeeded Tesla, it has at least been stimulating. After a period of obscurity, the one hundredth anniversary of his birth in July 1956 brought an international reawakening to the importance of the inventor's life and genius. Interest in his work, fired by a growing awareness of the riddles surrounding it, has been escalating ever since, almost as if he had been reborn in his true psychological age.

He was honored by centennial celebrations in America and Europe. The American Institute of Electrical Engineers dedicated its fall meeting in Chicago to a review of his life and inventions. Commemorative programs were arranged by the Institute of Radio Engineers, the Chicago Museum of Science and Industry, the Franklin Institute, and various universities, the Tesla Society playing an active role in such recognition. Permanent memorials in the form of scholarships and medals were proposed and exhibits presented by science museums. Special ceremonies were conducted at Niagara Falls, and a statue was later erected in his honor on Goat Island, a gift from the people of Yugoslavia. Chicago, reminded by attorney/author Elmer Gertz that it should be eternally grateful to him for having made the Columbian Exposition of 1893 the "wonder of the globe," dedicated a new public school to Tesla's memory.

The inventor's old colleagues of the AIEE journeyed to Europe to attend more celebrations, statue unveilings, and dedications in his honor. The International Electrotechnical Commission in Munich took formal action, making his name an international scientific unit, the tesla joining such historic electrical symbols as farad, volt, ampere, and ohm.[1]

As the exploration of space accelerated, so did interest in Tesla, especially from the standpoint of beam weaponry and microwave work. In America, Russia, Canada, and various other countries, projects in his name or derived from his pioneering, from weather-control to nuclear fusion, began to attract scientific attention. Some were just the shoestring efforts of loners, their laboratories old Quonset huts. Some were top secret and financed by enormous budgets.

Tesla's year of secret experiments at Colorado Springs in 1899 provided the basic impetus for much of this new exploration. His *Colorado Springs Notes,** when they appeared in English in 1978

*This book may be ordered from Nolit, Terazije, 27, Belgrade, Yugoslavia (about $40).

under the imprint of the Tesla Museum at Belgrade, were eagerly awaited by many scientists. But even this work left important questions unanswered.

The bulk of his papers having vanished from America, reliable information was harder to come by than the recurring rumors of conspiracy, espionage, and patent theft. Scientists thought it strange that some aspects of his Colorado Springs research found in scattered sources did not appear in the Yugoslav-published *Notes*. Only by piecing together fragmentary information could the magnitude of his experiments be comprehended.

Around 1928 O'Neill, by merest chance, had happened to see a legal advertisement in a New York newspaper announcing that six boxes placed in storage by Nikola Tesla would be sold by the storage warehouse for unpaid bills. Feeling that such material should be preserved, he went to the inventor and asked permission to try to obtain funds to reclaim the material.

"Tesla hit the ceiling," he recalled. "He assured me he was well able to take care of his own affairs.... He forbid me to buy them or do anything in any way about them."

Shortly after the inventor died, O'Neill got in touch with Sava Kosanović, told him about the boxes, and urged him to protect them. He was never able to get a positive statement from Kosanović that he had obtained the boxes and examined the contents. "He gave evasive assurances that there was no reason for me to worry..."

Others too were interested in the papers. A young American engineer engaged in war work consulted Tesla on a ballistics engineering problem because he could not get time on an overworked computer, and Tesla's mind was known to offer the nearest thing to it. Soon he became fascinated with Tesla's scientific papers and was allowed to take batches of them home to his hotel room where he and another American engineer pored over them each night. They were returned the next day, a procedure which continued for about two weeks prior to the inventor's death.

Tesla had received offers to work for Germany and Russia. After the inventor died, both engineers became concerned that critical scientific information might fall into foreign hands and alerted United States security agencies and high government officials.

The relevant records that I have obtained from federal agencies under the Freedom of Information Act reveal strange twistings and inconsistencies in the handling of the inventor's estate. Tesla left tons of papers, barrels and boxes full of them. But he left no will. He was survived by five nieces and nephews, of whom two lived in America at the time of his death.

Curiously, the FBI released his estate to the Office of Alien Property, which promptly sealed the contents. Since Tesla was an American citizen, the OAP's concern in the matter was hard to justify. After a court hearing, however, the estate was released to Ambassador Kosanović, one of the heirs.

Swezey, who also had hoped to write a biography of Tesla (his death intervened), received the following account in 1963 from a former aide of Ambassador Kosanović's:

"Back in 1943... when Tesla died, it was a matter of very short time when Mr. K was issued a certificate from or by the Office of Custodian of Alien Property conveying to Mr. K full rights to the Tesla papers.... he had them all packed up and sent off to the Manhattan Storage Company where they remained until ready for packing and shipping off to Yugoslavia in 1952. Mr. K paid for storage charges.... All this time the certificate from the Alien Property Office was in my possession (in case of need)....

"You will perhaps remember that a number of times Mr. K mentioned the fact that the custodian at the storage warehouse told him that some government guys were in to microfilm some of the papers.... when we opened the safe in the present museum building (in Belgrade, Yugoslavia) the bunch of keys, which was the last thing Mr. K flung into the safe at the New Yorker Hotel before the combination was re-set to a new combination, were not found in the safe, but in an entirely different box. Also the gold medal (the Edison Medal) was missing from the safe.... Anyway, for years and years Mr. K was bothered by the fact that Tesla papers had been gone thru and just before his departure from Washington in 1949-50(?) he decided to follow my suggestion to call Edgar J. Hoover [sic] and ask him. Mr. Hoover denied categorically that the FBI had gone into the papers...."

The aide said Tesla had told his nephew that "he wished to leave his works, property, etc., to his native country." (Not only is this uncorroborated but the papers were in English.)

Immediately after Tesla's death an exchange of telegrams flew between FBI Agent Foxworth, of the field division of the New York Bureau and the director of the New York Bureau of the FBI. The day following discovery of the body, Agent Foxworth reported:

"Experiments and research of Nikola Tesla, deceased. Espionage—M. Nikola Tesla, one of the world's outstanding scientists in the electrical field, died January seventh, nineteen forty three at the

Hotel New Yorker, New York City. During his lifetime, he conducted many experiments in connection with the wireless transmission of electrical power and ... what is commonly called the death ray. According to information furnished by X [name deleted], New York City, the notes and records of Tesla's experiments and formulae together with designs of machinery ... are among Tesla's personal effects, and no steps have been taken to preserve them or to keep them from falling into hands of people ... unfriendly to the war effort of the United Nations...." (The FBI was, however, advised by the office of Vice-President Henry A. Wallace that the government was "vitally interested" in preserving Tesla's papers.)

Bloyce D. Fitzgerald, "an electrical engineer who had been quite close to Tesla during his lifetime," continued Foxworth, "advised the New York office that on January seventh, nineteen forty three, Sava Kosanović, George Clark, who is in charge of the museum and laboratory for RCA, and Kenneth Swezey ... went to Tesla's rooms in the New Yorker [author's note: the correct date would have been January 8], and with the assistance of a locksmith broke into a safe which Tesla had in his rooms in which he kept some of his valuable papers.... Within the last month, Tesla told Fitzgerald that his experiments in connection with the wireless transmission of electrical power had been completed and perfected.

"Fitzgerald also knows that Tesla had conceived and designed a revolutionary type of torpedo which is not presently in use by any of the nations. It is Fitzgerald's belief that this design has not been made available to any nation up to the present time. From statements made to Fitzgerald by Tesla, he knows that the complete plans, specifications and explanation of the basic theories of these things are some place in the personal effects of Tesla. He also knows there is a working model of Tesla's, which cost more than ten thousand dollars to build, in a safety deposit box belonging to Tesla at the Governor Clinton Hotel, and Fitzgerald believes this model has to do with the so-called death ray or the wireless transmission of electrical current.

Tesla has also told Fitzgerald in past conversations that he has some eighty trunks in different places containing transcripts and plans having to do with experiments conducted by him. Bureau is requested to advise immediately what, if any, action should be taken concerning this matter by the New York Field Division."[8]

Kosanović later reported to Walter Gorsuch of the Office of Alien Property in New York that he first went to Tesla's rooms with the other men to search for a will. After the safe was opened, Swezey took from it a book containing the testimonials sent to Tesla on his seventy-fifth birthday, while Kosanović took from the room three pictures of Tesla. According to the manager of the New Yorker Hotel and Kosanović, nothing else was removed. The safe was closed under a new combination, which combination was in Kosanović's exclusive possession.

On January 9, Gorsuch of OAP and Fitzgerald went to the New Yorker Hotel and seized all of Tesla's property, consisting of about two truckloads of material, sealed it and transferred it to the Manhattan Storage and Warehouse Company. It was added to about thirty barrels and bundles that had been there since about 1934, and these too were sealed under orders of the OAP.

In addition to the question of the legitimacy of Alien Property's involvement in the case is the question of why Kosanović was allowed to have access to the safe's combination, from which he later claimed the Edison Medal had vanished. Tesla's American naturalization papers, which he so prized that he always kept them in his safe, may now be seen at the Tesla Museum in Belgrade; but it is not known what other papers or objects were in the safe.

The Washington Bureau of the FBI went so far as to advise the New York Bureau "to discreetly take the matter up with the State's Attorney in New York City with the view to possibly taking Kosanovich into custody on a burglary charge and obtaining the various papers which Kosanovich is reported to have taken from Tesla's safe." New York was also told to contact the Surrogate Court so stops could be placed against all of Tesla's effects, so that no one could enter them without an FBI agent being present, and New York was to keep Washington advised of all developments.[3]

The idea of arresting the Yugoslav ambassador was quickly dropped. And very soon the Washington headquarters made a curious decision. Edward A. Tamm of the FBI in Washington advised D. M. Ladd of that Bureau that the whole matter was being turned over to the Custodian of Alien Property; and Tamm noted, "There appears to be no need for us to mess around in it."[4]

Soon the well-known electrical engineer Dr. John G. Trump, who was serving as a technical aide to the National Defense Research Committee of the Office of Scientific Research and Development, was asked to participate in an examination of Tesla's scientific papers. Present at the Manhattan Warehouse & Storage Company in addition to Dr. Trump were Willis George, Office of Naval Intelligence, Third Naval District, Edward Palmer, chief yeoman, USNR, and John J. Corbett, chief yeoman, USNR.

Dr. Trump reported afterward that no examination was made of the vast amount of Tesla's property that had been in the basement of the New Yorker Hotel for ten years prior to his death, or of any of his papers except those in his immediate possession at the time of death. It should be remembered that Tesla's scientific reputation had been in eclipse for a number of years and that there had been many efforts to discredit his claims in radio, robotry, and alternating current. Dr. Trump was a busy man, just as the staff of the FBI was stretched thin by its preoccupation with investigating wartime sabotage.

"As a result of this examination," wrote Dr. Trump, "it is my considered opinion that there exist among Dr. Tesla's papers and possessions no scientific notes, descriptions of hitherto unrevealed methods or devices, or actual apparatus which could be of significant value to this country or which would constitute a hazard in unfriendly hands. I can therefore see no technical or military reason why further custody of the property should be retained."

He added: "For your records, there has been removed to your office a file of various written material by Dr. Tesla which covers typically and fairly completely the ideas with which he was concerned during his later years. These documents are enumerated and briefly abstracted in the attachment to this letter."

In closing Dr. Trump said: "It should be no discredit to this distinguished engineer and scientist, whose solid contributions to the electrical art were made at the beginning of the present century, to report that his thoughts and efforts during at least the past fifteen years were primarily of a speculative, philosophical, and somewhat promotional character—often concerned with the production and wireless transmission of power—but did not include new sound, workable principles or methods for realizing such results."

The file (of which Dr. Trump's notes were only an abstract) consisted apparently of either photostats or microfilm made by the naval officers present, and the original papers apparently remained in storage, later to be transmitted to Yugoslavia. The examination had failed to disclose any alien-owned property subject to the vesting power of the Alien Property Custodian under the Trading with the Enemy Act. Tesla's papers and personal effects were released in

February of 1943 for disposition by Kosanović, the administrator of his estate.

Dr. Trump's abstract included the following:

"*Art of Telegeodynamics, or Art of Producing Terrestrial Motions at Distance*—This document, in the form of a letter dated June 12, 1940, to the Westinghouse Electric & Manufacturing Co., proposes a method for the transmission of large amounts of power over vast distances by means of mechanical vibrations of the earth's crust. The source of power is a mechanical or electromechanical device bolted to some rocky protuberance and imparting power at a resonance frequency of the earth's crust. The proposed scheme appears to be completely visionary and unworkable. Westinghouse's reply indicates their polite rejection....

"*New Art of Projecting Concentrated Non-Dispersive Energy through Natural Media*—This undated document by Tesla describes an electrostatic method of producing very high voltages and capable of very great power. This generator is used to accelerate charged particles, presumably electrons. Such a beam of high-energy electrons passing through air is the 'concentrated nondispersive' means by which energy is transmitted through natural media. As a component of this apparatus there is described an open-ended vacuum tube within which the electrons are first accelerated.

"The proposed scheme bears some relation to present means for producing high-energy cathode rays by the cooperative use of a high-voltage electrostatic generator and an evacuated electron acceleration tube. It is well known, however, that such devices, while of scientific and medical interest, are incapable of the transmission of large amounts of power in nondispersed beams over long distances. Tesla's disclosures in this memorandum would not enable the construction of workable combinations of generator and tube even of limited power, though the general elements of such a combination are succinctly described.

"*A Method of Producing Powerful Radiations*—an undated memorandum in Tesla's handwriting describing 'a new process of generating powerful rays or radiations.' This memorandum reviews the works of Lenard and Crookes, describes Tesla's work on the production of high voltages, and finally in the last paragraph gives the only description of the invention contained in the memorandum.... 'Briefly stated, my new simplified process of generating powerful rays consists

THE MISSING PAPERS ←→ 276

in creating through the medium of a high-speed jet of suitable fluid a vacuous space around a terminal of a circuit and supplying the same with currents of the required tension and volume.'"

Long afterward in a letter to a colleague, Dr. Trump told what happened when he visited the Hotel Governor Clinton to examine the "device" stored in its vault, presumably the same box remembered by the messenger boy in Tesla's room.

"Tesla had warned the management that this 'device' was a secret weapon," said Dr. Trump, "and it would detonate if opened by an unauthorized person. Upon opening the vault and indicating the package containing the secret weapon, the hotel manager and employees promptly left the scene." The federal agents who had come along also pulled back, the better to give him the sole distinction of opening the parcel.

It was wrapped in brown paper and tied with a string. He remembered hesitating, thinking how beautiful the weather was outdoors, and pondering on why he was not outside too.

He lifted the parcel onto a table and, mustering his courage, snipped the string with his pocket knife. He removed the wrapping. Inside was a handsome polished wooden chest bound with brass. It required a final effort of courage to raise the hinged lid.

Inside stood a multidecade resistance box of the type used for Wheatstone bridge resistance measurements—a common standard item to be found in every electrical laboratory before the turn of the century!

Why had Tesla seen fit to terrify the staff and management of the hotel with this harmless object for so many years? Perhaps he had become so accustomed to having his hotel bills paid behind his back (believing that the hotels, honored to have him living there, had routinely dismissed the billings), that he was insulted when the Governor Clinton brashly demanded its $400.

Although the FBI closed its Tesla file in 1943, it didn't seem to want to stay closed. It was reopened in 1957 when an informant complained that a New York couple were issuing newsletters containing "information pertaining to flying saucers and interplanetary matters" and exploiting the inventor's name and fame. They allegedly claimed that Tesla's engineers, after his death, had completed a "Tesla Set," a radio device for interplanetary communication, that the device had been placed in operation in 1950 and since then Tesla engineers had been in close touch with alien spaceships. Once again the FBI decided no action was warranted and the file was closed.

THE MISSING PAPERS ←→ 277

Swezey had never put much credence in the "secret weapon" rumors and had written to an inquirer: "Because Tesla was a recluse, and himself liked to talk in mystifying terms during his later years, I think many legends have been built up about the dozens of ideas he had evolved but which were not permitted by others to see the light of day."

He said he had known the inventor well for two decades before his death: "Tesla's greatest genius flamed up during a dozen or so years just before and slightly after the turn of the century. What he did after that may have carried the germs of some of the developments we are witnessing today, but he had not carried any of them—at least on paper or in any other tangible form—to the point of practicality..."

Perhaps, but between 1945 and 1947 an interesting exchange of letters and cables occurred among the Air Technical Service Command at Wright Field, Ohio, in whose Equipment Laboratory much top-secret research was being performed, Military Intelligence in Washington, and the Office of Alien Property—subject, files of the late Nikola Tesla.

On August 21, 1945, the Air Technical Service Command requested permission from the commanding general of the U.S. Army Air Force in Washington, D.C., for Private Bloyce D. Fitzgerald to go to Washington for a period of seven days "for the purpose of securing property clearance on enemy impounded property."

On September 5, 1945, Colonel Holliday of the Equipment Laboratory, Propulsion and Accessories Subdivision, wrote to Lloyd L. Shaulis of the OAP in Washington, confirming a conversation with Fitzgerald and asking for photostatic copies of the exhibits annotated by Trump from the estate of Tesla. It was stated that the material would be used "in connection with projects for National Defense by this department," and that all of it would be returned in a reasonable length of time.

That was the last time that the Office of Alien Property or any other federal agency in the United States admitted to having possession of Tesla's papers on beam weaponry. Shaulis wrote to Colonel Holliday on September 11, 1945, saying, "The materials requested have been forwarded to Air Technical Service Command in care of Lt. Robert E. Houle. These data are made available to the Army Air Force by this office for use in experiments; please return them." They were never returned.

These were the full photostatic copies, not merely the abstracts. OAP has no record of *how many* copies were made by those who

THE MISSING PAPERS ⟷ 278

examined the files with Dr. Trump. The Navy has no record of Tesla's papers; no federal archives have a record of them.

Curiously, four months after the photostats had been sent to Wright Field, Col. Ralph Doty, the chief of Military Intelligence in Washington wrote James Markham of Alien Property indicating that they had never been received: "This office is in receipt of a communication from Headquarters, Air Technical Service Command, Wright Field, requesting that we ascertain the whereabouts of the files of the late scientist, Dr. Nichola [sic] Tesla, which may contain data of great value to the above Headquarters. It has been indicated that your office might have these files in custody. If this is true, we would like to request your consent for a representative of the Air Technical Service Command to review them. In view of the extreme importance of these files to the above command, we would like to request that we be advised of *any attempt by any other agency to obtain them.* [Italics supplied.]

"Because of the urgency of this matter, this communication will be delivered to you by a Liaison Officer of this office in the hope of expediting the solicited information."

The "other" agency that had the files, or should have had them, was the Air Technical Service Command itself! Colonel Doty's letter, which was classified under the Espionage Act, was declassified on May 8, 1980.

This embarrassing contretemps goes unexplained in the records. Perhaps it was handled orally with the Liaison Officer.

However, on October 24, 1947, David L. Bazelon, assistant attorney general and director of the Office of Alien Property, wrote to the commanding officer of the Air Technical Service Command, Wright Field, Dayton, Ohio, regarding the Tesla photostats that had been sent by registered mail on or about September 11, 1945, to Colonel Holliday at the latter's request.

"Our records do not reveal that this material has been returned," said Bazelon. He sent a description and asked that it be returned.

Obviously at least one set of Tesla's papers had reached Wright Field because on November 25, 1947, there was a response to the Office of Alien Property from Colonel Duffy, chief of the Electronic Plans Section, Electronic Subdivision, Engineering Division, Air Matériel Command, Wright Field. He replied: "These reports are now in the possession of the Electronic Subdivision and are being evaluated...." He believed that the evaluation should be completed by January 1,

THE MISSING PAPERS ⟷ 279

1948, and "At that time your office will be contacted with respect to final disposition of these papers."

There is no written record that OAP ever sought further to have the documents returned, and they were not returned.

For many years there have been rumors that these unpatented inventions or concepts of Tesla's found their way not only to the U.S. Army Air Force but to Russia and to private American defense industries, and ultimately into certain university research laboratories engaged in beam weaponry.

The Office of Alien Property experienced a very difficult problem over the years in explaining its role in connection with Tesla's papers. Between 1948 and 1978 it issued the following variations on a theme to many inquirers:

"While this Office participated in an examination of certain material owned by the late Dr. Tesla, our records do not disclose that any such material has been vested or is presently under the jurisdiction of this Office...."

"This Office has never had custody ... of any property of Nikola Tesla...."

"While the Tesla papers were in our custody..."

"Photostatic copies of certain documents, made while the papers were under our seal...."

"In 1943 this Office placed a seal on the property..."

"While the Tesla papers were in our custody..." etc., etc., etc.

As for what is now Headquarters Aeronautical Systems Division, Wright-Patterson Air Force Base, Ohio, they state: "The organization (Equipment Laboratory) that performed the evaluation of Tesla's papers was deactivated several years ago. After conducting an extensive search of lists of records retired by that organization, *in which we found no mention of Tesla's papers, we concluded the documents were destroyed at the time the laboratory was deactivated.*"[5] (Italics supplied. Response, under the Freedom of Information Act, dated July 30, 1980.)

Tesla's original papers, and the remaining models of his inventions—his magnifying transmitter, robot boats, early tube lighting, induction motors, turbine, exhibits shown at the Chicago World's Fair of 1893, such as the "Egg of Columbus," and others—left America in 1952 for Yugoslavia. His ashes were sent later. The artifacts may now be seen at the Tesla Museum in Belgrade, a dignified-looking building with a broad, well-proportioned facade at No. 51 Proleterskih

THE MISSING PAPERS ⟷ 280

Brigada, an avenue renamed after the war, but formerly known under the monarchy as Crown Street. The museum bears a plaque on a low wall, printed in the old Cyrillic alphabet.

Here Tesla's English writings have been translated into Serbo-Croatian—except, as the archivist admits, for the "unimportant" material, which remains, just as he wrote it, in the language of his adopted country.

30. The Legacy

The fact that Tesla's research notes and papers have not been easily available for western scientists has not, of course, meant that Teslian research is dead. On the contrary, the very mystery surrounding some of his unproved claims has served to goad numerous scientists into trying to duplicate his experiments. And since his aspirations were virtually limitless, there has always been a chance that the rewards of success would not be inconsiderable. But the single greatest stimulus to try to follow in Tesla's footsteps doubtless remains the example of the man himself—his stunning record of achievement and the enduring fascination of his mind. As one admiring German writer put it, "Tesla went beyond the borders of his exact science to foretell what lies in the future ... a modern Prometheus who dared reach for the stars...."[1]

Although a comprehensive summary of the state of Tesla-inspired research today would be beyond either the scope of this book or the intent of its author, no account of the inventor's life would be complete without at least some indication of what has become of a few of his major preoccupations. The record, as one might expect, is both mixed and incomplete, but it is no less impressive for that.

To begin, then, with Tesla's experiments with ball lightning: He had no idea what ball lightning might be useful for when he first encountered it in his Colorado Springs research; to him it was a nuisance, but it demanded an explanation. And so he set about determining the mode of formation of the strange fireballs and learned to produce them artificially.

The technical explanation runs like this: In the highly resonant transformer secondary comprising his magnifying transmitter, the entire energy accumulated in the excited circuit, instead of requiring a quarter period for transformation from static to kinetic, could spend itself in less time, at hundreds of thousands of horsepower. Thus, for example, Tesla produced artificial fireballs by suddenly causing the impressed oscillations to be more rapid than free ones of the secondary. This shifted the point of maximum electrical pressure below the elevated terminal capacity, and a ball of fire would leap great distances.

Yet strangely enough, modern plasma physicists with the best-equipped laboratories, have failed to produce plasmoids with anything near the stability of the true ball-lightning spheres that he created.

Why the fascination with this problem? First, of course, because it is there, an unknown. But second because among other uses, it may hold a vital key in the international race to achieve controlled nuclear fusion—potentially the greatest power source in history. Among those long interested in ball-lightning research are Peter Kapitza, the great Russian physicist, Lambert Dolphin and his colleagues in the radio physics laboratory at SRI International, Dr. Robert W. Bass of Brigham Young University, and Robert Golka, with whom Bass has collaborated on research.

Golka, a Massachusetts physicist, Tesla disciple, and lightning experimenter, has pursued the ephemeral fireball with the fervor of a hunter of snarks. Like Tesla in Colorado, he has done his research alone in a remote western laboratory in the Utah salt flats, and like Tesla, he has struggled to win the kind of federal support that usually goes only to enormous institutions or corporations.

In the largest hangar at the far end of the ghost base at Wendover, Utah, which was built by the U.S. Army Air Force during World War II, big spotlights are often burning as Golka conducts lightning tests. Here, under tightest security in the 1940's, the B-29 *Enola Gay* was housed and outfitted for delivering the first atomic bombs to Hiroshima.

Golka made two trips to the Tesla Museum to pore over the inventor's then unpublished notes and concentrated on replicating as exactly as he could in the old air base hangar the magnifying transmitter that Tesla had built in 1899 when investigating the lightning storms of Pike's Peak.

"He [Tesla] was 'way ahead of anything we have today in the equipment he built," Golka says. "Such as the high-powered switches and spark gap switches. The knowledge has been lost; we don't know how he did it. Some of it was in the diaries, but he kept much of this stuff in his head."

Golka built a magnifying transmitter at his "Project Tesla" that would discharge 22 million volts, creating almost twice as powerful a chain-lightning storm as the maestro himself had produced at Colorado Springs

THE LEGACY ⟷ 283

The relevance of ball lightning to fusion research has to do with the problem of confining plasma. The heart of the most common type of experimental fusion reaction involves taking isotopic hydrogen gas and both accelerating and superheating it until the hydrogen nuclei fuse to make helium nuclei, releasing, in the process, staggering amounts of energy. Along the way, while the hydrogen is being charged with vast amounts of kinetic and thermal energy, it enters an imperfectly understood material state known as plasma.* In the penultimate stages of the process, before fusion begins, the besetting problem is to maintain the plasma's coherence, to confine it within some kind of invisible electromagnetic "bottle."†

Since the strongest geometric shape is a sphere, Golka believes that ball lightning offers the best potential for containment of the unstable mass. He describes the odd lightning as "a glowing sphere of a variety of colors, a half-inch in diameter or as big as a grapefruit," and resembling an onion in its "layers and layers of alternate charged particles, positive and negative." It may bounce along through buildings, fall into water and set it boiling; and sometimes, as at the Hill Air Force Base in Utah, it may knock out the most sophisticated electronic equipment. In the summer of 1978, with the use of CO-2 laser beams, he finally managed to produce "bead" lightning, which he believes to be a form of ball lightning, and to photograph it in sequential frames.²

He then sought support from the U.S. Department of Energy for a major program of research for which he proposed to use a device called a pyrosphere, employing five laser beams to create thermonuclear fusion. In a "Fireball Fusion Reactor" only nonradioactive helium is created and, according to Golka, mathematical models indicate it can reach and hold temperatures above a billion degrees.

He also proposed to the Air Force another Teslian concept, a charged particle beam, but again one designed to employ laser technology. Such beam guns, he believes, would have a range of

*Until recent years plasma had no major industrial importance but was merely a laboratory curiosity. Richard L. Benin, executive vice president of International Plasma Corp., believes that the first practical application of plasmas came in the 19th century when "the glowing plasma produced by a Tesla coil was used to locate leaks in glass vacuum flasks."

†Teslian ideas are also involved in other aspects of fusion research. Superconducting magnetic coils, cooled to a few degrees above absolute zero, are used in magnetic containment devices; and, in a newly developed rival process, hydrogen fuel pellets are being bombarded by high-energy particle beams.

THE LEGACY ⟷ 284

6,000 miles and could melt and destroy ICBM-type missiles in the air. With a Tesla coil three times the size of his combined coils, Golka believed he could generate 200 million volts of electricity.

But he inherited the usual Teslian problems of a loner, and as he said, "The walls fall in on me when I work for corporations." His work reached a point where it could no longer progress with improvised equipment, but called for enormous investments. His competitors were large corporations and leading universities engaged in the nuclear-fusion race; and even some of the latter were being cut off from their federal grants. They too were deeply into laser technology, although Golka claims his system is different and unique. By no means the only scientist to have attempted to carry forward Tesla's work with ball lightning, he undoubtedly has been one of the most singleminded.*

Russia's Kapitza, who shared the 1978 Nobel Prize in physics with Arno Penzias and Robert W. Wilson of America for his work in magnetism and the behavior of matter at extremely low temperatures, acknowledges his debt to Tesla. "The efficient generation of super-high-frequency oscillations and their conversion back to direct-current electrical energy," he writes, "discloses possible solutions to the problem of transmitting electrical energy ... in free space. The transmission setup will, of course, be similar to that already considered but, instead of a wave guide, a highly directional beam must be used, which, as is well-known, only at short wavelengths will diverge little. Such a setup for the transmission of electrical energy, firstly thought by N. Tesla many years ago, has already been discussed.... Although ... possible in principle, it is tied up with the solution of a series of complicated engineering problems and therefore it can be implemented in practice only in such special situations in which other methods of energy transmission are inapplicable (for example, when energy must be supplied to a satellite)."[3]

In this field of wireless energy transmission, so directly concerned with the space race, there is progress nearer home. Richard Dickinson, who heads the Microwave Power Transmission project for Cal Tech's Jet Propulsion Laboratory in the desert near Barstow, California, traces his inspiration to the early work of Tesla. The concept of bringing electricity to Earth from an orbiting solar-power system via

*Lambert Dolphin says of Golka's replica of the Colorado Springs Tesla coil: "It is spectacular indeed, to either scientist or layman. I hope it ends up in a museum such as the Smithsonian where it can be appreciated." He too is a proponent of further research in ball lightning.

microwaves is daring, costly, romantic, and thoroughly in the style of the maestro.

"We beamed power from our transmitter at Goldstone a distance of one mile," Dickinson said of the NASA project initiated in the mid-seventies. "All of the microwave energy that fell within our target (of which we could only collect a portion with our existing apparatus), we converted 82.5 percent to useful direct current. Thirty-four thousand watts of direct current output carried a distance of one mile. We are well pleased. The next step is to look further into the technology and needs of the satellite power system of the future."[4]

William C. Brown of the Raytheon Company, who developed the rectenna used in this microwave-power research, also attributes the idea of sending electricity by radio waves to Tesla's pioneering in the fundamentals of radio broadcasting and wireless power transmission.

Theoretically, a city the size of New York could be supplied with five billion watts on a winter day by enormous satellite structures in the sky that would orbit synchronously with Earth at a height of 22,300 miles. But admittedly, the cost of such floating power stations would be many billions of dollars, and they would be highly vulnerable to enemy killer satellites, in the event of war.

Brookhaven National Laboratory, located just to the northeast of Tesla's old Wardenclyffe site at Shoreham, also feels a close link with the inventor through the advanced high-energy work being conducted at the laboratory. In 1976 it paid homage to him in a ceremony, and the Yugoslav government sent a plaque to be placed at the still-standing Wardenclyffe laboratory.

Canada, too, has long been a bastion of Tesla Energy System advocates, and because of the country's rich hydroelectric sources, through-the-Earth transmission—if it worked—could be a boon to areas of power shortage.

But—will it work? Several projects have been planned, and some partially implemented, in Canada, central Minnesota, and most recently in Southern California—to "pump" hydroelectric power wirelessly through the Earth to an area of need, employing the Tesla system as it is understood.[5] The U.S. Department of Energy has often been asked to fund projects based on Tesla's system.

Unfortunately, there is no evidence that the system ever worked for Tesla, and none that it could work for anyone else. One of the inventor's problems was that he improperly extended into the electromagnetic domain fluid and fluid-mechanical analogies. Tesla's patent No. 787,412 provides for the Earth to be excited by a carefully valued wavelength to establish a standing wave condition. Tesla believed the propagation path fell along a diameter. But according to much knowledge developed since 1899, the propagation path would not be along a diameter but, rather, along an ellipsoidal arc somewhere between the diameter and the spherical surface.

A fundamental aspect of wave propagation of power is that *no power is transmitted if the wave is standing*; power is transmitted solely with a traveling component. Boundary layer propagation, i.e., the mode of lossless propagation of waves at the boundary of two differing media (such as earth and sky), is a viable concept. However, the boundary plane must be smooth and the waves must be properly launched. At the frequencies Tesla was using, such launching apparatus would be an enormous structure. In examining the photographs of his experimental station at Colorado Springs, it is apparent to experts that he did not employ apparatus essential to the launching of such waves.

Tesla probably was mistaken at Colorado Springs in his interpretation of the lightning storms which he observed traveling away from him (eastwardly) across the plains, producing maxima and minima effects upon his instruments. This he interpreted as standing waves being set up in the Earth by the traveling storm, with the crests of the waves passing through his location as the storms advanced. It is believed he was seeing an interference effect caused by the reradiating surface of the frontal range of mountains to the west of his station. The results would have been the same on his instruments.

Dr. Wait, formerly senior scientist at the Environmental Research Laboratories, National Oceanic and Atmospheric Administration, in Colorado, describes himself as a "firm skeptic" of the Tesla theory. "The concept that electromagnetic energy penetrates 'through the earth,'" he says, "is valid only if the frequency is sufficiently low and if the distances are small. It's all tied up with 'skin-effect' phenomena; that means that the field is confined to the surface of a good conductor as in metallic wave guide."[6]

Dr. Wait even goes so far as to suggest that Tesla never really accepted the fact that electromagnetic waves could transport energy through the air. "Instead he thought of the earth itself as a conveyor and also thought of the possibility of a return conductor at heights of '15 miles above sea level.' The parallel of this idea to the earth-ionosphere wave guide at extremely low frequencies is striking (see IEEE *Journals of Oceanic Engineering*, Vol. OE-2, No. 2, April 1977). Also his proposed resonance of the system might be interpreted as the first disclosure of the earth-ionosphere cavity oscillations that have been associated from the early 1960s with W. O. Schumann, N. Christofilos, and J. Galejs, among others."[7]

With respect to wireless communication, the U.S. Navy's Project Sanguine/Seafarer of recent years has evolved from Tesla's Colorado experiments. In a thermonuclear war, conventional radio communication probably would be disrupted at certain heights and wavelengths. America's atomic submarine fleet might then be without a means of receiving messages. The U.S. Navy, seeing this danger, turned back to Tesla's nineteenth-century suggestion of employing 10 Hz signals (ELF or extra low frequency), to circle the globe and penetrate the deepest waters.

One of the headier speculations concerning Teslian science is a suggestion that Russia has been employing his theories on weather modification to interfere with the jet stream, causing droughts and extremes of hot and cold weather. However unlikely the charge, it is true that Tesla did do a good deal of theorizing (but very little experimentation) on weather control.

He wrote, for example, on the possible use of radio-controlled missiles and explosives to break up tornadoes and the use of "lightning of a certain kind" to trigger rainfall. Of the former he said, "It would not be difficult to provide special automata for this purpose, carrying explosive charges, liquid air or other gas, which could be put into action, automatically or otherwise, and which would create a sudden pressure or suction, breaking up the whirl. The missiles themselves might be made of material capable of spontaneous ignition." His proposal included a lengthy mathematical formula.[8]

As with much modern scientific exploration inspired by the maestro, the returns are still not in on weather changing. Scientist Frederic Jueneman, "Innovative Notebook" columnist for *Industrial Research* magazine, calls attention to the fact that Dr. Robert Helliwell and John Katsufrakis of Stanford University's Radio Science Laboratory, demonstrated that very low frequency radio waves can cause oscillations in the magnetosphere. With a 20-km antenna and a 5 kHz transmitter in the Antarctic, they found that the earth's magnetosphere could be modulated to cause high energy particles to cascade into our atmosphere, and by turning the signal on or off they could start or stop the energy flow.

"The theoretical implication suggested by their work," says Jueneman, "is that global weather control can be attained by the injection of relatively small 'signals' into the Van Allen belts—something like a super-transistor effect."

But Jueneman's speculations go further and are eminently

THE LEGACY ⟷ 288

worthy of Tesla: "If Tesla's resonance effects, as shown by the Stanford team, can control enormous energies by miniscule triggering signals, then by an extension of this principle we should be able to affect the field environment of the very stars in the sky...With godlike arrogance, we someday may yet direct the stars in their courses."[9]

No biography of Tesla would be complete without mention of his bright following of amateur physicists who build Tesla coils for their personal research, endeavoring to replicate his electrical magic; and the young inventors who pore over his basic patents and still find inspiration from them.

Durlin C. Cox, a Wisconsin physicist who has pondered Tesla's published writings, has built two Tesla coils, the second of 10 million volts. The reasons: "My own personal interest in high voltage engineering, especially in the field of high frequency rf transformers; to further my studies on the laboratory production of ball lightning; and because the University of Wisconsin at Madison asked me to submit a Tesla coil in their bi-annual Engineering Exposition in the spring of 1981." He and friends built one Tesla coil for a Hollywood studio for lightning effects, which has been a common use of them.

Electrical engineer Leland Anderson has summarized the major points in design that a coil builder might gain from reading Tesla's *Colorado Springs Notes*:

1. The Q's of the primary and secondary must be as high as practicable.
2. The Q's of the primary and secondary should be equal.
3. The length of the secondary winding should be one-quarter of the effective operating wavelength.
4. The technique of using an "extra coil" tank circuit (or a variation of it) in the secondary to magnify the voltage should be used.

"With these criteria in mind," he says, "the builder will find that hundreds of turns are not necessary for the secondary winding to achieve high voltages."

Last but not least, what about Tesla's death/disintegrator rays? Were his concepts sound? If they were found useful by the U.S. Army Air Force research team, whose top-secret project was rumored to have had the code name "Project Nick," it may be safely assumed that instead of being "destroyed," as reported, his papers are still highly classified.

Dr. Trump's evaluation and Swezey's assessment of Tesla's "secret weapons" have, however, received updated concurrence by

Lambert Dolphin, assistant director of the Radio Physics Laboratory at SRI International, who has studied the inventor's work and his ball-lightning research for two decades. He points out that the fields of knowledge of both physics and electrical engineering have grown exponentially since about 1930.

"Whole libraries are now required just to keep track of all the theory and experience that have unfolded since Tesla's time," he says. "Our mathematical and practical understanding of electricity, magnetism, electromagnetic theory, and radio communications has continued to grow explosively ever since 1950, or should I say 1970!"

Tesla, Dolphin believes, "may have had intuitive insight into lasers and high-energy particle beams as well as ultra-high voltage phenomena, but now that we understand all the physics much more, we can easily evaluate many of his extravagant later-life claims."[10]

In fact, there is no good evidence to suggest that Tesla anticipated lasers. His "teleforce rays" seem to have been concerned exclusively with high-energy particle beams. We still do not know precisely how he intended them to work, although, says Dolphin, the available evidence suggests that Tesla may not have paid sufficient attention to how greatly such beams may be absorbed or dispersed by molecules and atoms in the air. In any case, even if we did understand Tesla's intentions more clearly, we should be hard put to compare them to the current state of the art, much of which is hidden under high security classifications.

Nevertheless, Tesla's work with high voltages to accelerate charged particles does seem to have been decidedly in what is now the mainstream of physical research. "In this field," says Dolphin, "he anticipated modern linear and circular nuclear accelerators. Such machines today have energy levels of tens of billions of electron volts or at least 1,000 times greater energy levels than Tesla ever attained.

"I am sure his magnifying transmitters were spectacular.... He probably generated some interesting arcs and sparks that were what we now study as *plasmas*. The containment of plasmas is a huge area of modern physics. For example ... to see if small amounts of matter can be turned into immense amounts of electrical power in carefully contained plasmas." But Tesla's early discoveries and inventions, he concludes, were indeed ingenious and ahead of their time."[11]

As this book goes to press, the Pentagon is studying the creation of a new branch of the armed services, to be known as the U.S. Space Command, whose primary arsenal will consist of laser and particle-beam weapons fired from "space battleships." In prose not

THE LEGACY ⟷ 290

unlike Tesla's own, a Department of Defense fact sheet compares particle beams to "directed lightning bolts"—although without explicitly admitting that such a weapon has in fact been developed.

It is difficult to assess the current state of the beam-weapons program because virtually everything about it is heavily classified. Apparently the technology involved has proved to be complex and difficult, raising questions about the project's feasibility, but many experts nevertheless seem to be hard at work on the problem. At the same time, the activities of the other nations in this area have been monitored carefully by agencies of the federal government. Indeed the possibility of creating a family of particle-beam weapons has been a subject of serious discussion in this country for at least the past twenty-five years, and it is, in my opinion, of no little significance that as long ago as 1947 the Military Intelligence Service identified the writings about a particle-beam among Tesla's scientific papers as being "of extreme importance."

Since he had no laboratory in the later years of his life, Tesla was unable to develop his ideas. But it is undeniable that he described in general terms half a century ago what may prove to be one of the main weapons of the Space Age. And to the end of his days, Tesla the pacifist hoped that such knowledge would be used, not for war among Earthlings, but for interplanetary communication with our neighbors in space, of whose existence he felt certain.

Bibliographical Essay

Some of Tesla's own writing—lectures, articles, patents, papers, and letters—is now available in the United States. His most important lectures and his brief autobiography, in bound volumes, are listed in the prologue to the reference notes.

Citation of biographies of Tesla by O'Neill, Hunt, and Draper, and others may be found in the reference notes. The O'Neill manuscript and the Swezey Collection are to be found at the Smithsonian Institution, Dibner Library.

Serious Tesla scholars will wish to consult the annotated *Dr. Nikola Tesla Bibliography* by J. T. Ratzlaff, and L. I. Anderson (San Carlos, California, Ragusan Press, 1979), for it contains some 3,000 sources of writings by and about Tesla. "Priority in the Invention of Radio, Tesla v. Marconi," by Leland Anderson may be obtained through the Antique Wireless Association, Monograph New Series No. 4.

A new means of analyzing Tesla's inventions is provided in *Dr. Nikola Tesla: Selected Patent Wrappers from The National Archives*, by J. T. Ratzlaff (Millbrae, Ca., Tesla Book Co., 1980). These "file wrappers" provide explanations and correspondence between the patentee and the Patent Office, to overcome objections raised by the examiner.

Tesla's *Colorado Springs Notes, 1899–1900*, published in 1978 by the Tesla Museum, is available through Nolit, Terazije, 27, Belgrade, Yugoslavia.

The Library of Congress Manuscripts Division contains microfilm correspondence between Tesla and George Scherff, Robert Underwood Johnson, Mark Twain, members of the Morgan family, George Westinghouse, and the Westinghouse Electric and Manufacturing Company.

In addition original correspondence and photographs may be found at the Butler Library, Rare Books and Manuscripts, Columbia University, including letters between Tesla and Johnson, Scherff, and

4-22 (Rev. 1-83)

FEDERAL BUREAU OF INVESTIGATION
Records/Operations Sections

_____ 8/26 _____, 19 83

b7C

☐ Name Searching Unit, 4543, TL# 115
☒ ~~Service Unit, 4654, TL# 225~~
☐ Special File Room, 5991, TL# 122
☐ Forward to File Review, 5447, TL# 143
☒ Attention ████████████
☒ Return to ████ 4134, 232 ████████
    Supervisor, Room, TL#, Ext.

Type of Search Requested: (Check One)
☒ Restricted Search (Active Index - 5 & 20)
☐ Restricted Search (Active & Inactive Index - 5 & 30)
☐ Unrestricted (Active & Inactive Index)

Special Instructions: (Check One)
☐ All References (Security & Criminal)
☒ Security Search
☐ Criminal Search
☐ Main _____ References Only
☐ Exact Name Only (On the Nose)
☐ Buildup   ☐ Variations
☐ Restricted to Locality of _____

Subject SAVA KOSANOVIC
Birthdate & Place _____
Address _____

Localities _____

R# _____ Date 8-26 Searcher Initials /AS
Prod. _____

FILE NUMBER	SERIAL
100-346268-	2008ap9 ✓
100-345155-	20p9 ✓
65-72038-	8 ✓
138-4457-	83p69
65-58068-	3561p2 ✓
105-53786-	90ap9 ✓
Sava N	
65-58068-	3677X

Bu BD
NR

ALL INFORMATION CONTAINED
HEREIN IS UNCLASSIFIED
DATE 2-22-17 BY ███████

891 860

(1)

FBI/DOJ

4-22 (Rev. 1-83)

FEDERAL BUREAU OF INVESTIGATION
Records/Operations Sections

8/24, 19 83

- ☐ Name Searching Unit, 4543, TL# 115
- ☒ ~~Service Unit, 1054~~, TL# 225
- ☐ Special File Room, 5991, TL# 122
- ☐ Forward to File R█████████ 143
- ☒ Attention ███████████
- ☒ Return to ███████████
  Supervisor, Room, TL#, Ext.

Type of Search Requested: (Check One)
- ☒ Restricted Search (Active Index 5 & 20)
- ☒ Restricted Search (Active & Inactive Index 5 & 30)
- ☐ Unrestricted (Active & Archive)

Special Instructions: (Check One)
- ☒ All References (Security & Criminal)
- ☒ Security Search
- ☐ Criminal Search
- ☐ Main _____ References Only
- ☐ Exact Name Only (On the Nose)
- ☐ Buildup   ☐ Variations
- ☐ Restricted to Locality of _____

Subject __NIKOLA TESLA__
Birthdate & Place _____
Address __Classified, SA/ACGM__
Declassify on: OADR
Localities _____
#2 8460

R# _____ Date 8/24 Searcher Initials 4/4
Prod. _____

FILE NUMBER	SERIAL
100-2237 ✓	
190-23940 ✓	
62-115830-9986 ✓	
-24012 ✓	
-12392 ✓	
65-37367-608 ✓	
77-32591-20 ✓	
94-5-90140 ✓	
97-724-15B P18 ✓	
105-0-9401 ✓	
105-254522-7 ✓	
138-4457-83 P69 ✓	
190-13537-1	
190-26450-2	
190-27882-4	
190-26491-3	
190-20097-11	
190-█████-6	
-11	

ALL INFORMATION CONTAINED
HEREIN IS UNCLASSIFIED
EXCEPT WHERE SHOWN
OTHERWISE
(B)

FBI/DOJ

4-22 (Rev. 1-1-83)

FEDERAL BUREAU OF INVESTIGATION
Records/Operations Sections

8/26, 19 83

b7C

☐ Name Searching Unit, 4543, TL# 115
☒ ~~Service Unit, 4054,~~ TL# 225
☐ Special File Room, 5991, TL# 122
☐ Forward to File R████████ 143
☒ Attention ████████
☒ Return to ████████
Supervisor, Room, TL#, Ext.

Type of Search Requested: (Check One)
☒ Restricted Search (Active In██ █5 & 20)
☒ Restricted Search (Active & ████ ███ 15 & 30)
☐ Unrestricted (Active & ████████)

Special Instructions: (Check One)
☒ All References (Security & Criminal)
☒ Security Search
☐ Criminal Search
☐ Main _____ References Only
☐ Exact Name Only (On the Nose)
☐ Buildup   ☐ Variations
☐ Restricted to Locality of _____

Subject: **NIKOLA TESLA**
Birthdate & Place: 7-7-79
Address: Classified by SP1ACGM
Localities: Declassify on: OADR

R# _____ Date 8/26 Searcher Initials 4/9
Prod. _____

FILE NUMBER	SERIAL
100-2237	✓
190-23940	✓
62-115530-9986	✓
-24013	
-12392	✓
65-37367-608	✓
77-32591-20	✓
94-5-90146	✓
97-724-158 P18	✓
105-0-9401	✓
105-254522-7	✓
138-4457-83 P69	✓
190-15537-1	
190-26450-2	
190-27882-4	
190-26491-3	
190-20097-11	
190-26640-6	
-11	

ALL INFORMATION CONTAINED
HEREIN IS UNCLASSIFIED
EXCEPT WHERE SHOWN
OTHERWISE

FBI/DOJ

4-22a (Rev. 11-17-59)

JMEROUS REFERENCE

SEARCH SLIP

Subj: Nikola Tesla

Supervisor _____ Room _____
R# _____ Date 6/24 Searcher Initial ___
Prod. _____

FILE NUMBER	SERIAL
190-13713-1	
190-14591-1	
190-16504-1	
-6	
190-17311-2	
190-19581-1	
190-20720-1	
-5	
190-22369-3	
190-22527-3	
190-23039-3	
190-26491-3	
190-23029-4	
190-23890-3	
-4	
r 190-24043-4	
190-24882-4	
-1	
190-27882-1	
190-26624-7	
190-0-4157	
-1364	

FBI/DOJ

4-22a (Rev. 11-17-59)

NUMEROUS REFERENCE
SEARCH SLIP

Subj: Nikola Tesla

Supervisor _____ Room _____
R# _____ Date 6/26 Searcher Initial ___

Prod. _____

FILE NUMBER	SERIAL
190-13713-1	
190-14591-1	
190-16504-1	
-6	
190-17311-2	
190-19521-1	
190-20720-1	
-5	
190-22369-3	
190-22527-3	
190-23039-3	
190-26491-3	
190-23029-4	
190-23890-3	
-4	
190-24043-4	
190-24882-4	
-1	
190-27882-1	
190-26624-7	
190-0-4157	
-1364	

FBI/DOJ

4-22a (Rev. 11-17-59)

NUMEROUS REFERENCE
SEARCH SLIP

Subj: Nikola Tesla

Supervisor _____ Room _____
R# _____ Date 8/24 Searcher Initial LL

Prod. _____

FILE NUMBER	SERIAL
190-0-5723	
-6466	
-7681	
190-25594-4	
190-33622-1	
190-31983-2	
190-20097-10X	
190-35718-1X	
-3	
190-34282-1	
190-31983-X	
190-30539-2	
190-35718-1	
190-35567-1	
190-40081-1	
190-24043-5	
190-20097-18	

VAR/NIKOLI
SI

VAR/NOKOLA
SI

(4)

FBI/DOJ

4-22a (Rev. 11-17-59)

NUMEROUS REFERENCE
SEARCH SLIP

Subj: Nikola Tesla

Supervisor _____   Room _____
R # _____ Date 6/24   Searcher Initial _____

Prod. _____

FILE NUMBER	SERIAL
190-13713-1	
190-14591-1	
190-16504-1	
-6	
190-17311-2	
190-19521-1	
190-20720-1	
-5	
190-22369-3	
190-22527-3	
190-23039-3	
190-26491-3	
190-23029-4	
190-23890-3	
-4	
190-24043-4	
190-24082-4	

www.ingramcontent.com/pod-product-compliance
Lightning Source LLC
Chambersburg PA
CBHW080529170426
43195CB00016B/2517